DATE DUE

AP 22 '99		
MY 13 '99		
AG 5 '99		
OE 1 0 '00		
AG 9 '01		
OE 3 '02		
FE 13 '03		
OE 1 8 '03		

DEMCO 38-296

Character Development
and
Physical Activity

David Lyle Light Shields, PhD
Brenda Jo Light Bredemeier, PhD
University of California at Berkeley

Human Kinetics

loging-in-Publication Data

ity / David Lyle Light
Shields, Brenda Jo Light Bredemeier.
    p. cm.
  Includes bibliographical references and index.
  ISBN 0-87322-711-5
  1. Sports—Moral and ethical aspects.   2. Moral development.
3. Personality development.   I. Bredemeier, Brenda Jo. 1950-   .
II. Title.
GV706.3.S54   1994   94-7514
796'.01—dc20   CIP

ISBN: 0-87322-711-5

Acquisitions Editor: Richard D. Frey, PhD; **Developmental Editors:** Ann Brodsky and Anne Mischakoff; **Assistant Editors:** Ed Giles, Jacqueline Blakley, Anna Curry, Julie Marx; **Copyeditor:** Molly Bentsen; **Proofreader:** Karen Leszczynski; **Indexer:** Joan K. Griffitts; **Typesetter and Text Layout:** Yvonne Winsor; **Text Designer:** Keith Blomberg; **Cover Designer:** Jack Davis; **Printer:** Braun-Brumfield, Inc.

Printed in the United States of America

10   9   8   7   6   5   4   3   2   1

Human Kinetics
P.O. Box 5076, Champaign, IL 61825-5076
1-800-747-4457

Canada: Human Kinetics, Box 24040, Windsor, ON N8Y 4Y9
1-800-465-7301 (in Canada only)

Europe: Human Kinetics, P.O. Box IW14, Leeds LS16 6TR, England
(44) 532 781708

Australia: Human Kinetics, Unit 5, Raglan Avenue, Edwardstown 5039, South Australia
(08) 371 3755

New Zealand: Human Kinetics, P.O. Box 105-231, Auckland 1
(09) 309 2259

To Micah and Maya, our beloved children

Contents

Preface

Across centuries and cultures, sport has been one of the most powerful spheres in which moral values are presented and acted on. The sport player is both athlete and moral actor. This book is about the moral dimensions of experience in physical activity contexts, especially sport.

Despite the significance of morality in physical activity contexts, students and scholars interested in both sport and moral psychology have been handicapped for lack of a comprehensive introduction to the field. One main purpose in writing this book is to provide such a source. You will find here an introduction to the primary concepts and theories of moral psychology, a synthesis of empirical research relevant to the psychology of sport morality, and a review of practical efforts to promote moral aims through physical education and sport.

But the book offers more than a summary and synthesis of current theory, research, and application. We have sought to extend theory by elaborating a framework useful for understanding, investigating, and promoting moral action in sport. We have indicated numerous directions for future investigations as a means to stimulate new empirical research. And we have endeavored to enhance efforts to promote moral growth through physical activity experiences by offering specific moral education strategies that can be used by physical educators, coaches, sport administrators, parents, and others involved in the world of sport.

Though we review and draw from fairly diverse perspectives on moral psychology, we are intentionally partisan. We have drawn most heavily from social and developmental psychology, highlighting structural developmental approaches that emphasize social interaction. We find these approaches the most enlightening of the available models of morality and moral development.

We have written *Character Development and Physical Activity* for all those interested in issues of sport morality. Though some of the material is technical, we have sought to make the book accessible. In particular, professors and researchers in the social sciences of sport, together with their graduate students and perhaps advanced undergraduates, may find the book helpful.

The book is organized into three parts. Part 1 opens with a brief response to the question, Can research on morality be scientific? The subsequent four chapters introduce the major concepts and theories of morality and moral development.

Moral action is the topic of Part 2. The first chapter of the part presents our twelve-component model for understanding and investigating moral action. The model identifies four major processes and three major sources of influence that feed into moral action. Each of the ensuing chapters in Part 2 probes one of the four processes in greater depth. The last part takes up the topic of physical activity and character. What is character and does sport build it? Do physical education programs? If they do not do so automatically, how can coaches, teachers, and parents shape physical activity experiences to provide optimal settings for moral growth?

Acknowledgments

Our reflections on morality and sport have been informed by friends and colleagues too numerous to mention. We are grateful to participants at national and international workshops and conferences who responded to and enriched the ideas we presented and have incorporated in this book. In particular, it was a privilege to share a portion of this book in June of 1991 in Reykjavik, Iceland when the Council of Europe sponsored a meeting for its Committee for the Development of Sport. The meeting on young people and ethics in sport was designed to hear reports on an international study of sport morality, and to chart future directions for the cooperative project. We were honored to participate in the conference, and remain deeply appreciative of the support and advice we received.

We have profited also from discussions with graduate students who read early drafts of various chapters and offered steady encouragement throughout the birthing process of this book. We especially want to thank Leslee Fisher, Debby Getty, Kathleen Ryan, Gloria Solomon, and Dawn Stephens. Also, we are grateful to Steve Miller for helping gather materials for our bibliography of sport and moral psychology literature. The patience and loving support of these folks, together with other friends and family members, helped nurture this book from conception to birth.

We salute the staff at Human Kinetics and thank them for their assistance in preparing this manuscript for publication. Rainer Martens, Publisher and Rick Frey, Director of the Human Kinetics Academic division intuited the importance of this book from the beginning, encouraged its development, and allowed it time to ripen. We are grateful to Ann Brodsky and Anne Mischakoff for their work as developmental editors, and to Molly Bentsen for her copyediting efforts.

Introduction

One of the most powerful themes permeating all dimensions of North American culture is the need to strengthen the set of common values that have made us, in all our diversity, one people. Some public figures profess the desire to return to "traditional values," a bag of virtues they fear are being replaced by an assortment of "-isms": secular humanism, feminism, and multiculturalism, to name a few. Others claim their values oppose a different set of "-isms": sexism and heterosexism, racism, classism, and the like. Although media messages trumpet the need for a valuing of values, the disenfranchised ask, Which values? and the disadvantaged ask, Whose values? Community leaders caution that a lack of shared values among the citizenry is leading to increasing frustration, hopelessness, and alienation on both personal and societal levels, and they warn that the moral fabric of our society has begun to disintegrate.

As part of society, sport reflects the prevailing value trends of the broader culture. It is, in fact, a highly symbolic and condensed medium for cultural values, a vehicle by which many young people come to learn about the core values of their culture. Perhaps this is why the adage that sport builds character persists. Unfortunately, sport transmits the full range of prevailing values, producing and reproducing social practices and relations that have contributed to daunting challenges in a society fragmented by prejudice and discrimination, poverty and drug abuse, and inadequate education. While sport also serves as a site of resistance to many of these dominant cultural forces, most forms of resistance have been marginalized. In general, sport has done little to transform dominant social values to enhance personal development and promote social justice for a majority of participants.

Media coverage of sport, in fact, suggests that, more than ever, winning matters much more than how the game is played. Violence among players; parent brawls at youth sport events; discrimination based on nationalism, sexism, racism, or homophobia; illegal use of performance-enhancing drugs; abusive leadership styles and behaviors; and the taunting, baiting, and ridiculing of opponents—these stories and more are widely reported.

In light of the multiple and manifest problems in sport—from children's sport through elite and professional sport—some critics have claimed that sport impedes value learning. But in truth the problems that plague sport may reflect not a failure of participants to learn cultural values but their success in learning them all too well. Highly visible and symbolically potent, sport may reveal distorted value priorities and moral failings that saturate the broader culture.

Sport is at once a mirror and a molder of social values; it reflects society's potentials and limitations alike. But our concern is not primarily social criticism or a sociological analysis of sport. Rather our concern is with sport and physical activity as arenas for moral action, and our avenue of approach is primarily psychological and social psychological.

Despite the problems associated with contemporary competitive sport, sport is replete with opportunities to encounter, learn, transform, and enact moral values. The moral tension that participants often experience, for example, between the norms of fair play and the desire to win parallels tension in almost any conflictive moral situation. The main difference between sport and everyday life is that moral experience is condensed and exposed in sport. We believe this makes it a valuable context for moral education.

Furthermore, sport provides young participants an experience of a social structure that is generally accepted as fair and legitimate. Despite occasional charges of favoritism, most game officials are probably viewed as more fair than many judges. The ground rules of the game are viewed as more fair than the ground rules of society. Sport may be an ideal setting for introducing children to conventional moral thinking. Some have even suggested that society could benefit from emulating sport's predominantly equity-based justice system (Brickman, 1977; Mark, Bryant, & Lehman, 1983).

Most social scientists would probably agree that the sport experience is pervasive and poignant, yet its psychosocial impact is not well understood. Our research suggests that sport can both be an important catalyst for moral growth and pose a risk to psychosocial development. One reason for such countervailing possibilities, of course, is that sport experiences are not uniform. "Sport" is actually an abstraction until we talk about specific sports in specific contexts. In the real world, sport experiences are affected by the structural dynamics of the particular sport being played, the nature of the interpersonal relationships established, and the quality and style of the coaching, to name only a few of the more prominent influences. Rather than talk about the impact of sport, we need to talk about the impact of team and individual sports, contact and noncontact sports, youth and intercollegiate sports, women's and men's sports, and so on.

Questions about the moral adequacy of physical education and sport programs have arisen largely from critiques of the harsh competitive ethic of our contemporary North American culture. The roots of sport in the fertile soil of play may dry up when exposed to the heat of competition, and our vision of the human and humane potential of sport may blur when our eyes are on the prize more than the process. In response to such criticism and in recognition of the positive potential for physical education, the American Academy of Physical Educators published a position statement that identified moral development as one of the most important social issues facing contemporary physical educators (Park, 1983). If physical education and sport are to fulfill the academy's mandate of providing a context for moral learning, we need an adequate moral psychology of physical activity experiences.

Two key assumptions undergird our approach to the moral psychology of sport. The first is that we need to avoid mind–body dualism, the second that we need to avoid individual–social dualism. We believe in the need to reclaim the body as a theme for psychology and to tear down the iron curtain between individual psychology and social psychology. In concluding this introduction, we will amplify each of these points briefly.

In Piagetian epistemology, all thought is ultimately traced back to physical activity (Piaget, 1923). Jean Piaget proclaimed children's physical play to be the foundation for every cognitive advance, from quantum physics to interpersonal morality. Within the Piagetian tradition, however, physical activity is transformed into and superseded by the activities of the mind early in each child's development. The living, breathing, running, playing physical self is forgotten as quickly as wisps of smoke from candles blown out on a birthday cake. Part of our purpose in writing this book is to call attention to the need for psychology scholars to re-member the body. Nowhere is this more important than in the study of morality, and nowhere in the field of moral psychology is this more salient than in the contexts of sport and physical education. We posit in this volume that moral thoughts, motivations, and emotions are critical but that moral action—physical action—is the cornerstone of moral being.

In addition to promoting mind–body dualism, much of contemporary psychology severs individuals from their social contexts. Although the individualistic paradigm may serve a purpose in some domains of psychology, it clearly does a disservice to moral psychology, for all moral meaning is derived from social experience. Thus, our understanding of morality in physical activity contexts must be informed by an understanding not only of the participants but also of the social world in which they work and play. Although Piaget (1932/1965) emphasized the significance of social processes in shaping moral development, his division of social interactions into two types—unilateral restraint and cooperation—was far too simplistic to carry the field far. Similarly, Kohlberg's early work on moral development focused almost exclusively on individual moral reasoning. Only recently have scholars begun to carefully examine how social interactions and social contexts affect morality (Kurtines & Gewirtz, 1987, 1991a, 1991b, 1991c; Lind, Hartmann, & Wakenhut, 1985). Kohlberg's Just Community Programs (Power, Higgins, & Kohlberg, 1989) and his devoted involvement in them exemplify his later efforts to influence social structures, processes, and methods of interpersonal decision making and to modify the power and authority relationships between teachers and the taught (Higgins, 1991).

One major impetus for focusing on the social dimension of psychology has come from feminist theory. In the early 1980s, Carol Gilligan gave voice to the belief that the social category of gender, and the different gender-specific experiences that accompany it, produce distinctive gender-associated ways of thinking about moral issues. Gilligan's writings were one visible sign of a dramatic transformation in psychology in general and moral theory and research in particular. Her work is one illustration of the feminist scholarship that has helped spur a trend toward studying how social processes relate to individual development and to personal and group behavior.

In this book we seek to promote an understanding of the dynamics of moral action in physical activity contexts—especially sport—and to elucidate the possibilities that sport presents for moral educators. We do so drawing from diverse theoretical perspectives, with particular concentration on social and developmental psychology, especially social cognitive and structural developmental theories. In brief, social cognitive theorists maintain a model of causality in which human behavior, cognition and other personal factors, and environmental events interact to determine each other. Central to social cognitive theories is the tenet that behavior is purposeful and is regulated by forethought. Structural developmentalists likewise emphasize the purposefulness of human activity. The unique feature of these theories is their emphasis on qualitative developmental changes and the reality-responsive and reality-constructive properties of human cognition and affect. In our analysis of the moral dimension of sport experience, we have sought to avoid the common pitfalls of mind–body and individual–social dualisms. We see this book as an invitation to dialogue about the theory and practice of moral psychology, and we invite you, the reader, to join us in an effort to promote moral development through physical activity.

Part I
Theory

In Part I, we introduce the major theories of moral development. Before we discuss the psychology of morality, however, we'll address a common question: Can research on morality be scientific?

The person who asks this may have several issues in mind, such as whether morality isn't just a matter of personal opinion. Another issue pertains to moral development: Is it really possible to designate some forms of moral reasoning as more mature—and "better"—than others? Yet a third issue is the supposed value neutrality of scientific investigation. How can "objective" scientists study such a value-laden topic as morality without sacrificing their scientific posture? We deal with each of these three issues in turn.

Morality and Opinion

How is morality grounded? How does one determine right from wrong? It has become common in North American culture to believe that moral perspectives are a matter of personal preference and cannot be justified by reason. Morality, accordingly, is a matter of opinion. An opinion connotes a belief that lacks certainty yet is sometimes held with conviction as if known to be true.

The cognitive status of morality has long been debated, with two streams of thought paramount. Some philosophers and psychologists are emotivists in their view of morality, believing that morality is rooted in the emotions and cannot be rationally justified. The psychoanalytic and social learning perspectives in psychology share this emotivist stance. In chapter 2 we discuss these perspectives more fully.

We have found more convincing the perspective of the cognitivists, who hold that behavior is to be considered moral only if it is motivated, at least in part, by moral reasons. If an athlete helps an opponent up after a fall because he thinks that doing so will give him an emotional edge that can later be exploited, whereas a second athlete does the outwardly identical act for altruistic reasons, only the second athlete would we say acted morally.

According to the cognitivist position, moral norms are not reducible to the irrational. For most of us, for example, it seems quite logical to have prescriptions against killing and stealing. Similarly, there is a logic underlying the complex web of moral norms and understandings that permeate human social life. This does not mean that emotion is irrelevant to morality—far from it! Emotions such as empathy, shame, guilt, and love are indispensable to moral functioning. But a hallmark of morality is the cognitive component that yields a defensible sense of "ought." This brings us to the question of moral development.

Morality and Development

If morality is defensible on rational grounds, then it is logical to assume that various moralities can be distinguished in terms of their greater or lesser moral adequacy. Just as children do not understand the complexities of algebra before grasping the concepts of elementary arithmetic, so they might fail to comprehend the complexity of some moral perspectives until they thoroughly understand less complex ones. This is the assumption that has guided research in the development of moral reasoning.

An illustration may help here. Damon (1975, 1977, 1980) has investigated the development of children's understanding of positive justice. He found that before about age 4, children view an act as fair or just if they want it. Beginning around age 4, children start to offer reasons other than personal desire to justify a particular act. They have come to realize that it is inadequate to simply equate desire with "the right" because desire does not provide any mechanism for negotiating "the fair thing to do" among people whose desires conflict.

But in their first attempts to transcend desire, children appeal to external characteristics of the actors involved (e.g., sex, size, age) in a rather self-serving way. Thus, an act is viewed as fair or just if desired by the older (or bigger, or . . .) child (usually the self). The child's recognized need to offer justification beyond simple desire is an improvement, but the self-serving appeal to observable realities that have little moral significance does not advance the child far. Usually by about age 5 children have perceived the difficulties inherent in the earlier approach and begin to resolve the problem of fairness through a strict appeal to equality: An act is considered fair if everyone gets the same. Later, further refinements are added: Concepts of merit begin to be integrated around age 6, the concept of special need around age 8, and concepts of equity that balance need and merit around age 10. With each step, there is a logical reason to abandon a particular way of approaching moral problems and adopt a more sophisticated perspective.

Morality and Scientific Inquiry

But doesn't the study of morality commit the investigator to a particular moral perspective, sacrificing scientific neutrality in the process? This is a complex question, and we will be able to provide only the contours of an answer.

The place to begin a response is with the antiquated but still persisting tenet that scientific investigation should be value-neutral. There is a growing consensus among philosophers of science that science never has been value-free and never can be (Fiske & Shweder, 1986; Habermas, 1973; Hanson, 1958; Kuhn, 1970). All scientific investigation is infused with values, including moral values. Truthfulness, for example, is a moral value, and it is hard to imagine a legitimate science that does not depend on its community adhering to the value of truthfulness.

The particular questions that scientists choose to address, the way they pose them, the procedures they use to collect data, and how information is distributed and used—all these are influenced by values. Furthermore, scientists do not exist in a vacuum. They do their work within institutions that serve various functions and whose values permeate the scientific enterprise. It is not surprising, then, that many psychologists have come to recognize the value-laden quality of their field of study (Haan, 1982; Howard, 1985; Kurtines, Alvarez, & Azmitia, 1990; Manicas & Secord, 1983).

So we see that scientific inquiry indeed involves values. But adopting values does not necessarily undercut objectivity. The old objective–subjective dualism whereby objectivity required eliminating everything subjective has been generally discarded in light of the realization that there is no neutral, objective vantage point from which to view the world. To the extent that objectivity is desirable and possible, it is reached not through "objective" observation but through subjective consensus about the meaning of multiple observations.

At one time the correspondence theory of truth was in vogue—that a theory, observation, or statement was true to the extent that it accurately matched or corresponded to its referent external reality. Let us say that I theorize the following: Aggression in sport, being an effective catharsis, will reduce aggression outside of sport. According to the correspondence theory, the statement is "true" if a complex set of events "actually happen" just as claimed. The fundamental problem with the correspondence theory of truth is that there is no neutral vantage point from which to check the degree of correspondence. Consequently, most contemporary theories of truth, of which there are many variants, subscribe to a more probabilistic and pragmatic notion of truth.

We have found Habermas's work (1971, 1973, 1979, 1983, 1988, 1990) particularly helpful to understanding the relationship between truth and normative commitments. According to Habermas, truth is defined pragmatically as the consensus reached through dialogue. But not every such agreement can be considered truth-identifying; it is possible for a false consensus to emerge. Consequently a test must be implemented to distinguish apparent consensus from true consensus. For Habermas, only when the dialogue that produces the consensus meets certain procedural conditions can the outcome—the consensus—be considered true: The dialogue must be free of all forms of domination and control, and it must implement conditions of freedom and equality. Thus the moral values of freedom and equality are indissolubly united with the quest for truth.

Haan (1982) noted that it is precisely the norms of freedom and equality that lie at the heart of the scientific enterprise. Why do scientific publications, for example, use the process of blind peer review? It is a mechanism for promoting the equal consideration of all evidence regardless of the particular reputation or stature of the researcher. The scientific community has attempted to progress beyond dogmatism and authoritarian dictates not through the use of reason alone, but through the implementation of moral norms in the processes of scientific inquiry and deliberation.

Research on morality can be as objective as any other research, Haan argues, because investigators need not (though some do) make any additional value commitments beyond those already inherent in scientific inquiry. Commitment to freedom and equality, values already implicit in the procedures of science, is the extent of value commitment necessary to investigate human morality.

We turn now to reviewing the major theoretical approaches to morality. As we will see, theorists approach the topic from differing vantage points and arrive at different conclusions. This need not disturb us. There is not a single area of scientific investigation where researchers all agree. We can hope that through the dialogue inspired by different approaches and conclusions, new evidence will emerge that will help us to better understand this complex topic we call morality.

Chapter 1
Coming to Terms With Morality

ORLA: *I don't know, Evette—everyone else is doing it. Why shouldn't I?*

EVETTE: *Not everyone is doing it. I don't. It's against regulations; and who knows what long-term effects those drugs have on your body. Do you really think it's worth the risk?*

ORLA: *Right now, it's hard to look down the road. I'm just interested in winning this year's nationals. And when the judges sit there and look at each contestant, they don't care one bit about whether some of us have taken steroids and others haven't. All they care about is muscle definition and a pretty face.*

EVETTE: *That may be, but there's more to life than winning contests. And it really isn't fair to those of us trying to do it clean.*

> **ORLA:** *Don't preach to me about fairness. You know very well the whole sport reeks of unfairness. What's so fair about a group of men sitting around deciding what feminine beauty is? What's fair about Elaine offering favors for votes? I'll tell you what's not fair; it is having to compete against others who are using drugs to enhance their performance. I just want to have the same advantages they have to win contests and endorse products and pose for magazines. Fair's fair.*

> **EVETTE:** *Maybe. But if you try the drug route, you give up a lot of yourself—more than I'm willing to give up. It comes down to what kind of person you really want to be, what your basic values are.*

Moral values. That is what this book is about. But what can psychologists tell us about human morality? What can scholars reveal about the structure of moral thinking like Orla's and Evette's, or the developmental course that brought them to their current perspectives, or the external influences that may lead them to act in one way as opposed to another? Addressing questions like these is our focus.

In the first section of this chapter, we place morality in a widened perspective by considering how it relates to beliefs, attitudes, and values. We then discuss morality specifically, and distinguish moral values from other values. Finally, we narrow the focus by briefly characterizing moral concepts that are particularly relevant to sport: fair play, sportspersonship, and character.

Beliefs, Attitudes, and Values

Are Orla and Evette talking about a moral issue? If so, what specifically makes the issue moral? Unfortunately, there is no single definition of morality shared by all social scientists, much less all philosophers. One strategy for clarifying a difficult concept is to examine how it relates to a set of related concepts—for morality, we relate it to beliefs, attitudes, and values.

Beliefs

A *belief* may be defined simply as an idea held to be true. Apparently, for example, Orla believes that taking steroids will enhance her likelihood of winning competitions. This simple definition, however, blurs the complexity inherent to the belief construct. Beliefs are complex psychological phenomena with multiple aspects. Beliefs always contain a cognitive component—an *idea* held to be true—but the idea may be ''held'' with a great deal of affect, and an idea may be the blueprint for action.

In *Beliefs, Attitudes, and Values*, Milton Rokeach (1968) helps to order the various meanings of the word "belief" by distinguishing among three different types. First, there are descriptive, or existential, beliefs, capable of being empirically evaluated and designated as true or false. Evaluative beliefs are those that contain a positive or negative judgment about the object of belief. Finally, there are prescriptive or proscriptive beliefs. These beliefs reflect a judgment of desirability or undesirability toward some means or end of action.

A person's moral reasoning makes use of all three types of belief. For an athlete to decide, for example, to cheat in order to win, she first must believe that the behavior is against the rules (a descriptive belief), that the goal of winning is desirable (evaluative belief), and that the use of illegal means to obtain the goal is OK, all things considered (prescriptive belief). Obviously, the last of these beliefs is the most directly tied to moral judgment, but the other forms of belief are clearly implicated as well.

Rokeach (1968) classifies beliefs not only by type but also by their location in what he calls "regions of the person." The point of his metaphoric language is to highlight that some beliefs are more critical, more foundational, and more central to self-identity than others. Blasi and Oresick (1987) write in a vein similar to Rokeach when they suggest that

unlike any other human behavior or process, beliefs seem to act as links connecting actions to the self. . . . Not all beliefs, however, have the same value and the same effects. Some are only peripherally related to our identity. If one acts against such beliefs, one is inconsistent, but in a weak sense. On the other hand, certain beliefs are so central to one's identity that one is compelled to act in accordance with them by psychological necessity; if one fails to do so, one is inconsistent in a strong sense. (p. 72)

Blasi and Oresick (1986, 1987) go on to argue that it may be the development of central beliefs in such ideals as faithfulness, integrity, and fidelity that is crucial to mature moral formation.

Beliefs do not exist in isolation; they cohere in more or less organized systems. Central beliefs, or what Thomas Green (1971) calls core beliefs, are foundational to belief systems. According to Green, core beliefs define the most fundamental features of personality. As one moves up from the roots of the belief tree (from core beliefs, to branches of intermediate beliefs, all the way out to peripheral beliefs that, like leaves of a tree, drop off easily in response to the shifting winds of life) one moves from central motivating beliefs to less significant ones. Thus, an athlete who has a core belief that the world is a dog-eat-dog place where only the strong survive is more likely to expect that all sport competitors will seek to advantage themselves unfairly. Such a moral perspective will in turn influence the athlete's behavioral choices.

Green makes another important point for those interested in sport morality: People have an incredible capacity to hold strongly to beliefs that are inconsistent. People often isolate one set of beliefs from another, so that beliefs about what constitutes moral behavior in a specific arena may be isolated from more general moral beliefs, even if there are clear contradictions. For example, it is not uncommon for athletes to espouse nonviolence in most spheres of life yet to defend intentional injurious behavior in the context of sport.

Attitudes

Although beliefs have cognitive, affective, and behavioral components, they are most readily characterized by the first. In contrast, attitudes, which also have a cognitive dimension, are more affective in character. Researchers have not agreed on a precise definition of the attitude concept, but there is enough overlap in the way it is used to offer a general description: *Attitudes* are dispositions or tendencies to make evaluative judgments concerning objects or events (Eagley & Himmelfarb, 1978).

After surveying the various approaches to attitudes, McGuire (1985) found that most researchers agree that attitudes relate an "object of thought" to a "dimension of judgment." For example, an attitude researcher might investigate basketball fans' acceptance (a dimension of judgment) of participation in competition by athletes who are HIV-positive (an object of thought).

Moral attitudes are only one small subset of the totality of attitudes, but attitudes are certainly important to the field of morality. Attitudes toward the law, human rights, political rivals, and people of other ethnicities, religions, or sexual orientations are but a few illustrations of important moral attitudes.

Attitude research has gone in and out of psychological vogue. The field of social psychology was dominated by attitude research from early in the century to about 1970. When Milton Rokeach wrote *The Nature of Values* (1973), he complained that "empirically oriented social psychologists have paid considerably more attention to the theory and measurement of attitudes than to the theory and measurement of values" (p. 17). However, by the time Rokeach's statement was published, the popularity of attitude research was already waning. In part, the decline reflected the failure of the grand attitude theories to yield as much empirical dividend as was once hoped. Equally important, however, the decline in attitude research was simply a by-product of new interests that caught the attention of researchers, including an interest in values.

Values and the Valuing Process

Of beliefs, attitudes, and values, it is values that are most directly tied to morality. In the next section we will work on discriminating between moral and nonmoral values, but first we will describe more generally the nature of *values*.

In broad terms, two general approaches to values have gained prominence. The first approach highlights values per se and their role in human psychology. The second approach moves away from an explicit analysis of values to the valuing process. To keep our discussion manageable, we highlight one classic work from each of these perspectives. Milton Rokeach's *The Nature of Human Values* (1973) will illustrate the role of values in psychology, whereas *Values and Teaching* by Louis Raths, Merrill Harmin, and Sidney Simon (1966) will represent the process approach.

Values Per Se

According to Rokeach (1973), a value "is an enduring belief that a specific mode of conduct or end-state of existence is personally or socially preferable to an opposite or converse mode of conduct or end-state of existence" (p. 5). Rokeach maintained that values are the most critical component of the human motivational system. In contrast to the large number of attitudes, there are only relatively few values, and they are culturally universal.

Values are subsets of what Rokeach labels prescriptive or proscriptive beliefs. Like beliefs, values have cognitive, affective, and behavioral components. A value contains a cognition about the desirable, either desirable means or desirable ends. And a person who has a value feels an affective bond to what is valued; this bond primarily accounts for the motivational significance of values. Finally, a value leads to action when it is sufficiently strong and activated.

According to Rokeach (1973), values play a central role in our affective and motivational life because they are intimately connected to basic human needs. Rokeach theorized that "values are the cognitive representation and transformation of needs" (p. 20). The biological need for sex, for example, may get transformed and represented in a valuing of love and intimacy. Perhaps most importantly, values serve our need for self-esteem. By our commitment to particular values, we come to value ourselves.

Values reflect not only the transformation of personal needs but the cognitive transformation of societal and institutional needs. In fact, a person's values can be said to result from a dialectical exchange between and merging of personal and social concerns. Society, through its various institutions, socializes the individual to appreciate certain end-states and modes of behavior that are deemed for the common good. But the individual does not passively internalize these values; the content of the socialization process merges with and is transformed by the individual, who brings a unique history and experience to the value formation process.

The valuing of sport success offers an example of the way personal needs are modified and transformed through social processes, and vice versa. There probably are innate needs to feel competent and to esteem oneself, but how these needs are experienced and expressed can be interactively modified by the social context in which we live. In our culture, these needs are frequently embodied (especially for males) in efforts to demonstrate superiority in sporting contexts. Such a transformation is not surprising given the competitive underpinnings of our capitalistic society. In contrast, members of subcultures less enmeshed in capitalism may resist this competitive orientation in favor of a more communal approach. For example, when Allison (1979) studied European American and Navajo high school students, she found that the Navajos were more likely to use sport as a means of reaffirming their relationships with others and were less likely to try to dominate their opponents in sport contests.

Rokeach distinguished between two types of values: *instrumental values*, which concern desirable modes of conduct, and *terminal values*, which concern desirable end-states of existence. He also divided values into the personal and social. The intersection between these classifications produces the following grid:

	Instrumental	Terminal
Personal	Competence values	Personal terminal values
Social	Moral values	Social terminal values

According to Rokeach's scheme, personal terminal values, like inner harmony and prosperity, pertain to desired personal end-states; social terminal values, like equality and world peace, pertain to desired end-states of an interpersonal character. Moral values, including such things as forgiving, helping, and loving, are interpersonal in focus and pertain to the means to bring about desired end-states. Finally, competence values, such as ambition, logic, and intelligence, are means to obtain personal ends.

For a person to deem something valuable, she need not believe that it is desirable for everyone. As Rokeach notes, "a person who informs us about his values may (or may not) intend to apply them differentially to young and old, men and women, blacks and whites, rich and poor, and so on. They may be shared or not shared and thus employed as single or double (or even triple) standards" (1973, p. 10). Rokeach goes on to speculate that "competitive conditions will encourage the employment of values as double standards, whereas cooperation will encourage their employment as single standards" (pp. 10-11). We will discuss the competitive–cooperative issue in more depth in chapter 6, but for now it is interesting to note that competition may shift the way values are employed by the valuer.

The Valuing Process

A quite different approach to values was developed by the educationally oriented team of Raths et al. (1966). The theme of their work is portrayed in the following passage:

> In this book we shall be less concerned with the particular value outcomes of any one person's experiences than we will with the process that he uses to obtain his values. Because life is different through time and space, we cannot be certain what experiences any one person will have. We therefore cannot be certain what values, what style of life, would be most suitable

for any person. We do, however, have some ideas about what *processes* might be most effective for obtaining values. These ideas grow from the assumption that whatever values one obtains should work as effectively as possible to relate one to his world in a satisfying and intelligent way. (p. 28)

Raths et al. (1986) were particularly concerned about the apparent difficulty many children and youths have forming meaningful and satisfying values. They believed several factors had made the formation of values problematic: the bewildering array of choices available to contemporary people, the loosely structured nature of modern community life, frequent travel, and the knowledge boom, facilitated by mass media, that makes the world of human diversity available even to young children. These forces combined had left many children confused, apathetic, and uncommitted. What Raths et al. hoped to do was provide a process approach to values that would help educators in their effort to provide experiences that would lead to value formation.

According to Raths et al. (1986), the valuing process (summarized in Table 1.1) involves three components: choosing, prizing, and acting. Collectively the three components define valuing, and results of the valuing process are called values.

As a definition for value, this description of the valuing process leaves much to be desired, as even supporters of the approach acknowledge (e.g., Kirschenbaum, 1977). There are ambiguities in every process. What is the definition of "freedom" used in the first process of choosing? How many alternatives need to be considered before something is considered a value? Must all the consequences of each alternative be "thoughtfully" considered? How "happy" must a person be with a value candidate before it is a genuine value? And so on. Despite such ambiguities, the processes contain some utility as educational guides, and Raths et al. launched a significant movement, known as values clarification, based on their conception of the valuing process.

Table 1.1   The Valuing Process

Values are based on three processes: choosing, prizing, and acting.

Choosing:	• freely,
	• from alternatives, and
	• after thoughtful consideration of the consequences of each alternative.
Prizing:	• cherishing, being happy with the choice, and being
	• willing to affirm the choice publicly.
Acting:	• doing something with the choice
	• repeatedly, in some pattern of life.

From *Values and Teaching* (p. 30) by L.E. Raths, M. Harmin, and S.B. Simon, 1966, Columbus: Charles Merrill Publishing. Copyright 1966 by Louis E. Raths, Merrill Harmin, and Sidney B. Simon. Reprinted by permission.

Morality

The concept of morality is closely linked to the concept of values. When people are trampled to death in a mad rush for the gates at a soccer match, many of us are morally outraged because we place a high value on human life. Similarly, many are offended when an athlete's drug test turns up positive because we value health, fairness, and honesty. The motivating power of values fuels our moral engines. But how are moral and nonmoral values to be distinguished?

Moral and Nonmoral Values

I may value my bicycle, but that does not make my intent to keep it functioning a moral concern. Many types of values are present in human experience besides the moral—aesthetic, cultural, economic, educational, political, and religious values, to name just a few.

Most theorists would agree that moral and nonmoral values are generally distinguishable. As we discussed earlier, Rokeach (1973) distinguishes moral values from other types:

> The concept of *moral values* is considerably narrower than the general concept of values. For one thing, moral values refer mainly to modes of behavior and do not necessarily include values that concern end-states of existence. For another, moral values refer only to certain kinds of instrumental values, to those that have an interpersonal focus which, when violated, arouse pangs of conscience or feelings of guilt for wrongdoing. Other instrumental values have a personal rather than interpersonal focus and do not seem to be especially concerned with morality. (p. 8)

In our opinion, Rokeach's method for distinguishing moral from nonmoral values is unacceptable, for two reasons. First, it rests on a dualism between means and ends. Morality, for Rokeach, is concerned only with means. But as John Dewey (1929) long ago pointed out, means and ends are relative concepts. Something that is viewed as an end from one perspective may be viewed as a means from another. Winning, for example, may be viewed as an end by competitors during the process of competition. But viewed from another vantage point, winning may be defined as a means to other ends, like buttressing self-esteem or obtaining an athletic scholarship. Even if means and ends could be neatly separated, it is counterintuitive to suggest that morality pertains only to means. Such terminal values as equality and world peace are deeply rooted in concepts of morality, but they are defined outside the moral realm by Rokeach's definition of moral values.

Our second concern with Rokeach's distinction is his intrapersonal versus interpersonal dichotomy. According to Rokeach, only interpersonal values are moral. But why should concern for everyone except oneself be moral? Why splinter off the self and deny it the right of moral consideration? The probable reason is the underlying assumption that self-regard is a threat to truly moral behavior.

Many people, including, apparently, Rokeach, equate morality with altruism, or other-regard. From this perspective, it seems reasonable to conclude that selfish action is a constant threat to moral action. But two lines of argumentation can be mounted to counter this perspective. The first has to do with the concept of "moral character." Certainly one legitimate concern of the moral agent is to cultivate what might be called personal moral virtue; this certainly involves an appropriate focus on intrapersonal values. Secondly, many moral theories focus on one or another interpretation of justice or fairness. What is required to be just or fair is not self-denial, but a balancing or coordination of self-interest with the interests of others. Again, intrapersonal values have a place in this perspective on morality.

The Moral Domain in Cognitive-Developmental Theory

Advocates of the cognitive-developmental approach to psychology have offered another avenue for separating morality from other spheres of life. They believe in the importance of integrating philosophical analysis with psychological investigation. Borrowing heavily from what is called the formalist tradition in ethics, they suggest that a set of formal criteria separate the moral domain from other domains.

Lawrence Kohlberg, whose work we will discuss in detail in later chapters, remains the best known and most influential cognitive-developmental theorist. According to Kohlberg (1976), some values—life, property, authority, conscience, rules, and truthfulness, for example—are universally recognized as important. What separates moral values from nonmoral values, however, is the point of view, or frame of reference, used to reason about them. The "moral point of view" can be characterized as informed by criteria of prescriptivity, impersonality, and universality. When people reason about such values as life, property rights, and truthfulness, for example, they often think in terms of shoulds or oughts (prescriptively), feel all people should be treated the same (impersonally), and believe that people everywhere should follow the same prescriptions (universally). In such cases, people are adopting the moral point of view.

The criteria of prescriptivity, impersonality, and universality are probably the most common ones appealed to by contemporary Western philosophers and psychologists seeking to differentiate the moral domain. But several philosophers (e.g., Blum, 1980; Friedman, 1985; Hampshire, 1983; Noddings, 1984; Philibert, 1987) and psychologists (e.g., Gilligan, 1982; Haan, Aerts, & Cooper, 1985; Kurtines & Gewirtz, 1984; Vine, 1984) have raised serious questions about the adequacy of this perspective. One controversial dimension of the formalist ethical tradition is the claim of universality.

The relativist–universalist debate in moral philosophy is centuries old. In brief, relativists believe that morality is socially determined and that what counts as moral in one context or culture may not be seen as moral in another. In contrast, universalists believe that despite the appearance of moral relativity, there are underlying universal features to morality. A review of this controversy would require a book in itself, so let us simply summarize our own position.

We believe that morality has both universal and relative components. Such fundamental values as human life, health, liberty, and honesty, for example, are universally recognized, if not universally observed. And there is a coherent and universal approach to basic issues of justice and fairness.

The fact that other cultures may develop moral norms that deviate from our culture's way of preserving moral values does not mean that the values themselves are not affirmed. As Turiel (1983) has pointed out, cross-cultural diversity in moral norms is not direct evidence for moral relativism. For example, suppose human sacrifice—to take an extreme—is viewed as acceptable in a particular culture. It cannot be assumed from the existence of human sacrifice that human life is not viewed as highly valuable and that the preservation of life is not taken as a moral norm in that culture. It only means that another value is given higher priority under certain, probably very well defined and delimited, circumstances.

But if some moral values are found in every culture, that does not mean that all or even most moral thinking is reducible to prescriptive, impersonal, and universal reasoning about those values. First, there may be other values that are regarded as moral by a particular group that are at the same time recognized as limited to that group. Human collectives, whether friendship groups, families, sport teams, cultural subgroups, or societies as a whole, may place a particularly high value on something or some mode of conduct yet not believe it should be universalized as a moral norm. A sport team, for example, may develop a moral norm prescribing that team members endorse a charitable cause because "that is part of who we are," but they may well believe that it is not necessary for athletes on other teams to do the same.

Similarly, we hold that some aspects of moral reasoning are appropriately impersonal while others are appropriately personal. We find no compelling reason to exclude from the field of morality, as Kohlberg does, interpersonal agreements that are too contextual and too personally nuanced to be readily universalized. For example, two athletes may over time work out an informal agreement about how they will share training equipment. Wanting to be fair (i.e., moral), the athletes come to agree that one athlete gets the equipment for more time during a less desirable part of the day. Because of the unique needs, interests, schedules, and personalities of the athletes, that agreement is mutually satisfying. But there is no reason to believe that all people under similar circumstances would or should come to the same resolution. Nonetheless, the athletes' agreement takes on the character of a set of morally binding reciprocal obligations that cannot be violated without warrant or discussion.

Morality and Convention

Another cognitive-developmentalist, Elliot Turiel (1983), has focused on the distinction between morality and *convention*. Turiel argues that some of the values Kohlberg includes under the umbrella of morality are more properly considered conventional values. For example, the value of authority may be relative to specific institutional contexts and serve conventional needs more than moral needs. Similarly, some rules, such as prohibitions against stealing, lying, or arbitrary hurting, may be viewed as pertaining to morality, but many others, such as the classroom rule to raise one's hand before speaking, have no such compelling moral underpinnings and function simply to provide order to social systems. It would not make sense to include the social rules under the category of morality, and the two are thus distinguished. We will have occasion to return to Turiel's important work in chapter 8.

Characterizing the Moral Domain

Augusto Blasi (1987, 1990) has offered three criteria that we find helpful and workable to define the moral realm as distinct from other realms. His framework is less rigid than most others and incorporates a broader range of concerns. Blasi has suggested that for the purposes of psychological research, a behavior or practice can be considered moral "if it is intentional, a response to some sense of obligation, and if the obligation is a response to an ideal, even if vaguely understood" (1987, p. 86).

First, moral action is intentional action. Accidental behaviors with good or bad outcomes are not moral action. Second, morality is experienced as prescriptive; a sense of ought or necessity accompanies the belief that an action comprises the "moral thing to do." Finally, the sense of prescriptivity arises from a more or less clearly perceived ideal, from a conception of the nature of good and right relationships among humans, and—potentially—between humans and the totality of creation. In this book we are concerned with a broad range of phenomena that fit this loose approach to morality.

Morality in the Context of Sport

To close this chapter we consider sport as a moral practice. It is important to begin by stating clearly what we do not intend to say. We are not claiming that the purpose of sport is to promote moral development, nor are we suggesting that sport participants frequently frame their activity in moral terms. We do maintain, however, that morality is as relevant to sport as to other spheres of life. Blasi's description of the moral domain fits sport quite nicely. Certainly many actions in sport are intentional. Furthermore, many reflect a sense of obligation arising from a clearly or dimly perceived "ideal sport contest."

Our basis for claiming that sport is a moral practice also reflects three main lines of argument, which can be only hinted at here. First, participants in sport are real people with genuine interests. Putting on a sport uniform does not demand disrobing one's status as a moral agent. Although sport may be described as "nonserious" from one standpoint, participants are serious about their desire to strive hard, seek victory, and avoid being "cheated."

Evidence that sport is a moral practice also comes from the fact that participants and observers alike sometimes employ moral categories to evaluate sport behavior. Some behavior in sport is deemed praiseworthy, other behavior evokes moral condemnation. If sport were not a moral practice, moral categories could not be applied to applaud or challenge sport behaviors.

Finally, and perhaps most important, sport is a moral practice because the moral concepts of fairness and freedom undergird its very foundations. Sport is a physical contest in which contestants choose to engage. Sport is an activity freely chosen, and it is specifically and explicitly designed as a "fair" contest. To undermine the fairness built into the structure and process of sport would be to annihilate its authenticity as a mode of human self-expression and enjoyment.

If sport is a moral practice, in whole or in part, we should expect there to be a vocabulary that reflects an understanding of sport morality. We'll introduce here three terms that we will use and elaborate on in other parts of the book: *fair play, sportspersonship*, and *character*.

Fair Play

Sport is a form of contest, and all contests depend on fair competition. Competition is often viewed as the opposite of cooperation, but it actually can be seen as a special form of cooperation. In a contest, two or more competitors cooperate, each providing the other with a worthy challenge that enables each participant to exhibit her or his best performance. Determination of a "winner" requires that all cooperate in upholding the conditions of fairness. *Fair play* necessitates that competitors understand and abide by not only the formal rules of play but also the spirit of cooperation needed to insure a fair contest.

The concept of fair play has spawned many valuable efforts to restore or maintain the integrity of sport. A 1963 seminar sponsored by the International Sports Press Association and the International Council of Sport and Physical Education (ICSPE), for example, was an important catalyst for the promotion of a European fair play movement. The purpose of the seminar was to address developments, particularly violent behaviors, that were detracting from the integrity of sport. The meeting led to the initiation of International Fair Play Trophies, awarded to athletes and teams in recognition of extraordinary demonstrations of a "sporting spirit." The seminar also paved the way for the development of the International Committee for Fair Play in the mid-1960s.

In the early 1970s, the International Committee for Fair Play, seeking to enlarge and decentralize its action, urged the creation of national fair play committees that would work in close cooperation with national Olympic Committees, sport organizations, and the sport media. The French Committee for Fair Play published an influential brochure on fair play in 1971, and UNESCO commissioned the

ICSPE, in cooperation with the International Olympic Committee, to draft a similar document that could be disseminated internationally. After the brochure's publication, an ad hoc "commission of experts," including representatives from a variety of countries and international sport organizations, then published a revised document: the "Declaration on Fair Play." The Declaration summarizes the concept of fair play in the following terms:

> [Fair play] requires as a minimum that [the competitor] shows strict, unfailing observance of the written rule. This will be the easier if [the competitor] appreciates the purpose of the rule and if [the competitor] recognizes that beyond the written rule there is a right spirit in which to engage in competitive sport. (p. 2)

The document goes on to identify specific behavioral responsibilities associated with 10 different roles in the sport context and recommends specific strategies for encouraging fair play in sport.

Building on these fair play efforts, the Council of Europe, an international organization of 25 democratic countries, in 1989 invited its Committee for the Development of Sport to launch a coordinated research project among member countries, conducting parallel studies in order to develop common policies and lines of action to encourage fair play. Though this research group has yet to publish its findings or recommendations, we look forward to the continued theoretical, empirical, and practical work of the Council of Europe.

In conclusion, let us emphasize that fair play is not relevant only to sport participants. It is equally central to everyone who has an impact on the formation, structure, and practice of sport: coaches and officials, spectators, parents (in youth sports), journalists and broadcasters, sports organizations, business people, and so on. It is neither fair nor practical to put the entire weight of fair play on the shoulders of athletes.

Sportspersonship

Another vital sport term with significant moral importance is sportsmanship, or as we prefer, *sportspersonship*. The concept has a rich history (cf. Chambers, 1984) and has spurred considerable, if somewhat problematic, empirical research.

James Keating (1964) is the sport philosopher most responsible for modern reflection on sportspersonship. Keating defines it as behavior becoming of a sportsperson. Behind this seemingly straightforward assertion is a complex set of ideas that need to be unraveled, with Keating's distinction between sport and athletics being paramount. Keating reserves the term *sport* exclusively for recreational activities that are engaged in for diversion and fun, and sportspersonship refers to the spirit of moderation and generosity that is appropriately exercised in such contexts. The virtue of sportspersonship is oriented toward maximizing the enjoyable experience of all participants.

Athletics, unlike sports, says Keating, are competitive activities where the primary goal is winning the contest. Rather than being infused with a spirit of fun, athletics are characterized by dedication, sacrifice, and intensity, and the appropriate virtue is fair play. It would be too much to expect sportspersonship in athletics, according to Keating.

In chapter 10 we elaborate a somewhat different view of sportspersonship. While retaining Keating's emphasis on a connection between sportspersonship and a spirit of play, we disagree with his radical separation of sport and athletics. In fact, it is precisely when competition is heated, when winning matters, that the concept of sportspersonship is most relevant. In brief, we maintain that sportspersonship involves the simultaneous dedication to the internal goals of sport and a play spirit; only this conjunction will allow ethical behavior to be chosen when it conflicts with success strategy.

Character

"Sport builds character" has been a popular claim for decades. Whatever its empirical status, the sentiment points to the importance that has been attached to sport as an institution of positive socialization.

The term *character* for most people has moral overtones—one desires to have "good" character, not "bad." But character, as a construct, is one of the most murky in the field of psychology. It has been defined in incredibly broad ways and still has not garnered anything approaching consensus, let alone operational definition. But despite these heavy limitations, the character-building potential of sport continues to be heralded.

One of our purposes is to identify four critical processes that function together in the promotion of moral action. We then use the four processes to define a conception of character that may be incomplete and diverge from other conceptions at crucial points but that at least has enough specificity to allow empirical investigation. In short, we suggest that character can be considered in terms of four virtues: compassion, fairness, sportspersonship, and integrity. Elaboration on these terms must await the laying of groundwork in subsequent chapters.

Summary

In this chapter we have sought to briefly survey the terrain of moral psychology, describing how beliefs, attitudes, and values intersect but do not define the moral domain. We have mentioned Kohlberg's influential work on "a moral point of view" and have highlighted Blasi's broader conceptualization of the moral realm. Finally, we indicated some of the ways sport is a moral practice, grounded in principles of fairness and freedom. In the remainder of the book we attempt to fill in details of the map we have sketched. To do this adequately, we need to offer our historical perspective on the field of moral psychology. To this task we now turn.

Chapter 2
Moral Development: The First Generation

Malia is a star college tennis player, greatly respected both for her high national ranking and her scrupulous honesty on the court. For example, on a crucial point in the championship game at last year's nationals, she called her opponent's serve good even though the line judge indicated it was out. When asked why she risked losing the match by contradicting the line judge's call, Malia talked about the importance of fair play and the role of honesty in all human relationships. Malia has a well-developed sense of morality, one that is integrated into her personality and guides her behavior, on and off the tennis court. But how did Malia develop such moral maturity? What processes are involved in moral growth and development? That is the issue addressed in this part of the book.

Dizzying detail might be presented in a summary of a century of research on moral development. To keep our presentation focused and manageable, we have concentrated only on the major research traditions that have gained significant following. Also, we do not give equal space to all major theories; favoring those that lay the foundation for later units in the book, we emphasize structural developmental theories. With these two caveats in mind, we have worked to present an accurate and useful overview.

In this chapter, we examine three of the earliest approaches to moral development, highlighting the work of Freud, Hartshorne and May, and Piaget. In chapters 3 and 4, we review more recent developments in the field of moral psychology, which build on the pioneering work reviewed in this chapter.

Freud and the Psychoanalytic Approach

How does an essentially selfish, impulse-ridden infant mature into a socialized, moral individual? Besides revealing Sigmund Freud's assumptions about human nature, this question guides his theory of moral development. In Freud's view (cf. Freud, 1933/1965, 1959), moral development bridged the gap between two sets of conflicting demands—those of instinct and society. Freud posited that individuals are motivated by life instincts (eros) and death instincts (thanatos) to engage in sex and aggression. Because these essentially self-serving behaviors create a natural antagonism among individuals, society must protect people from one another and preserve cultural achievements by curbing instinctual expression or channeling (sublimating) it into activities that support social aims. If our sexual and aggressive appetites were not curbed by social processes, Freud maintained, civilization quickly would be overrun and destroyed by unruly and unrestrained pleasure-seekers.

Moral development, for Freud, was a battle that must be fought anew by each parent, seen as representing society, with each infant in a regular sequence of events. Typically it is not a conscious battle, but the warfare image is appropriate because of the threat to civilization that the unsocialized child represents. Let us trace Freud's hypothesized process for an imaginary child, Ali.

Sex and aggression, the two basic instincts fundamental to Freud's theory of psychosexual development, both play an important part in Ali's moral development. During infancy, Ali is controlled by these and other biologically rooted instincts. When an instinct is aroused, it motivates and guides Ali's behavior until it is satisfied, returning him to a state of constancy.

According to Freud's theory, Ali will pass through a regular sequence of stages in the nature and focus of his sexual instinct, centering first on oral satisfaction, shifting next to the anal region, and then moving to the genital region during what Freud called the phallic stage. During this period an important transition occurs: The focus of Ali's sexual interest shifts from himself to another person. The desired object of sexual gratification generally becomes the mother for boys and the father for girls (Freud did not theorize about nontraditional family units). As Ali becomes sexually interested in his mother, he comes to view his father as a rival. Logically enough, Ali's aggression instinct becomes focused on his father, whom he views as vying for the attention of the parent he desires, his mother. The stage is now set for the decisive battle: the Oedipal conflict.

Freud claimed that the Oedipal conflict is waged within the psyche of a young child from about 4 to 6 years of age. Caught in a powerless position, Ali finds himself in a state of inner tension and turmoil. Due to the highly energized nature of his sexual and aggressive instincts, neither of which are finding their desired route to gratification, Ali's experience of conflict is quite intense. Furthermore, he is caught in a web of ambivalence because of his continuing emotional attachment to his father, who is now also the object of his aggressive intent. The turmoil leads to a variety of unpleasant fantasies, thoughts, and affects, including Ali's fear that his father may physically hurt him (castration anxiety).

Given no possibility of winning the Oedipal conflict through direct instinctual expression, Freud postulated a rather amazing series of processes that transform the dynamics of the child's psychological life. In brief, the Oedipal conflict is resolved through a suppression of the sexual desire for the other-sex parent and an identification with the same-sex parent (If you can't beat 'em, join 'em). Unable to compete successfully with his father, Ali instead identifies with him. This identification leads Ali to internalize his father's values and standards, which in turn leads to the formation of a new psychic structure—the superego. Ali's superego features two subsystems, the conscience and the ego ideal. The conscience has a basically negative function, operating as a repressor of instinctual desire, a dream sensor, and a punisher of the ego—the conscious component of the individual—for deviations from dictates of the superego. Ali's ego ideal incorporates a set of moral standards or values—adopted from his father—that Ali now embraces and seeks to personify.

From a social perspective, the formation of Ali's superego reflects the victory of society over the unsocialized individual. But just as society needs a police force to insure that its norms are followed, so the individual needs an internal mechanism to keep the instincts under control. This is accomplished through a major transformation of the aggression instinct. Rather than focusing on his father, Ali turns his aggression inward, and when he deviates from the internalized standards of his superego, the aggression instinct gets expressed as guilt.

Freud maintained that the Oedipal conflict and the resultant identifications, internalizations, and transformations all go on below the level of conscious awareness. But this does not mean that they are invisible to the careful observer. The themes of the Oedipal conflict, according to psychoanalytic theorists, are reenacted in numerous contexts, such as in children's play (Bettelheim, 1977). Thus, children often work through the dynamics of their own moral development through the symbolic medium of playful physical activity.

To summarize, morality, according to Freud, is an outgrowth of the emotional turmoil connected to the Oedipal conflict. Thus, moral issues are at root emotional issues, and moral behavior is equivalent to integrated drive-satisfaction. Correspondingly, immoral behavior can erupt from unconscious motivations despite the presence of apparently sound moral reasoning, for moral reasoning is simply seen as rationalization.

The psychoanalytic approach to moral development has been challenged along a number of lines. First, it is difficult to submit the theory to empirical verification. The highly speculative nature of the underlying psychodynamic processes that are hypothesized makes the theory as a whole difficult to either verify or refute. The theory is flexible enough that in the hands of an imaginative and skillful theorist almost any empirical finding can be made consistent with the basic thrust of the approach.

A second concern is that Freud's theory emphasizes the experience of males, resulting in a distorted and negative view of female morality. It is no accident that we depicted a male child in our illustration. The female journey toward moral maturity is less clearly articulated by Freud and is based on a male-as-normative model (Freud, 1905/1962, 1925/1961). Because girls do not come into the world with a penis, Freud reasoned, they have no reason to fear its castration. But castration anxiety is for Freud crucial to the successful resolution of the Oedipal complex and the formation of the superego. Consequently, women do not develop a strong superego, and their morality cannot be held to the high standards of male morality.

A final critique is that the nature of morality is fundamentally misrepresented by Freud's view, in which morality is equated with an irrational commitment to internalized social norms, a perspective that led Heinz Hartmann (1960) to observe that psychoanalysis can produce an integrated personality but not a good person. Moral cognitions are irrelevant from the psychoanalytic perspective; in fact, moral reasoning is dismissed as defensive rationalization. But in their everyday experience most people believe that their moral behavior reflects reasons, not irrational, subconscious processes. Of course, they may be mistaken. But before we discard such a fundamental and commonsense understanding, we need clear evidence of its inadequacy. In fact, as we shall see, there is ample support for a cognitive interpretation of morality.

Hartshorne and May and the Moral Trait Approach

Early in the century Hugh Hartshorne and Mark May, together with their colleagues J.B. Maller and F.K. Shuttleworth, conducted a highly influential series of studies on moral character, published between 1928 and 1930 in three volumes: *Studies in Deceit, Studies in Service and Self-Control*, and *Studies in the Organization of Character*.

Hartshorne and May wanted to find out whether morality was a general character trait. Congruent with the psychological perspectives of the time, ''good character'' was equated with a set of moral virtues; that is, moral people were seen as honest, fair, helpful, and the like. The desirable moral virtues were in turn hypothesized to consist of a coherent and integrated set of beliefs, attitudes, and behaviors. A moral person was someone who knew right from wrong (belief), was disposed to view moral violations as reprehensible (attitude), and acted accordingly (behavior).

Two questions in particular guided Hartshorne and May's research: Are moral virtues demonstrated consistently across situations? (For example, are people who are honest in one situation honest in others?) And can people's moral behavior be predicted by knowing their moral attitudes and beliefs?

Hartshorne and May frequently used game and sport contexts to assess morality among children. In *Studies in the Nature of Character* (Vol. 1), they described using a school athletic contest to assess girls' and boys' honesty. In this study, 2,175 girls and boys in grades 4 through 10 were told that their school was holding a "physical ability contest" and that specific handicaps had been arranged to give all a chance to win a badge in each of four events: grip strength, lung capacity, pull-ups, and the standing long jump. For each of the four events, the examiner first demonstrated the task and then directed the student to do a specific number of trials. After being "coached and urged" by the examiner to achieve a good practice trial score, the student was instructed to perform a specified number of "contest" trials when alone and report the best performance. Hartshorne and May assumed that if any self-recorded score was higher than the best practice trial score, deception had taken place.

When Hartshorne and May compared the athletic contest results with data from other measures of honesty, they found only low correlations between tests. Concluding that there was little evidence for a general trait of honesty, they proposed the "doctrine of specificity." Virtues like honesty, they wrote, should be viewed not as unified character traits but as specific behaviors that correspond to specific life situations. Individual behavior is a function of the environment, not of internal processes.

These monumental studies were highly discouraging to those interested in the development of moral character. Following the publication of Hartshorne and May's conclusions, the topic of morality almost disappeared from psychology journals. Moral research was temporarily banished to the sidelines as behavioristic approaches to psychology moved into center court in the middle of the century. If all behavior is under the control of environmental contingencies, then there is little place for special study of morality.

From a vantage point improved by 60 years of continued theoretical and empirical developments in the social sciences, we can now see numerous difficulties in Hartshorne and May's studies. One critique centers on methodological concerns. For example, a simple reevaluation of the data, grouping similar behaviors into a single measure rather than treating them separately, has been shown to yield more positive results than Hartshorne and May found (Rushton, 1980).

Perhaps the most telling flaw, however, stems from an inadequate theory of moral reasoning. Hartshorne and May hoped to find a high correlation between moral thought and moral action, but thought was tapped only at the level of specific belief. In other words, if a child said "cheating is wrong" and then cheated in a particular test of honesty, Hartshorne and May arrived at the understandable conclusion that the child was inconsistent. Based on this approach, they found inconsistency to be the norm. But what they ignored was another commonsense observation, namely that most people, while believing that honesty is right generally, accept dishonesty as morally appropriate in some circumstances. In other words, Hartshorne and May did not take account of reasoning patterns that underlie specific moral beliefs and behavior.

In 1976, Turiel administered "moral knowledge" tests similar to those used by Hartshorne and May to subjects between 10 and 16 years of age. Most earlier studies had been done with younger children, with the general conclusion that by the time children reach the second grade they obtain high scores on such tests. With older subjects, however, Turiel found that as age increased, test scores actually declined. The most probable interpretation is not that moral knowledge degenerates with age, but that as children get older they become aware of mitigating circumstances that might call for more qualified and complex moral judgments. It is this kind of underlying process of reasoning that went unstudied by Hartshorne and May.

Ironically, the weaknesses of Hartshorne and May's approach to the moral consistency question were being addressed by an independent investigator in Switzerland at the same time as Hartshorne and May were publishing their disconcerting conclusions.

Piaget and the Structural Developmental Approach

In the school athletic contest, Hartshorne and May left their subjects alone to complete their trials. Across the Atlantic, Jean Piaget was down on his hands and knees playing marbles with children (Piaget, 1932/1965). Their different physical locations symbolize their theoretical approaches. Hartshorne and May were not interested in understanding morality from the child's point of view. What they wanted to know was whether the children understood moral rules as enunciated by adults and to what extent the children followed those rules. Their approach paralleled that of intelligence investigators who designed tests for children and then evaluated the young test takers' responses according to the extent to which they produced the answers that adults consider right. It was in fact intelligence tests that first interested Piaget in children's reasoning.

Piaget wanted to discover why children answered some IQ test questions incorrectly. He found that children's mistakes were not random—there was a regular pattern to their errors. Furthermore, after interviewing children about their understanding of the test items, Piaget found that from the logical outlook of children, the answers made perfect sense. He discovered that children's thinking can be distinguished from adult thinking not only in terms of the amount of knowledge in their grasp but also according to the way that knowledge is organized. Children differ qualitatively, not just quantitatively, from mature reasoners.

Thus, when Piaget turned his attention to children's morality, he engaged children in discussion and joint activity so that he could understand morality from their perspective.

Cognitive Development

Before summarizing Piaget's key findings about morality, we will highlight the major tenets of his general theory of cognitive development. Piaget, a main architect of the structural developmental approach in psychology, held that there is an underlying cognitive structure to manifest thought and behavior. People do not simply internalize their experience, they seek to interpret it and organize it into meaningful patterns by activating structures of cognition that have arisen out of previous interactions with the environment. Thus, Piaget advocated a *constructivist epistemology*, a belief that knowledge is constructed out of one's interactions with the physical and social environment. This perspective stands in stark contrast to the unidirectional, stimulus–response concept of mental formation espoused by behaviorists, some social learning theorists, and trait theorists like Hartshorne and May.

Piaget distinguished two interdependent aspects of the thought process—the figurative and the operative. The figurative aspect of thought, which refers to its content, is primarily descriptive and representational. The following, for example, are figurative schemas (i.e., cognitive representations): a mental picture of a softball, a rule about manners, a number, a name. In contrast, the operative aspect of thought refers to the underlying rules by which figurative schema are combined, transformed, or otherwise "operated" on.

According to Piaget, children's first source of knowledge is their physical experience in the environment. Children's early behavioral interactions with physical and social objects are the foundation on which all their later cognitive abilities are built. Through such interaction, children expand their repertoires of figurative schemas and develop increasingly complex operative schemes (i.e., mental and physical action blueprints). Piaget characterized the older child's "operative" cognitive activity as interiorized action. In other words, the developing child learns to perform mental actions with symbols that are extensions and refinements of the kinds of physical actions that could be done directly with physical objects.

The process through which cognitive structures are developed and transformed is *equilibration*. Piaget, whose first writings were in biology, saw equilibration as the process of cognitively adapting to the environment. Equilibration in turn comprises two interdependent components: assimilation and accommodation. By *assimilation* Piaget meant that process whereby the child comprehends something in the environment by using existing structures of understanding. Assimilation does not force internal cognitive change, because the environment is made to fit existing meaning structures.

Many of a child's experiences, on the other hand, do not neatly fit the expectations arising from existing cognitive structures. They are not easily assimilated. Instead, they require *accommodation*—a modification, refinement, reorganization, or transformation of existing cognitive structures. Through assimilation the child modifies experience to fit existing structures of meaning, and through accommodation the child modifies mental structures to fit experience. In reality, assimilation and accommodation are usually engaged simultaneously, and experience is partly assimilated and partly results in accommodation. Through assimilation and accommodation, the developing child's cognitive structures become increasingly complex and integrated.

Piaget maintained that assimilation and accommodation inevitably lead to a regular sequence of age-related changes in the structures of cognition, proposing that the growing child passes through an orderly hierarchy of stages in cognitive development. The stage concept is crucial to Piagetian theory, and we will detail it before moving on to Piaget's theory of moral development.

Two distinctions are important to the stage concept. First, it rests on a distinction between the content of thought (the figurative aspect) and its underlying structure (the operative aspect). The stage structure itself is content-free, is rarely conscious, and can only be inferred from a series of observations regarding the organization of various contents. Second, the stage concept rests on a distinction between competence and performance. One's current stage of development defines one's competence at a given class of tasks, but one's actual performance in any given instance may deviate from one's maximum competence due to a multitude of personal and situational factors.

Three other concepts also are important for understanding Piagetian stage theory. First, stages imply an *invariant sequence*. Every child in every culture passes through the same sequence of stages, step-by-step. Not every child attains the highest of the stages, nor does every child progress through the stages at the same rate, but to get to any particular stage, each prior stage must have been passed through in the specified order. Each succeeding stage builds on insights gained during the preceding stage, reorganizing those insights into a more complex and sophisticated perspective. For example, a child will grasp the concept of number before the principles of arithmetic, which in turn precede an understanding of algebraic functions, and so on.

Second, stages define *structured wholes*—they reflect coherent organizations of thought that cut across a variety of content areas. In Piaget's early work stages were defined so globally that almost all cognition was included in a single structural organization (Piaget, 1923). Later, recognizing that the child develops differentiated types of knowledge, Piaget modified the structured wholes characteristic of the stage concept. For example, he separated stages of logical-mathematical understanding from stages of comprehending physical concepts (Piaget, 1970a, 1970b, 1977; Turiel, 1983).

Finally, stages are *hierarchical integrations*. Each succeeding stage in the progression is more adequate than the preceding one. Piaget's concept of adequacy is based in the biological idea of adaptation: Each higher stage is better able to deal with the complexities of experience and is therefore more adapted to the environment. Specifically, each succeeding stage is more differentiated (able to take account of finer distinctions and more pieces of information) and more integrated (able to coordinate and synthesize information).

Moral Development

With these comments as background, we can now summarize Piaget's key findings about moral development. You will recall that Hartshorne and May concluded that no general trait of morality existed and that moral behavior was situationally determined. This conclusion reflected their two-fold observation that children who were honest in one situation were not necessarily honest in others and that children who scored high on a moral knowledge or attitude test did not necessarily act morally in a behavioral test. Piaget's major contribution was to demonstrate that surface inconsistencies may reflect a deeper consistency.

Piaget conceived of morality as rule-governed behavior (1932/1965). He believed that the essence of moral development could be best understood by studying how children at different ages respect rules of the social order and interpret justice—a sense of the rights of people stemming from considerations of equality, social contract, and reciprocity in human relations. Because games are governed by rules and are easily observed, Piaget decided to use marble games as one context for studying children's conceptions of morality (1932/1965). As Swiss children between the ages of 5 and 13 played marbles in the streets of Geneva, Piaget quizzed them about such things as where the rules came from, whether or not it would be all right to change them, and whether the rules had changed over time. Piaget found that younger children and older children had very different ideas about rules.

Under about 6 years of age, children thought rules were unalterable and the result of adult authority. For these children, notions of right and wrong were tethered to externally determined, authority-based rules. Ironically, although children at this stage believe in the importance of rule conformity, they often violate the rules when playing games. The apparent paradox dissolves, however, when one discovers, as Piaget did, that the children were acting according to how they understood game rules, not in accordance with how adults (or older children) interpreted them. Piaget labeled this phase of moral development *heteronomous morality*. He believed that its essential features involve a natural outgrowth of two interacting forces: the child's egocentrism and the child's unilateral respect for and emotional attachment to adults.

Piaget postulated that *egocentrism*, thinking that is unable to move beyond the limits of direct, individual experience, is a global characteristic of young children's thinking. One consequence of egocentrism is a confusion between subjective and objective reality. Thus, children in early development believe that dreams actually happen, that the sun follows them, and that social rules are like physical laws. They see moral rules as an intrinsic part of the physical operation of the world. Violation of a moral rule, in young children's thinking, will invariably result in something bad happening—a belief that Piaget labeled *imminent justice*.

In addition to egocentrism, a second dynamic is operative in early childhood. Most of the child's social interactions are characterized by an exchange among unequals. Because children have at best a rudimentary understanding of growth and development, it appears to them that the world contains two classes of people: children and adults. Adults know the truth about the world, and children respect and follow the dictates of adults. Piaget called this a relation of constraint. Such a view of social reality leads the child to believe that what the adult says about moral rules is intrinsically right and invariant. This belief, in turn, buttresses similar conclusions that originate from the child's egocentrism, and thus the two forces of egocentrism and constraint are mutually reinforcing.

Between the ages of about 6 and 12, however, children experience changes in the two processes that are the structuring principles of heteronomous morality. First, a process of *decentering* leads to the abandonment of egocentrism. The child comes to appreciate multiple perspectives, can differentiate subjective experience from objective realities, and distinguishes clearly the social and physical realms. In the social realm, peers become important, and cooperative relationships supersede relations of constraint as the reference point for an understanding of social norms. These advances lead to a major reshuffling of the child's moral perspective. Rules come to be seen as alterable by consensus, as originating in cooperative activity, and as having a history of change and development. Piaget labeled this phase *autonomous morality*, or a morality of cooperation.

Piaget's moral investigations were not limited to children's perspectives on the rules of marbles. He also focused on their conceptions of justice, developing a questioning technique he referred to as the ''clinical interview'' to probe the underlying structure of children's moral reasoning. Typically, he would tell the children a pair of stories that differed in some crucial aspect and then ask them about the differences. For example, in one famous story pair he told first about a girl who accidentally broke a whole tray of cups as she was carrying them to the dining room to set the table, then described a second girl who broke a single cup while climbing a kitchen counter in pursuit of a forbidden treat. After telling the stories, Piaget would ask, ''Which child do you think was naughtier?'' Depending on the response, he would follow up with additional questions to reveal more about the child's underlying structure of reasoning.

Piaget's conclusions about children's justice reasoning generally conformed to the pattern exhibited in his investigation of their understanding of the rules of marbles. Younger children's reasoning was structured by the twin dynamics of egocentrism and unilateral respect, whereas older children's judgments were based on an understanding of cooperative relations. Responding to the cup stories, younger children said that the girl who broke more cups was naughtier, whereas older children identified the child who broke one cup in the process of doing something wrong as the more culpable.

Piaget's influence on the study of moral development has been enormous. The single work he published on the subject was the spark that ignited a multitude of studies by others. As Piaget's conclusions underwent careful scrutiny, several significant criticisms emerged and many of the details of his moral theory have been discarded. A complete review of these critiques and revisions is neither necessary for our purposes nor feasible, so we will offer only a sampling (see Lickona, 1976b, for a more complete review).

The issue of rule flexibility has been extensively studied. Epstein (1965) conducted one of the more interesting investigations, discussed by Lickona (1976b) in a review of Piagetian moral literature. Epstein found it crucial to investigate children's comprehension of rules before directly analyzing their view of whether rules can be changed. Young children often confuse the issue of changing a rule and breaking it. Once children can make that differentiation, however, they believe that changing rules within the spheres of activity over which they have control is OK but that rules that mediate between subordinates in a hierarchy are unchangeable by the subordinate. Thus, children at a relatively young age accept that the rules of a game among equals can be changed, but this flexibility is not generalized to students' changing classroom rules or teachers' changing rules passed down from the principal. Turiel (1983) elaborates this insight further by developing a sophisticated categorization of types of rules and the domains of cognition to which they relate.

One of the most important critiques of Piaget's theory has to do with his stage concept. Observing that aspects of heteronomous and autonomous morality coexist within the same child, Piaget suggested that the stages be viewed as overlapping. Still, his stage concept implies that the various aspects of morality should cohere in some form of organized whole. This hypothesis, however, has not received much support (Lickona, 1976b).

Despite these and similar critiques, Piaget's work continues to be a source of innovation and inspiration in the field of moral development. One of Piaget's permanent contributions was his emphasis on studying morality from the child's point of view. From this perspective, the moral quality of a given behavior is not determined by whether it conforms to adult standards (à la Hartshorne and May) but rather by the meaning that the behavior has for the actor. Piaget also provided methodological innovation by developing his clinical interview technique, which was a breakthrough in psychologists' ability to investigate the underlying structures that pattern children's thought.

Summary

The complementary efforts of Freud, Hartshorne and May, and Piaget helped to shape a foundation of psychological theorizing on moral development. Freud concluded from his therapeutic work with adults that morality is an irrational but socially desirable artifact of the affective turmoils of early childhood. Hartshorne and May studied children's overt behavior in various contexts, concluding that children's moral behavior is not consistent; they advanced the doctrine of specificity, contending that morality is specific to the situation, not to the person. Piaget studied children's reasoning and proposed that beneath surface inconsistencies in children's verbal or behavioral responses is a coherent structure of reasoning.

In the next two chapters we build on this first generation of moral theorizing by examining the contributions of a second generation of theorists. Chapter 3 focuses on theories reflecting an internalization approach, the belief that what is moral is what a given society defines as moral and that moral development is synonymous with internalizing dominant cultural values. In chapter 4 we discuss the constructivist approach, which encompasses those structural developmental theorists who advance a more active, knowledge-constructing role for the individual.

Chapter 3
Internalization Approaches to Moral Development

There are two main contemporary approaches to the psychological investigation of morality, each resting on different fundamental assumptions about the person, the nature of morality, and the dynamics of moral learning. According to the *internalization* approach, people are driven by irrational (or nonrational) forces, morality is equated with existent social mores, and the processes of moral learning pertain to the mechanisms by which moral norms and prosocial behavioral propensities are internalized. In contrast, *constructivist* theorists posit a truth-seeking and reality-forming human agent; define morality as a domain of social cognition grounded in conceptions of just, fair, and caring relations; and envision moral development as a process of constructing an increasingly sophisticated grasp of how moral action is situated within a web of human interdependency. In this chapter, we will focus on internalization approaches. Constructivist approaches are taken up in chapter 4.

The concept of internalization is central to two major theoretical perspectives in psychology: psychoanalytic and social learning. These two approaches differ radically, yet they share common assumptions about moral development. Three of these assumptions are critical. First, both psychoanalytic and social learning theorists characterize moral development as a process of moving what is initially outside the individual to the inside. Moral growth occurs as a child is socialized to embrace social norms. Second, in both approaches morality is essentially nonrational; whether a cultural value or norm is reasonable is immaterial. In fact, the question, Is cultural practice X right? is meaningless. Theorists define culture as the ultimate moral reference point. Third, both psychoanalysts and social learning theorists see moral learners as relatively passive vis-à-vis moral content. Psychoanalytic theorists emphasize instinctive drives and unconscious mental agencies, and social learning theorists point to the role of socializing agents in modeling and reinforcing prosocial behavior. Neither approach emphasizes a reflective, reasoning, creative human.

We begin by examining the post-Freudian psychoanalytic approach, then turn to social learning theory. We conclude with the eclectic theory of Martin Hoffman, who combines aspects of several approaches but still highlights the process of internalization.

Post-Freudian Psychoanalytic Theory

Several developments have occurred in the psychoanalytic movement since the time of Freud. A number of reviews of contemporary psychoanalytic perspectives on morality are available, and the interested reader may wish to consult them (Ekstein, 1978; Emde, Johnson, & Easterbrooks, 1987; Holder, 1982). Here we limit our discussion to noting a few significant trends.

Various theorists have modified Freud's account of the formation of the superego, often finding pre-Oedipal roots to superego formation (Holder, 1982; Kennedy & Yorke, 1982; Spitz, 1958). Scholars have also proposed new or revised psychodynamic mechanisms to account for the complexity of moral consciousness. Spitz, for example, has posited that during their second year toddlers acquire a "semantic no" that becomes a tool for expressing aggression against parents. Later, children transform the principle of negation into the moral potential of self-criticism.

Another psychodynamic mechanism, attachment, was introduced by Bowlby (1958, 1969), who suggested that children seek to maintain a sense of security through maintaining physical proximity to a caretaker. The importance of attachment, a concept operationally defined by Ainsworth et al. (1978), is accepted by many contemporary developmental scholars. Sroufe (1983) demonstrated through longitudinal studies that attachment in infancy is linked with empathy and control of aggression in the preschooler.

In a provocative book titled *Freud, Women, and Morality*, Eli Sagan (1988) argues that Freud's notion of the superego arose from his ambivalence about women and that he missed the more central psychic structure of morality—the conscience—precisely because it originates in the infant's relationship to its mother. In contrast to the Oedipal dynamics, the compassionate and nurturing maternal relationship provides a nonconflictual space for moral internalizations, according to Sagan.

Arguably the most thorough revision of the psychoanalytic perspective on morality was developed by Erik Erikson (1962, 1964), who postulated that the human life cycle can be divided into eight phases, each defined by a crisis structured by two opposing possibilities. The successful resolution of each life crisis depends on the development of a particular virtue. Together, the virtues that emerge from the struggles of each phase contour the person's moral character. In order of development, these virtues are hope, will, purpose, competence, fidelity, love, care, and wisdom.

Other changes in the psychoanalytic perspective have come about as the metatheory gradually shifted from a focus on drive reduction to a concern with the person as an adaptive, self-regulatory system (Gill & Holtzman, 1976). This changing conceptualization, heavily influenced by systems theory, extends the theoretical boundaries of moral issues beyond the limits of emotional conflicts originally imposed by Freudian theory. Morality is often imaged by contemporary psychodynamic theorists as a form of self-regulated, internalized, rule-governed behavior.

Social Learning Theory

Both the social learning and psychoanalytic approaches feature the processes of socialization and internalization, but they approach them very differently. Rather than speculate on internal mechanisms, social learning theorists concentrate on observable behavior. Stated succinctly, the focus of social learning theorists is the learning principles that define how behavior is acquired, maintained, modified, or extinguished through the contingencies operating in the social environment.

The social learning approach encompasses a variety of specific theories, each emphasizing different learning principles and outcomes. Despite this variability, several key tenets shared by most advocates have clear implications for those interested in morality. First, as we mentioned, social learning theorists are interested in the regularities of learning that predict observable behavior. Thus, it is *prosocial* behavior, not moral reasoning or judgment, that concerns them. Second, people are viewed as highly pliable; thus, no age-related sequence of moral stages is accepted. To adopt a stage model of development would imply too great a role for internal constraints on moral thinking and acting. Third, all behavior is responsive to the same learning principles; thus, moral behavior is learned in the same way as is, say, playing Frisbee. Finally, morality is socially defined and therefore culturally relative.

Rather than review a number of specific theories, we will summarize some of the more important findings of social learning theorists, then review one theory in more detail. Major findings about which there is reasonable consensus can be grouped under four points.

First, there is ample evidence for the effectiveness of classical, or Pavlovian, conditioning. This learning principle states that when one stimulus is paired with another, the learner will come to respond as if the second stimulus were present when the first is encountered. Through this learning mechanism, emotional responses to various stimuli can be learned. In one classic experiment, for example, Aronfreed and Paskal (1965) paired a neutral stimulus (an adult saying "There's the light") with an emotionally positive stimulus (a child receiving a hug). In later trials, the child preferred to press a lever to hear an adult say "There's the light," even though the child did not receive a hug, than to press a lever and receive candy.

The efficacy of reinforcement contingencies in shaping behavior is equally well established. Behavior that is positively reinforced is likely to be repeated, whereas behavior that meets with continual punishment is likely to decrease. Between the poles of continual reinforcement and continual punishment are a variety of reinforcement schedules, each with its own consequence for subsequent behavior. Intermittent reinforcement, for example, is the most powerful schedule for maintaining behavior (Bandura, 1969, 1977). The application of this learning principle to morality is clear: If prosocial behavior is reinforced (especially if reinforced intermittently), then it will become strengthened and stabilized as an action tendency.

Modeling is another well-documented learning process. Social learning theorists have demonstrated, for example, that children who observe someone act in a prosocial way are more likely to act prosocially themselves, particularly if the model is similar to themselves, is a person of status, or has her or his behavior rewarded (Rushton, 1982). Similarly, the amount of exposure to a model and the consistency with which behavior is modeled affect the likelihood that the behavior will be replicated. Of course, modeling is equally effective in teaching antisocial behaviors.

The final set of findings concerns the role of cognitive processes. Although disputes persist regarding the precise role of cognition, most social learning theorists concur that behavior is often intentionally directed rather than simply responsive to immediate environmental influences. One issue central to the debate involves the relationship between comprehension and reinforcement efficacy. There is some evidence, for example, that reinforcement can impact behavior without a person's awareness of the rationale for the reinforcement (cf. Hefferline, Bruno, & Davidowitz, 1970). But when people do understand why they receive reinforcements, the reinforcements are much more potent (e.g., Spielberger & DeNike, 1966). This learning principle suggests that when people are informed about the moral precepts that are socially valued, the effects of modeling and reinforcement on prosocial behavior will be amplified.

Probably the most influential social learning theorist to address morality is Albert Bandura, who recently (1986, 1991) proposed a "social cognitive theory" of morality. According to this approach, moral cognitions, affective self-reactions, moral behavior, and environmental factors are interacting determinants that influence each other bidirectionally.

Bandura has posited that moral cognitions play a vital role in moral functioning. The moral judgments that one makes will determine, in interaction with other factors, one's behavior. Moral judgments, in turn, involve two separate processes: One must select from a multitude of situational cues the relevant moral elements, and one must prioritize the selected elements by applying moral rules. With increasing experience and cognitive competence, one's moral reasoning evolves from simple rules to highly complex ones.

Bandura recognizes that there are culturally invariant patterns in the development of moral cognition. These patterns are at the heart of stage theories of morality, but unlike stage theorists Bandura attributes these regularities to uniformities in the types of biopsychosocial changes that occur with increasing age in all cultures. For example, in moral reasoning young children universally focus on external constraints, whereas older children appeal to the reasons behind the constraints. Bandura explains this invariant pattern by suggesting that parents universally use external and physically oriented restraints on toddlers but that as children mature parents increasingly offer explanations in their discipline.

The relationship between moral cognition and moral action is mediated, according to Bandura, by *moral agency* (Bandura, 1986, 1991). In turn, two constructs are central to Bandura's definition of moral agency. The first is *self-regulatory mechanisms*, which function in combination with social sanctions to inhibit transgressive behavior and promote prosocial behavior. Self-regulatory mechanisms are affective reactions to one's behavior or contemplated behavior. For example, a high school shot-putter, knowing that there will not be a weigh-in, might think about using a shot that is underweight. In the face of this temptation, however, she may experience anticipatory guilt, which might function as a self-regulatory mechanism leading her to use a shot of proper weight. Positively, the self-regulatory affects of self-satisfaction and self-respect also motivate the person to act prosocially.

To use self-regulatory mechanisms effectively requires not only well-established affective reactions but strong belief in one's capabilities to achieve personal control. *Perceived efficacy* in self-regulation is the second major construct defining moral agency. According to Bandura, the stronger their perceived self-regulatory efficacy, the more people will persevere in the effort to maintain moral conduct in the face of social pressures or personal desires to behave otherwise.

The selective activation and disengagement of moral control is another important component in Bandura's theory. According to Bandura (1991), self-reaction influences do not operate unless they are activated, and there are many processes by which self-sanctions can be disengaged from conduct, facilitating inhumane behavior. A person can avoid self-censure for inhumane behavior by reconstruing conduct, obscuring causal agency, disregarding or misrepresenting injurious consequences, or blaming and devaluing victims.

Bandura's theory is comprehensive, and many of its key constructs have received empirical support. The main weakness, in our view, is the failure to maintain the "cognitive interactionist perspective" (Bandura, 1991) as promised. Bandura emphasizes cognition in his theory but never truly presents a view of cognition that is active, reality responsive, truth seeking, and innately organizing of experience. Rather, cognition ultimately seems to be swallowed by affect or environmental factors. For example, when discussing the origins of moral cognitions, Bandura invariably traces them back to familial modeling. Similarly, he recognizes that patterns of cognition change with age; not, however, because there is an innate tendency to restructure cognitive understandings in response to perceived realities but because the nature of the social influences change. In our view, this is an abridged view of cognition that ultimately collapses it into the environmental pole of the interaction.

Hoffman's Empathy-Based Theory of Morality

Martin Hoffman (1970, 1975a, 1975b, 1981, 1982, 1984, 1987, 1990) has developed a comprehensive theory of moral socialization that borrows from several theories while maintaining consistency with the internalization approach. For Hoffman, moral development involves three processes: learning moral precepts, coming to view the moral precepts as self-generated, and becoming motivated to act on one's moral precepts. To explain these processes, Hoffman focuses on how internalization is related to parental discipline and the development of empathy.

Internalization and Parental Discipline

Children sometimes misbehave. How a parent typically responds to a child's misbehavior is key to the future course of that child's moral development, according to Hoffman. Different discipline styles tend to produce different types of moral orientations. A discipline style that relies heavily on pointing out the human consequences of misbehavior, a technique called *inductive discipline*, is most effective in producing an internalized moral orientation: The child accepts the parental moral values, attributes them to the self, and is motivated to act on them. Authoritarian discipline, particularly the extensive use of physical force, tends to produce a child with an "external" moral orientation.

When a child does something that hurts another, the parent by employing inductive discipline can direct the child's attention to the other's distress and explain the connection between that distress and the child's own behavior. Helping the child attend to such consequences engages the child's capacities for empathy, heightens the ability to perceive moral cues, and deepens the sense of responsibility. In addition, because the child's attention is directed to the impact of her or his behavior on others, the parent becomes a background figure. This low salience of the parent in the discipline encounter is crucial; it enables the child to later attribute positive behavior to internal sources (e.g., her or his own empathy) rather than to parental force.

Inductive discipline, however, cannot be used exclusively. Reasoning itself lacks the potency for optimal affective arousal. For inductive discipline to be effective, Hoffman has recommended that it be combined occasionally with the affectively charged techniques of power assertion or love withdrawal, or both. In this way the child comes to know that the parent feels strongly about moral issues and consequently is likely to attend to the message contained in the inductive discipline.

Imagine that Arik, a toddler, keeps throwing sand at his playmate while they build sand castles. Arik's father explains how that action could hurt the other child, but to no avail. Then his father moves over and places a hand firmly on Arik's shoulder and says sternly, "I want you to hear my words. If you throw sand one more time, we will pick up our things and go home." The combination of such power assertion with inductive discipline is likely to be effective, especially if power assertion is used with considerable discretion. Frequent use of power assertion or love withdrawal will provoke anxiety, resentment, anger, or other negative emotions and heighten the saliency of the parent. The child may then come to view prosocial behavior as compliant behavior, done for the sake of the parent, rather than empathically responsive behavior.

Hoffman's Theory of Empathy

In our discussion of parental discipline, we made mention of empathy. According to Hoffman's theory, empathy and a constellation of related affects (sympathy, guilt, empathic anger, and empathic injustice) jointly form the main source of moral motivation and provide the foundation for moral judgment.

Hoffman defines *empathy* as "an affective response more appropriate to someone else's situation than to one's own" (Hoffman, 1982, p. 279). But empathy is not a simple, unitary response. Hoffman adopts a developmental approach to empathy and suggests that although it is a primary response that need not be mediated by complex cognitive functioning, as children mature their developing cognitive capacities allow for the formation of more complex empathic responses.

Hoffman's model identifies four primary forms of empathy. Each form combines a mode of empathic arousal with a particular level of social-cognitive development. To summarize his theory, we identify the modes of empathic arousal, then the parameters of social-cognitive development that are central to Hoffman's theory, and finally the four primary forms of empathy.

Empathy can be aroused through one or more of five means. It can arise from a simple *automatic reaction* (such as when a baby cries at the sound of another's distress), from *mimicry* of the other (such as when a child physically replicates another's behavior), and from *conditioned affect* (such as when negative stimuli have become associated with visual cues of harm to another). These three modes of empathic arousal are relatively nonvoluntary and automatic. In addition, empathy can be aroused through two means that involve higher order cognitive processes. Thus, empathy can be mediated by *language* (as when someone tells about the plight of another) and *role taking* (as when one imagines being in another's situation).

The main parameter of social-cognitive development that Hoffman employs is self–other differentiation. In early precursors to empathy, the child is unable to distinguish between self and other, but with development the child first differentiates the other as a physical entity, then as a psychological entity, and finally as an other with a unique history and stable personality configuration. Each increased level of self–other differentiation allows for more sophisticated forms of empathy.

The resulting coalescence of mode of empathic arousal and social-cognitive development yields four levels of empathy:

- Global empathy
- Egocentric empathy
- Empathy for another's feelings
- Empathy for another's life condition

Global Empathy

Infants may experience empathy through any of the nonvoluntary and automatic modes of empathic arousal. None of these require significant self–other differentiation, and the resultant empathy is global and diffuse in nature. This form of empathy does not invite further moral reflection because the respective needs of self and other are not differentiated.

"Egocentric" Empathy

The child can now recognize that the other is a distinct physical self and that it is the other, not the self, that is in distress. But the child's empathy is limited by an inability to perceive that the other has an independent psychological life; thus the child may act to relieve the other's distress through behaviors more appropriate for relieving self-distress. For example, Hoffman has related a story about a 13-month-old who offered a distressed adult the child's favorite toy.

Empathy for Another's Feeling

Around the age of 2 or 3 the child separates the self and other psychologically and recognizes that other people's feelings may differ from one's own. At the same time, language development dramatically extends the range and depth of emotion that can be experienced empathically. With further development, the child is able to empathize with complex and conflicting emotions and with the likely emotions of someone who is absent. The attainment of skill at this form of empathy dramatically improves the child's ability to interpret situations and to accurately predict the likely consequences of different behavioral choices.

Empathy for Another's Life Condition

The final level of self–other differentiation involves recognizing the other as a person with a unique history and stable identity consisting of a complex set of physical and psychological characteristics. This development enables the person to empathize with others not only in their immediate situations but in their chronic life circumstances. With the development of formal operational thought in early adolescence, empathy can be extended from the individual to classes of individuals, and one can empathize with entire groups, such as minorities, women, the poor, and others.

Empathy and Moral Cognition

Recently Hoffman (1989, 1991) has extended his theory of empathy in an effort to provide a comprehensive moral theory. Hoffman's original model was based on a bystander paradigm (the emotional response of someone witnessing another in distress). But Hoffman has proposed that the model is not limited to such situations, suggesting that when people consider such issues as abortion, affirmative action, gay rights, or child pornography, the essential features of the bystander model still pertain. Furthermore, Hoffman has posited that there is a congruence between empathy and the moral principles of caring and justice.

The relevance of empathy to caring is rather obvious, and we will say nothing more about it. More controversial is Hoffman's claim for a congruence between empathy and justice. Hoffman begins his argument by noting that there are three somewhat contradictory principles of distributive justice: Goods and services can be distributed based on need, strict equality, or merit (equity). The choice of a principle in a particular situation may depend on how one imagines the consequences of various distribution systems for certain people. If one empathizes with poor people, for example, one is likely to argue that any distribution system must protect the most vulnerable members of a society from exploitation by the powerful. Alternatively, one may empathize with those who work hard and expect rewards to be contingent on effort or output (an ideology certainly supported in the sport milieu). In actuality, most people empathize to some extent with a diverse range of people to varying degrees, and they seek compromises and checks among the principles.

Hoffman argues that empathic affects develop long before the maturing individual considers moral principles and that the empathic sensitivities one develops partly determine the principles that one eventually embraces. Even after moral principles have been constructed, empathic skills play a significant role in decision making. Hoffman (1989) writes,

I am arguing that most moral dilemmas in life may arouse empathy because they involve victims—seen or unseen, present or future. Since empathy is closely related to moral principles, the arousal of empathy should activate moral principles, and thus—directly, and indirectly through these principles—have an effect on moral judgment and reasoning. (p. 66)

Hoffman's claim that empathy activates moral principles is dwarfed by his much more radical claim that empathy alone is sufficient for moral decision making. To make this claim more convincing, he has attempted to address the frequent criticism that empathy lends itself to "empathic bias"—the tendency to give undue weight to the interests of those individuals for whom one feels the greatest affection or who are closest at hand. In our view, Hoffman's response is not entirely satisfying. He admits that empathic morality lends itself to bias, argues that the cognitivist morality of Kohlberg is also biased, and suggests that empathic bias can be minimized by a moral education that stresses the common humanity of all people (Hoffman, 1989, 1991).

We believe that empathy and its related affects are essential affective components in moral functioning but that empathy alone is insufficient for moral judgment. Empathy probably aids in identifying key moral issues and energizing the moral agent to seek a solution, but ultimately if the act is to be a moral one it must be carefully *thought* through as well, using the best moral reasoning of which the agent is capable.

Hoffman, from our perspective, has not adequately appreciated the self-corrective nature of a constructivist epistemology and has overemphasized the potential for bias in reasoning while minimizing the same concern for affectivity. That does not mean, however, that we believe cognition is not susceptible to bias. It certainly is, and moral cognition is perhaps more prone to bias than most other types. Indeed, Haan (Haan, Aerts, & Cooper, 1985) found that people who scored high in Kohlberg's moral system also tended to score high on defensive intellectualization (or rationalization).

What we find intriguing (and hopeful) is that the biases of the cognitive and empathic approaches tend to move in different directions; the two approaches, therefore, may complement one another (cf. Gibbs, 1991). The ethicist William Frankena (1973) has argued that the moral life must invariably be guided by two irreducible principles—a principle of justice (based on impartiality and "universalizability") and a principle of beneficence (based on care and a concern for maximizing good over harm). We find the cognitive and empathic moralities similarly irreducible complements in the moral life.

Summary

Internalization approaches to morality have much to offer. Modern psychoanalytic theory has focused on a number of early learning processes that provide insight into the early precursors of moral behavior, and they continue to remind us of the human propensity to self-deception.

Social learning theorists remind us that in the area of morality, as in all other areas of life, people act (at least in part) on what they believe will bring personal gain, defined in terms of material advantage, social approval, or self-satisfaction. Moral behavior in sport, for example, is often motivated by a desire to win rewards in the form of public acclaim, a coach's acceptance, or self-praise. Social learning theorists have also identified important learning dynamics, such as modeling, that need to be taken into account in a comprehensive approach to moral development. Similarly, Hoffman's work has highlighted important learning dynamics related to the development and employment of empathy, a critical moral affect.

But we believe that the internalization model misrepresents the nature of the cognitive function. This is particularly important in the area of morality. A defining mark of moral action is that it is intentional behavior congruent with a reasoned moral perspective. The most prominent alternatives to the internalization approach are offered by constructivist theorists, who assume that morality has a cognitive dimension and that cognition itself is in the service of truth seeking. Having alluded to this approach many times already, we now examine it more closely.

Chapter 4
Constructivist Approaches to Moral Development

All structural developmental theorists, whatever their differences, agree on three fundamental points. At the heart of their consensus is a focus on an interactionist, or constructivist, epistemology. According to this perspective, the person and the environment are coparticipants in the construction of meaning, and neither can be reduced to the other. The environment provides the concrete substance of experience, and the developing child contributes an innate tendency to interpret, organize, and synthesize experience.

The next two points are corollaries to the constructivist epistemology. First, structural developmental theorists hold that beneath an individual's manifest thought and behavior in a particular domain of action/experience is a coherent mental structure that can be characterized by a set of conceptual presuppositions and logical rules. The individual typically is aware of the content that comprises thought but not of the structure that gives coherence and order to that content. For example, when we speak we are aware of our words but rarely of the complex set of grammatical rules—the grammatical structure—that we employ to generate and organize our words.

Finally, these theorists advocate a robust view of development. For structural developmentalists, the concept of development implies that the maturing individual passes through a series of distinct, qualitatively different phases, stages, or levels (the terminology and conceptualizations differ) on the way toward maturity.

In this chapter, we summarize the theory of Lawrence Kohlberg, together with extensions and modifications of his theory made by former students and colleagues. The theories of Gilligan and Haan are singled out for extended review because of the importance of their theoretical contributions and because of their use in sport psychology.

Kohlberg's Theory of Moral Development

Until his death in 1987, Lawrence Kohlberg was the unrivaled leader in moral development research. The cognitive developmental theory that he elaborated remains the most carefully articulated theory of moral development in existence. Even following his death, Kohlberg's influence remains unparalleled through the many students, friends, and colleagues whom he inspired (cf. Kurtines & Gewirtz, 1991a).

Kohlberg's theory rests on the claim that what makes a particular act moral is the reason motivating it. Let's take an example. Suppose Fiona is in the middle of an open-water swim in a long course triathlon, and she notices a competitor suddenly break stroke and start gasping. Though leading, she stops to help, giving up any chance of winning. She has acted morally.

Or has she? What if her thinking process went something like this: ''What's wrong with Liam? Forget it, that's his problem. Wait a minute, if I stop and help, that could boost my media visibility. People will notice my heroic act. Besides, I probably won't win anyway. I didn't pace myself well and I'm tiring too quickly. Here's a chance to turn defeat into a different kind of victory.'' If Fiona's act were thus motivated, most readers, we believe, would concur that its moral character was compromised. Morality entails reasons.

Kohlberg never maintained the implausible idea, however, as some critics have suggested (e.g., Bandura, 1991), that an action is right just because a person believes it to be right and uses a moral principle to justify it. Moral reasoning, like all other reasoning, can be misguided or put to self-serving ends. Any moral claim is subject to scrutiny by all interested parties. Moral rationalization is revealed as such when subjected to the canons of consensual validity testing. The fact that a person can twist a principle to justify an inhumane behavior does not discount the cognitive theory of morality.

Methodology

Kohlberg's methodology is relatively well known. He invented short hypothetical stories that pit one person's moral claims against another's. In his most famous story a man's wife is dying of a kind of cancer for which a druggist recently discovered a cure. The man, however, cannot afford the drug. After exhausting other possibilities, he breaks into the pharmacy and steals it. Kohlberg then asks the interviewee whether the man did the right thing.

Kohlberg presented his moral dilemmas to people and probed the reasons for their opinions. The actual decisions respondents advocated were relatively insignificant because they were an aspect of moral content, not structure. People at each stage of moral development, Kohlberg argued, could take either side of a dilemma. What really interested him were the reasons people gave for their choices. By analyzing the presuppositions in people's reasoning and how various reasons related one to another, Kohlberg reconstructed the basic parameters of the underlying moral stage structure.

Key Concepts

Four key concepts are central to Kohlberg's theory of development: moral claims, orientations, stages, and principles. After discussing each in turn, we present Kohlberg's understanding of how moral reasoning stages relate to moral behavior.

Moral Claims

People organize themselves into families, communities, organizations, and societies to enhance their mutual lives. But the benefits of social life, like the blossoms of the rose bush, do not come without some thorns. Social living inevitably raises questions about the types of claims that people can make on one another and the norms for distributing the benefits of social organization. Morality, for Kohlberg, involves the coordination of moral claims in a social context.

Moral claims arise from the assignment or recognition of rights and duties. These are not simply assigned arbitrarily but rather arise from the universal moral values discussed in chapter 1. People's rights are derived from society's need to protect those qualities of social life that are essential to human integrity and social cooperation. When we say that someone has a right, it means that he or she can make a particular demand on society or relevant individuals. When we say that someone has a duty, it means that she or he has an obligation to others to act or refrain from acting in a particular way.

But conflicts between rights are inevitable. For Kohlberg, "the area of the conflicting claims of selves is the area of morality" (1984, p. 73). Thus, for example, if a player is asked by a coach to violate a rule, the coach's claim of authority may conflict with the player's claim to rule obedience. The adjudication of moral claims is the central task of a person's cognitive moral structure.

Moral Orientations

To clarify what is involved in moral thinking Kohlberg (1976) isolated four basic types of *moral orientations* (approaches to dealing with moral conflicts) advocated

Table 4.1   Moral Orientations

---

1. *Normative order*: This orientation defines the moral with reference to the operative rules and roles in a situation. In the realm of sport, for example, a person following normative order might define clipping in football as morally wrong because it violates the rules of the game.

2. *Utility consequences*: This orientation defines the moral by referring to the consequences, positive or negative, of action. From the utility perspective, clipping is wrong not because it violates the rules but because it is potentially harmful to the opponent.

3. *Justice or fairness*: This orientation defines the moral by referring to relations of liberty, equality, reciprocity, and contract. Clipping viewed from this perspective is wrong because it unfairly advantages one player or team, would not be condoned by the actor if the roles were reversed and the actor was the recipient of the action, and violates the informal contractual agreement between players to limit their behavior to that prescribed or not proscribed by the rules or informal norms of play.

4. *Ideal-self*: This orientation defines the moral by referring to an image of the actor as a good self, or as someone with conscience, and to the self's motives or virtue. It would be wrong to clip from this perspective because clipping reflects an egocentric motive and would demean the actor.

Note: Adapted from Kohlberg, 1976.

by different traditions of moral philosophy. Each orientation focuses on a critical element that can be used to differentiate right from wrong. The four moral orientations, together with illustrations of how someone using each might define the wrongness of the act of clipping in football, are presented in Table 4.1.

It is easy to see how the four basic moral orientations might all come into play in many sport settings. Certainly, rules hold a preeminent place in sport. Concern for consequences—particularly the welfare implications for behaviors like aggression—constrain action in certain ways. The structure of the game is designed to ensure fairness and equal opportunity, and some players may rely on this dimension, the "spirit of the game," for their moral guidance. Furthermore, some athletes may resolve moral decisions by appeal to ideals of sportspersonship associated with images of the ideal athlete.

Kohlberg's theory is deeply embedded in his conviction that the justice orientation is the most adequate. Only the justice orientation, Kohlberg maintained, can lead to the formulation of a moral principle that can be used to decide fairly among competing moral claims. Rules can conflict. The consequences to one person or group may conflict with those of another, and, furthermore, consequences often cannot be foreseen with clarity. Conscience, contrary to the popular adage, is too contaminated by cultural idiosyncrasies to be the best guide. According to Kohlberg, only the justice orientation can lead to an impartial and universalizable mode of resolving moral disputes.

Moral Stages

Kohlberg hypothesized an invariant, culturally universal six-stage sequence of moral development. A summary of the stages is presented in Table 4.2. His stages reflect different reasoning structures, organized into a developmental hierarchy, for dealing with conflicting claims.

Over the years the precise definitions of the stages underwent several revisions as Kohlberg sought to more carefully distinguish structure from content. In general, scoring of stages became tighter. In fact, Stage 6 was dropped from the scoring manual entirely, though it remained part of the theory as the theoretical terminus of potential moral growth. The hypothetical Stage 6 helps define the domain of morality, in Kohlberg's view, but it is no longer seen as an empirically demonstrated stage.

The fundamental idea behind the stage scoring system is what Kohlberg calls the *sociomoral perspective*, "the characteristic point of view from which the individual formulates moral judgments" (Colby et al., 1987, p. 15). There are three developmental levels of sociomoral perspective: the concrete individual perspective, the member-of-society perspective, and the prior-to-society perspective. These three levels undergird preconventional (Stages 1 and 2), conventional (Stages 3 and 4), and postconventional (Stages 5 and 6) morality, respectively.

The details of Kohlberg's stages are quite complex, but the general course of development can be outlined. In the first two stages, a person has little conception of the nature or purpose of social cooperation and correspondingly approaches moral problems through an individualistic or egocentric perspective. The limited amount of social cooperation that a person does understand is interpreted in a framework of instrumental exchanges between individuals. For example, Phoumara may keep his promise to Joseph because Phoumara doesn't want Joseph to break a promise to him on some later occasion. Kohlberg called this the *preconventional* level because the person does not yet comprehend the way social norms and rules impact moral responsibility.

The next two stages comprise the *conventional* level. People reason at these stages from a perspective informed by membership in social units. In general, a person at Stage 3 takes on the perspective of personalized social units, like the family or friendship group, whereas a person at Stage 4 adopts the perspective of social systems with impersonally defined rules and roles. In both cases, what is right is defined by the norms of a reference group.

Finally, at the *postconventional level*, moral disputes are resolved not by appeal to specific cultural or institutional norms but by applying a universal moral principle that is valid regardless of social context. We will elaborate further on the concept of moral principle shortly, but first let us outline Kohlberg's discussion of moral types.

Moral Types

Within each stage, Kohlberg identified Type A and Type B (or Substage A and Substage B) forms of moral reasoning. These were initially derived from

Table 4.2   Kohlberg's Stages of Moral Development

Level and stage	Content of Stage		Social perspective of stage
	What is right	Reasons for doing right	
Level I—Preconventional Stage 1—Heteronomous morality	To avoid breaking rules backed by punishment, obedience for its own sake, and avoiding physical damage to persons and property.	Avoidance of punishment, and the superior power of authorities.	*Egocentric point of view.* Doesn't consider the interests of others or recognize that they differ from the actor's; doesn't relate two points of view. Actions are considered physically rather than in terms of psychological interests of others. Confusion of authority's perspective with one's own.
Stage 2—Individualism, instrumental purpose, and exchange	Following rules only when it is to someone's immediate interest; acting to meet one's own interests and needs and letting others do the same. Right is also what's fair, what's an equal exchange, a deal, an agreement.	To serve one's own needs or interests in a world where you have to recognize that other people have their interests, too.	*Concrete individualistic perspective.* Aware that everybody has his or her own interest to pursue and these conflict, so that right is relative (in the concrete individualistic sense).
Level II—Conventional Stage 3—Mutual interpersonal expectations, relationships, and interpersonal conformity	Living up to what is expected by people close to you or what people generally expect of people in your role as daughter, brother, friend, etc. "Being	To need to be a good person in your own eyes and those of others. Your caring for others. Belief in the Golden Rule. Desire to maintain rules and	*Perspective of the individual in relationships with other individuals.* Aware of shared feelings, agreements, and expectations which take

	good'' is important and means having good motives, showing concern about others. It also means keeping mutual relationships, such as trust, loyalty, respect and gratitude.	authority which support stereotypical good behavior.	primacy over individual interests. Relates points of view through the concrete Golden Rule, putting yourself in the other guy's shoes. Does not yet consider generalized system perspective.
Stage 4—Social system and conscience	Fulfilling the actual duties to which you have agreed. Laws are to be upheld except in extreme cases where they conflict with other fixed social duties. Right is also contributing to society, the group, or institution.	To keep the institution going as a whole, to avoid the breakdown in the system ''if everyone did it,'' or the imperative of conscience to meet one's defined obligations.	*Differentiates societal point of view from interpersonal agreement or motives.* Takes the point of view of the system that defines roles and rules. Considers individual relations in terms of place in the system.
Level III—Postconventional, or principled Stage 5—Social contract or utility and individual rights	Being aware that people hold a variety of values and opinions, that most values and rules are relative to your group. These relative rules should usually be upheld, however, in the interest of impartiality and because they are the social contract. Some nonrelative values and rights like *life* and *liberty*, however, must be upheld in any society and regardless of majority opinion.	A sense of obligation to law because of one's social contract to make and abide by laws for the welfare of all and for the protection of all people's rights. A feeling of contractual commitment, freely entered upon, to family, friendship, trust, and work obligations. Concern that laws and duties be based on rational calculation of overall utility, ''the greatest good for the greatest number.''	*Prior-to-society perspective.* Perspective of a rational individual aware of values and rights prior to social attachments and contracts. Integrates perspectives by formal mechanisms of agreement, contract, objective impartiality, and due process. Considers moral and legal points of view; recognizes that they sometimes conflict and finds it difficult to integrate them.

(continued)

Table 4.2 (continued)

Level and stage	What is right	Reasons for doing right	Social perspective of stage
Stage 6—Universal ethical principles	Following self-chosen ethical principles. Particular laws or social agreements are usually valid because they rest on such principles. When laws violate these principles, one acts in accordance with the principle. Principles are universal principles of justice: the equality of human rights and respect for the dignity of human beings as individual persons.	The belief as a rational person in the validity of universal moral principles, and a sense of personal commitment to them.	*Perspective of a moral point of view* from which social arrangements derive. Perspective is that of any rational individual recognizing the nature of morality or the fact that persons are ends in themselves and must be treated as such.

categorizing people's responses to moral dilemmas according to the four moral orientations. In Kohlberg's view, everyone uses all four orientations, but each person has a clear preference for using either a combination of the normative order and consequence orientations (which he called Type A) or a combination of the justice and ideal self orientations (Type B).

As Kohlberg elaborated his notion of *moral types*, he found the Piagetian distinction between heteronomous and autonomous morality useful (Kohlberg, 1984). Drawing from Piaget, Kohlberg identified nine characteristics that distinguish heteronomous from autonomous morality. Type A moral reasoning conforms to the characteristics of heteronomous morality—a concern for such values as legality and authority. In contrast, the autonomous concerns for rights and welfare are characteristic of Type B.

Kohlberg's discussion of moral types is relatively independent of his stage theory. The moral types do not exhibit the same logical tightness and inner consistency that characterize the moral stages. Still, some developmental progression is often evident, with people moving from Type A to Type B.

Kohlberg found the type distinction helpful in explaining why some people at an early stage of development seem to be able to intuit the same moral judgment as is articulately stated by postconventional reasoners. He suggested that Type B reasoners who score at Stages 2 to 4 dimly perceive the critical moral issues that are finally integrated in a self-conscious way by those at the postconventional level.

Kohlberg's conceptualization of moral types may have particular relevance to sport. We have found that many athletes use a unique form of "game reasoning" in response to moral dilemmas set within sport. Perhaps one element in this game reasoning pattern is a shift away from Type B moral reasoning to Type A. The world of sport is structured by rules and artificially created goals, hierarchy and organization are central concerns, and authority figures are highly salient. It is likely, then, that the values and norms of heteronomous morality will be prominent in an athlete's reasoning about issues in sport-specific contexts. As yet, however, this interpretation has not been investigated empirically.

Moral Principles

Kohlberg originally claimed that his theory of moral development was comprehensive and complete, normatively defining the relationships among all four major moral orientations and the evolution of each. More recently, he adopted the more modest claim that his theory describes the universal development of justice reasoning (Kohlberg, 1984). Still, Kohlberg's theory is deeply embedded in his conviction that only justice reasoning can yield consistent and defensible moral principles. A moral principle, for Kohlberg, is "a mode of choosing that is universal, a rule of choosing that we want all people to adopt always in all situations" (Kohlberg, 1981, p. 39).

Two characteristics define a moral principle. First, it is a method of choosing between seemingly plausible moral alternatives. This characteristic helps distinguish moral rules from moral principles. Moral rules are specific codes. Thus,

Don't steal is a moral rule that protects property rights. Don't cheat is a moral rule protecting fair competition. But moral rules can come into conflict and, consequently, they must allow exception. For example, Don't steal might in some circumstances oppose another moral rule: Preserve life.

In contrast to moral rules, moral principles define a method for establishing moral priorities. That is, a moral principle enables a person to distinguish an order of moral precedence when moral claims conflict, and this ordering should be observed in all similar circumstances when the same moral issues arise.

Kohlberg drew from the formalist tradition in moral philosophy for criteria that can be used to distinguish more-adequate from less-adequate moral principles. In brief, Kohlberg argued that better moral judgments are more "reversible" than less-adequate ones. What Kohlberg meant is that a sound moral principle will yield a judgment that would be viewed as fair by all parties in a dispute if each took the role of the others. In Kohlberg's view, the principle of justice satisfies the criterion of reversibility better than any other moral principle.

To better describe what Kohlberg meant by justice, we present an illustration featuring Maggie, an athletic director who reasons at Kohlberg's Stage 6. Maggie must decide how to respond when members of her university's women's basketball team complain because the men's team gets first choice of practice times in the gym. The men, on the other hand, claim that because they bring more financial resources to the school they have a right to preferential treatment. The thinking that Maggie, as a Stage 6 reasoner, goes through might be described as moral musical chairs (Kohlberg, 1981). In her imagination she alternately takes the role of everyone in the dispute—including those not directly represented, such as fans and alumni, who are still affected by whatever decision is made— putting herself in their shoes to identify the moral claims that each party could make. Then Maggie imagines that she actually might become any one of those people, without yet knowing which.

From that vantage point—similar to what Rawls (1971) called the "original position" behind a "veil of ignorance"—Maggie decides whose claim takes priority. Because Maggie has imagined the equal possibility of being each person, she will be able to justify her choice from every viewpoint. Thus, Maggie has reached a reversible judgment. Maggie's judgment is reversible because she would arrive at the same decision even if she were to trade identities (i.e., reverse roles) with any of the other parties. Of course, Stage 6 reasoners need not literally go through this exact sequence of mental gymnastics, but the structure of their reasoning will conform to the structural properties of the moral musical chairs exercise, or what Kohlberg called "ideal role taking" (1981). The ideal role-taking procedure leads to moral conclusions that are impartial and universalizable.

Thought and Action

One of the earliest critiques of Kohlberg's work was that he neglected moral action. To some extent the critique was unfair. First, Kohlberg took account of action in his epistemological foundation. Following Piaget, he maintained a reciprocal causal model in which thought and action are mutually determining. For Kohlberg, "moral judgment arises out of moral action itself, although there is no single causal direction. A new stage of moral judgment may guide new behavior, whereas a new action involving conflict and choice may lead one to construct a new stage of moral judgment" (Kohlberg & Candee, 1984, p. 53). Secondly, Kohlberg clearly had a theory of moral action itself—in brief, that the more mature a person's moral reasoning, the more reliably reasoning and action would cohere and the more likely the action choice would be morally defensible. Kohlberg's theory rested on his view that moral cognitions are moral motives: We are motivated by the appeal of those principles of morality that we fully comprehend.

An overly simplistic model of the thought–action relationship would suggest that people's behavior can be predicted from their stages of moral reasoning. Kohlberg himself never entertained such a model, but several of the early studies of moral action that used Kohlberg's framework were based, at least in design, on such an assumption. There are several problems with such a model. Most importantly, because each stage can be used to support different action choices, it is not possible to predict action from knowledge of stage. It also is clear that moral reasoning is not the only cognitive-affective processing that goes on in a moral situation. A person will interpret a situation in terms of prudential considerations as well, for example. The coordination of these different interpretations, and the different motives they activate, inevitably creates disparities between thought and action.

In his later work Kohlberg elaborated a model of moral action that identifies two types of moral judgments that mediate between stage structure and action (Kohlberg, 1984). The first of these is the *deontic judgment*, which reflects what a person believes to be morally right. As noted before, two people reasoning at the same stage may take opposing views on a particular dilemma. The actual decision that someone makes about what is the right action is the deontic judgment.

Kohlberg also hypothesized that a *responsibility judgment* serves as a mediating factor. After the actor has determined that a particular act is the morally correct one, she or he must make a second judgment, independent of the first, and decide whether it is her or his responsibility to perform the act. Merrika might believe, for example, that it would be right to stand up and speak out against the unreasonable practice schedule of her coach (deontic judgment), but Merrika also may decide that it is not her responsibility to take such a stand (responsibility judgment).

Kohlberg (1984) posited that moral action often fails to keep pace with mature moral reasoning because people use various "quasi-obligations" or morally rooted excuses to avoid a responsibility judgment that parallels their deontic one. For example, the quasi-obligation of team loyalty may keep a player from turning in a steroid-using teammate. In this connection, Kohlberg has noted that it is likely that someone who uses predominantly Type B moral reasoning will offer fewer excusing quasi-obligations than someone using Type A reasoning.

Kohlberg's Theory Summarized

Because Kohlberg has defined the debate in moral psychology, let's review the main presuppositions and conclusions that are fundamental to his theory. First, Kohlberg offered a *phenomenalistic* approach to morality, which requires that people's reasons and judgments be taken as meaningful on their own terms; they cannot be reduced to epiphenomena of irrational affects, unconscious motives, or environmental contingencies. A person's moral reasoning is a reflection of moral reality as that person perceives it (Colby et al., 1987).

A related presupposition is Kohlberg's constructivism. Following Piaget, Kohlberg believed that the individual actively constructs moral meaning (but see Haan et al., 1985, p. 58). The growing child is a budding moral philosopher.

Kohlberg's approach is also structural, analyzing moral reasoning at two levels—content and structure. The structure refers to the form of reasoning, or the pattern of reasoning, in contrast to the specific norms, values, or beliefs that are expressed.

Finally, Kohlberg's approach is cognitive-developmental. He concluded that moral cognition develops through an invariant, culturally universal sequence of stages. Each stage of development defines an integrated meaning-system through which the person interprets moral reality. Kohlberg was not unconcerned with such issues as affect, motive, or action, but he believed that the cognitive structure undergoes regular transformations in the process of development and that these structural transformations largely determine what affects are elicited, what motivational pulls are most influential, and how action choices are conceptualized.

Critical Appraisals

No moral development theory has received more attention than Kohlberg's. As Rest (1979) noted, volumes of empirical research have been marshaled to support the main outlines of Kohlberg's theory. But central aspects of Kohlberg's philosophy, methodology, and theoretical constructions also have been criticized by many (see Modgil & Modgil, 1985, for an excellent collection). We will first note some of the more common critiques and then examine models of morality that have been inspired by Kohlberg's work but have redefined it in significant ways.

Perhaps the most frequent critiques focus on Kohlberg's philosophical commitments. Many have argued that his twin claims to have isolated the universal features of morality and to have established justice as the ultimate moral principle are spurious. Some of these scholars have suggested that Kohlberg's description of justice is not as universal as he claims (e.g., D. Locke, 1979; May, 1985; Rosen, 1980; Shweder, 1982; Simpson, 1974; Sullivan, 1977; Vine, 1984). Others have disputed the normative commitments that undergird his theory (e.g., D. Locke, 1979, 1980). Some anthropologists, most notably Levi-Strauss (1969), object to the whole idea of more-adequate and less-adequate moral principles. Other social scientists accept the distinction between immature and more mature moral reasoning but believe that additional moral principles need to be added to justice to make the moral category system complete (e.g., R.E. Carter, 1980; Gilligan, 1982; Puka, 1991).

Kohlberg's methodology also has been challenged. He used hypothetical dilemmas removed from everyday life to minimize the likelihood that idiosyncratic associations might influence responses. The technique was designed to help people convey their optimal capacity (i.e., competence) for moral reasoning. But Bandura (1991) has criticized Kohlberg's reliance on a few moral dilemmas that sample only a narrow range of moral conflicts. Gilligan (1982) has argued that the use of abstract, hypothetical dilemmas does not facilitate the expression of the moral principles most important to women (e.g., care and responsibility).

Other critics challenge Kohlberg's concentration on the cognitive dimension of morality (cf. Gibbs, 1991; Haan et al., 1985; Hoffman, 1991). Drawing from Piaget, Kohlberg maintained that cognitions and affects are really flip sides of the same mental events (e.g., Kohlberg, 1984; see also Cowan, 1982, for an updated Piagetian view of cognitive-affective relations). There are no cognitions that are unaccompanied by affect, however slight; nor are there affects that are not cognitively structured. But, for Kohlberg, it is the cognitive side of moral experience that defines it as distinctively moral and that potentially renders it rational, impartial, and imperative (Kohlberg, 1969, 1971).

Also criticized are Kohlberg's thesis that "cognitive disequilibrium" is the mechanism of stage progression (Haan, 1985; Kupfersmid & Wonderly, 1982; Zimmerman & Blom, 1983), his claim of structural wholeness (Rest, 1979; Turiel, 1983), and specific stage descriptions (Keller, Eckensberger, & Von Rosen, 1989).

Extensions and Modifications of Kohlberg's Theory

Broadly speaking, there are two basic types of revisions within the Kohlberg tradition. Former students and early research colleagues have offered modifications of Kohlberg's work that leave the major scaffolding of his theory intact. We briefly summarize three, and a fourth is reflected in the work of Turiel, discussed in chapter 8. Other theorists offer approaches reflecting major reconstructions and departures from Kohlberg's theory. Two in particular stand out: Carol Gilligan and Norma Haan. We review their work in the concluding sections of this chapter.

James Rest (1979) has offered a very influential modification of Kohlberg's theory, proposing a "layer cake" approach to moral development. According to Kohlberg, as an individual progresses through the moral stages, each new stage displaces the previous one. However, there appears to be evidence that people use different stages of reasoning in response to different situations (e.g., Higgins, Power, & Kohlberg, 1984; Sobesky, 1983). Rest resolves the problem by abandoning Kohlberg's claim to internal consistency. Rest maintains that during each period of development, people have access to and continue to use several stages.

His measure of moral development, The Defining Issues Test, reflects this perspective. Bandura (1991) has argued that Rest's position undermines the fundamental premises of structural-developmental theory.

John Gibbs (1977, 1979, 1991) has posited that Kohlberg's preconventional and conventional moral stages are genuinely developmental but that his postconventional stages are not. Full moral maturity, which Gibbs has reinterpreted as an ability to perceive the underlying purpose beneath moral regulations, is available at both Stages 3 and 4. In support of his view, Gibbs cites Snarey's (1985) review of cross-cultural research on Kohlberg's theory. Snarey concludes that Kohlberg's Stages 1 through 4 are represented in a wide range of cultural groups but that there is little evidence for the cultural universality of postconventional reasoning.

Finally, Bill Puka (1986, 1991) offers a startling reinterpretation of Kohlberg's work. One of the key reasons that Kohlberg advanced the field of moral psychology was his insight into the importance of turning to philosophy to define a conception of ultimate moral adequacy. With such a conception in hand, Kohlberg maintained that the task of the psychologist was to trace the psychological trajectory that leads toward that conception. For Kohlberg, a particular theory of justice defined the end point of moral maturity. But his commitment to a formalist ethic also caused him problems. Over the years Kohlberg's critics charged him with various forms of bias, and he responded with increasingly sophisticated philosophical defenses. From Puka's perspective, two decades worth of debate, refinement, and writing was all wasted effort. Despite Kohlberg's intense commitment to a particular ethical stance, what both Kohlberg and his critics overlooked is that his philosophy is really quite irrelevant to the basic empirical work that led to stage descriptions. Puka suggests that Kohlberg's theory can be cut loose from its philosophical moorings without loss. The relative adequacy of the different stages of development, one to another, can be established without appeal to any final "end point" of development.

We turn now to the comprehensive revisions of Kohlberg's theory offered by Gilligan and Haan.

Justice and Care as Distinct Moral Orientations

Carol Gilligan (Brown, Debold, Tappan, & Gilligan, 1991; Brown & Gilligan, 1990; Gilligan, 1982; Gilligan & Attanucci, 1988; Gilligan, Brown, & Rogers, 1990; Gilligan, Ward, & Taylor, 1988) has authored one of the most popular revisions of the Kohlberg model. Her central thesis is that Kohlberg's theory is inadequate because his focus on justice neglects the equally important themes of care, relational responsiveness, and responsibility. Gilligan maintains that these themes are more prevalent in girls' and women's life experience than in boys' and men's.

According to Gilligan, two distinct, universal human experiences lie at the root of the two "voices" of justice and care. All children necessarily experience themselves as both *attached* and *unequal*. The experience of attachment promotes a focus on relationships and connection. The accompanying fear is separation and abandonment. In contrast, the experience of inequality promotes a focus on the separate self who is concerned for fairness and justice. The accompanying fear is exploitation.

Both males and females experience attachment and inequality. But boys experience a disruption in their attachment. Drawing from the psychoanalytic work of Nancy Chodorow (1978), Gilligan observes that in a culture where women are still the primary caretakers of young children, boys must go through a process of individuation and separation when establishing their sense of gender identity. Girls, on the other hand, can establish identity through affirming their connection and attachment to their caretakers. This differential early experience plants the seeds for boys' developing emphasis on autonomy and justice and girls' developing emphasis on relationship and care.

The early experiences of individuation and inequality on the one hand and attachment and connection on the other contour different understandings of the self, responsibility, and relationship. The first set of experiences leads to a sense of self as separate, responsibility as commitment to obligations, and relationship as hierarchical or contractual. The experiences of connection and attachment, on the other hand, promote an understanding of self as interdependent, responsibility as responsiveness, and relationship as networks created and sustained by attention and care.

For Gilligan, a *justice orientation* reflects a moral perspective informed by impartiality, a strong sense of the autonomous self, a definition of responsibility as obligation, and a contractual approach to relationships. In contrast, a *care orientation* centers on particularity, an interdependent sense of self, a definition of responsibility as responsiveness, and a nurturant web approach to relationships.

An example may further clarify the justice and care orientations. Suppose Marquita is using performance-enhancing drugs and Rona, another athlete, becomes aware of the situation. Should Rona tell the coach? A justice reasoner may put himself or herself in the role of each person and conclude that the right thing to do is tell. In the first place, Rona has an obligation to the norm of truthfulness that is not superseded by any moral claim with higher priority. Second, from the vantage point of each athlete, including Marquita, the conditions for fair competition are being undermined because of Marquita's activities. Third, the coach can make a legitimate claim to information directly relevant to a player's well-being and athletic performance. A care reasoner may argue, on the other hand, against Rona's turning Marquita in, again for several reasons. Turning Marquita in may jeopardize the support network that may be necessary for long-term recovery, it may undermine their own relationship, and it may nullify any potential that Rona may have to influence Marquita. Of course, justice and care reasoners may respond quite differently than just described, but we have offered these scenarios as illustrations of the two perspectives.

From Gilligan's standpoint, Kohlberg's theory may reflect relatively well the developmental progression that occurs in the sphere of justice. As justice reasoning proceeds toward the principled level where claims are arbitrated fairly and objectively, the dangers of oppression are progressively minimized. But the strength of one moral vision is revealed as a weakness when seen from the vantage point of the other moral vision. The very objectivity, detachment, and distance required to enact fairness are threats to connection and relationship. The virtue of relational responsiveness is lost behind the blindfold of justice. Similarly, Gilligan acknowledges that the moral vision centered on care and responsiveness may lose sight of the need for fairness. For Gilligan, both moral visions are needed, and mature morality recognizes moral ambiguity as intrinsic to the complexities of moral life.

Kohlberg responded to Gilligan's work by acknowledging the morality of care, but he subordinated it to a morality of justice (Kohlberg, 1984). For Kohlberg, justice defines one's minimal obligation to others, but an ethic of care, rooted in particular relationships, may transcend justice, nurturing a broader sense of responsibility for others than justice alone would demand (Nunner-Winkler, 1984). Kohlberg also has denied Gilligan's (1982) claim that his theory is biased against women, and Walker (1984, 1991) has marshaled considerable evidence to support the contention that Kohlberg's theory lacks any systematic gender bias. Walker argues that justice and care considerations, rather than reflecting generalized orientations, are elicited by the type of dilemma presented, an interpretation disputed by Gilligan (Gilligan, Ward, & Taylor, 1988).

Friedman, in a critique of Gilligan, proposes that justice and care are interwoven and largely inseparable emphases. This can be seen in the various ways personal relationships of caring involve justice. As an illustration, the trust and intimacy that characterize some coach-player relationships creates special vulnerabilities, opening people to possible emotional damage that does not exist in less personal relationships. For example, a coach's care may degenerate into the injustice of exploitation ("You must meet with the newspaper reporter regardless of your final exam schedule") or oppression ("If you don't lose 3 pounds by next week, you won't be in the starting lineup"). In these cases, justice becomes a matter of righting the wrong a coach might have done to her or his athlete within the relationship of care. The inseparable nature of justice and care is also evident in Kohlberg's own biography. Kohlberg's dedication to justice arose from his deep compassion and caring for victims of injustice (see Noam & Wolf, 1991).

Despite the popularity of Gilligan's theory, the research base on which it rests is relatively weak, and many of her claims have remained unsubstantiated. Furthermore, the shifting definitions of key terms has made problematic any testing of her theory (see Rest, 1994). We believe Gilligan has correctly identified an aspect of moral consciousness not adequately incorporated in Kohlberg's formulation; but Gilligan's notoriety may be due more to her ability to articulate legitimate feminist grievances against mainstream psychology than the soundness of her own moral theory. Additional work is needed to clarify the relationship between the themes of justice and care.

Haan's Model of Interaction Morality

Another important theory is offered by Norma Haan (1977a, 1977b, 1978, 1985, 1986, 1991; Haan et al., 1985). Haan began her career as a child psychologist trained in the psychoanalytic tradition. When she moved into research psychology, however, she became increasingly interested in the Piagetian framework. With the eruption of the 1960s free speech movement on the Berkeley campus where Haan was working, she focused on the moral dynamics of the protesters and turned to Kohlberg for assistance. She both collaborated with him on research and used his model (Haan, 1971, 1975; Haan, Langer, & Kohlberg, 1976; Haan, Smith, & Block, 1968). Soon, however, she became discontent with the philosophical underpinnings of Kohlberg's theory and his exclusively cognitive interpretation. She came to believe that psychologists could elucidate more fruitfully the process dimensions of morality rather than solve philosophical issues of a "best" morality.

To understand Haan's conceptualization of morality, it is helpful to see her moral research as part of a larger project. Before her work on morality, Haan had developed a model of "coping and defending" ego processes that brought together insights from the psychoanalytic and constructivist positions. From the Freudian tradition she learned to appreciate the human tendency to resort to processes of psychological defense—such as repression, rationalization, and projection—in order to see ourselves as moral. "Freud's theory of the ego defenses depends on the single observation that humans will resort to all means of self-deception to fortify their view of themselves as moral" (Haan et al., 1985, p. 38).

But Freud's focus on psychopathology prevented him from giving equal attention to the problem-free and nondistorted ways people interact. Haan found the Piagetian tradition much more useful for understanding the processes of normal, accurate human psychological functioning. To bridge the gap between the two approaches, she developed her model of coping and defending ego processes.

Starting with the 10 classic ego defenses identified in the psychoanalytic tradition, Haan asked a straightforward question: If the ego defenses represent distortions, what are they distortions of? What are the corresponding processes of psychological accuracy from which the defense mechanisms deviate? In answer, Haan (1977b) proposed a model of 10 "coping" processes that correspond to the 10 defenses. Projection, for example, is a distortion of the coping process of empathy. Both empathy and projection are efforts to understand the inner experience of another. Empathy carries out that process successfully, whereas projection distorts it.

Coping and defending represent the process side of psychological functioning. Haan believed that people also develop structural competencies for understanding their environment in much the way Piaget describes. Morality is one domain of structural competence, though moral structures, in Haan's view, do not exhibit the same degree of internal coherence and hierarchical organization that strictly cognitive structures do. Haan became convinced that Kohlberg was too enamored with the liberal philosophical tradition of individualism and autonomy to capture the intricacies of people's everyday moral experience. Consequently, she set out to develop her own moral psychology.

Key Concepts

Haan was not particularly interested in how people reason about abstract moral issues. Rather, she focused on how people in actual life situations construct moral agreements and resolve moral disputes. For Haan, morality refers to that aspect of practical human interaction that seeks to coordinate people's desires and needs through explicit or implicit appeal to concepts of fairness or "the good" (or both).

Haan's basic constructs were derived from structural analysis of people's behavior in simulation games (Haan, 1978). Thus, her theory is an attempt to describe moral structures underlying action. Five major concepts are at the heart of Haan's model of morality: moral balance, dialogue, truth, levels, and secondary moral structures. We discuss each in turn, then discuss Haan's understanding of the relationship between moral levels and moral action.

Moral Balance

The *moral balance* is a complex notion with several nuances of meaning. Stated most simply, a moral balance is an interpersonal agreement (tacit or explicit) about respective rights, privileges, and responsibilities. When people are in moral balance, an agreement exists—usually informal and unstated—about what should or should not be done and by whom. In a game of basketball, for example, competitors may be described as in moral balance if there is basic agreement about the formal and informal norms of play. Similarly, a player and a coach are in moral balance if they share an understanding about such issues as the amount of practice required, the type and quality of the coach's input, and the amount of the player's game time.

But moral balance is not just a static interpersonal psychological state. At the same time it is a dynamic process. Achieving moral balance represents less a finished accomplishment than a moment in an evolving process of equilibration— because people's perceived needs and interests vary with circumstances, moods, changing insights, and a host of related factors.

People are in moral balance when they agree about respective rights, privileges, and responsibilities and believe that each party is giving in an equalized manner. But the moral balance does not require that at any one moment in time or in any one set of circumstances each person must give equally. Short-lived imbalances—and under exceptional circumstances, extended lopsided giving—may be accepted without upsetting the moral balance because the participants recognize that in a complex world we each need to give or receive more or less from others depending on our internal and external circumstances. Participants in a moral balance implic- itly recognize that the pattern of give and take generally balances over time.

What is important is not objective equality but a reciprocal recognition of balanced commitment to the relationship and the moral exchange. This sense of balanced commitment allows giving patterns to be responsive to fluctuations in resources and needs.

The concept of moral balance connotes a particular understanding of fairness. For Haan, what is fair is not determined by appeal to an abstract, universalizable moral principle. Rather, what is fair in any instance is the product of a unique, contextually conditioned negotiation that is carried out in light of a relationship that has both a particular past and an anticipated future. Suppose Joshua wants to play marbles with his sister, Dana, but she would rather play catch with the football. A Kohlbergian might conclude that the children should flip a coin to determine which game to play. That solution respects each person equally. But the solution is flawed. In this particular instance, it may be more fair for the children to play catch because just before this exchange Dana helped Joshua with his math homework, and playing her choice of games would be a way to show appreciation. Obviously, the details of this example could be extended and complicated so that determining what is fair becomes a much more complex process with an indeterminate outcome. The point is that the historical flow in which a decision occurs influences the processes and outcomes of fairness decisions.

The concept of moral balance also implies that fairness be particularized. Fairness does not require impersonality, impartiality, or blindfolded justice. Who people are—their interests, needs, foibles, and strengths—is relevant. Let us imagine that Laura spends a significant amount of time offering valuable advice and assistance to Steve about bicycle safety. At first glance, what might seem fair would be a reciprocal offering on the part of Steve. But suppose Laura gets irritated whenever Steve offers suggestions. Certainly, fairness does not require Steve to return behavior that Laura would view as offensive. What is fair is particular to the individuals. Furthermore, fairness often involves trade-offs of goods, favors, or services that cannot be easily compared or objectively balanced, and fairness must be tied to their personalized meanings.

Before leaving the concept of moral balance, we should make two other points. First, the concept of moral balance implies that it can be a tricky proposition to negotiate the dynamics of relational exchange. Just how much can I expect from those around me? How much should I give psychologically or materially to others? It is as easy to upset the moral balance by giving too much as by failing to give enough. We all know people who tend to give too much. Sometimes such overgiving is done deliberately or semiconsciously to make the recipient feel gratitude and obligation, feelings that can then be manipulated. Other people tend to habitually give too little. Both over- and undergivers violate the moral balance. The problem is that defining over- and undergiving is necessarily particular to the individuals involved and their context.

Second, our illustrations of moral balance all have been drawn from the realm of personal relationships. But it is equally appropriate to discuss the moral balance between or among collectives, such as teams, communities, and nations.

Obviously, additional complexities arise in such instances, but the fundamental dynamics are strikingly similar. For example, arms control negotiations often involve intricate efforts to balance nonequitable forces in light of perceived fears and hopes. In such negotiations, there is no external standard of fairness to which all rational people would assent. What is fair is what the parties decide is in their mutual interest.

A corollary to the concept of moral balance is moral imbalance. When two or more people or collectives disagree about mutual rights, responsibilities, and privileges, they are experiencing moral imbalance. Moral imbalances occur frequently because interpersonal life is characterized by shifting expectations, selective perceptions, and subtle changes in mood and behavior. A moral imbalance could arise between a player and a coach, for example, simply because the player believed she should have received more game time than the coach allowed. Moral life can be described as a process of fluctuation between moral balance and imbalance.

Haan also described moral imbalances that are socially legitimated. A clearly unequal pattern of psychological and material exchange exists, for example, between parent and child. Because the child cannot enter the moral exchange on equal footing, the parent—with greater emotional, cognitive, and material resources—is expected to take greater responsibility and give disproportionately to the exchange. Similar forms of legitimated imbalances might be found between teacher and student, coach and athlete, veteran player and rookie. In legitimated imbalances, the person with greater resources assumes greater responsibility. Even in these relationships, however, the person with greater resources can "overgive," creating in the recipient unhealthy dependency or a burdening sense of indebtedness, guilt, or resentment.

Moral Dialogue

Given the complexities of moral exchange, most people are likely to experience periodic breaks from the moral balance. When imbalances occur, people use various means to try to reestablish moral balance. Haan collectively defined these efforts as *moral dialogue*.

The most obvious and clearest instance of moral dialogue is open, verbal negotiation, as in the effort by representatives of a professional athlete and a team to reach a contract through negotiation. But moral dialogue can take many other forms. If a soccer player is tripped by another player, in violation of both the rules and informal player norms, then the two players are in moral imbalance. Under such circumstances, moral dialogue may take the form of the offended player's hitting the offender with extra force during a later play to communicate "I didn't like what you did to me—don't do it again." The result may be a restored moral balance. If the communication is unsuccessful at restoring balance, further "dialogue" may continue until balance is achieved or the relationship ends. In sum, any communication—direct or indirect, verbal or nonverbal—that is intended to convey information about one's needs or desires in an effort to establish, maintain, or restore moral balance is an instance of moral dialogue.

Moral dialogue typically evolves through phases. Following moral disruption, dialogue occurs that reflects a mutual exploration of the facts, emotions, and parameters of the moral issue at hand. Initially, parties often make fumbling awkward statements of their positions. People are frequently surprised when someone else does not see a moral situation in the same way, and the initial antithesis results in both parties' offering condensed and emotionally charged defenses of their viewpoints. A process of elaboration and clarification follows. People frequently step back in an effort to define the parameters of the dispute, the meanings being attached to words and actions, and the motives for stances taken. The dialogue often concludes when the issues are newly simplified and a new balance is achieved.

People cannot long tolerate moral imbalance. Even if it is impossible to confront someone directly in a moral dispute, dialogue with that person often goes on in one's own head. If there is no effort at mutual resolution over an extended period of time, interest in the relationship tends to wane.

Moral Truth

The effort to establish equalized relationships results in moral balances that are particularized, historically sensitive, and often preconscious. But Haan did not contend that every agreement that is reached is morally adequate simply because the parties implicitly or explicitly endorse it. According to Haan, there can be corrupt or inadequate moral balances.

The problem of defining moral grounds—the moral norms or ideals that undergird one's theory—is invariably controversial. Haan wished to avoid two paradigms: Kohlberg's model of grounding moral psychology in a preferred tradition of moral philosophy, and the internalization approach that begs the question of moral grounds by simply deferring to society. We find Haan's solution intriguing. She saw moral grounds as tethered to the moral dialogue, not to moral solutions. Haan grounded her theory in a procedural approach to fairness rather than a substantive one. In other words, she did not claim that there is an ultimate ''right'' moral theory identifiable by psychologists but believed that psychologists can distinguish processes of moral dialogue that are legitimate from ones that are not. In short, she described a dialogue as fair when it includes as participants all who will be affected by its conclusions, there is no domination, all have equal access to relevant information, and all hold powers of veto. For Haan, *moral truth* is defined as any pragmatic conclusion reached through a moral dialogue that meets these procedural criteria for fairness. Haan believed that these procedural principles of fairness are universally recognized, though she did not claim to have empirically verified this.

Moral Levels

Initially, Haan proposed a model of moral development based on a description of five developmental levels of moral maturity (Haan, 1977a, 1978; Haan et al.,

1985). Later (Haan, 1991) she reframed the levels as incremental increases along a continuum of improved moral adequacy and sensitivity. Essentially, each level reflects a different approach to the structuring of the moral balance. The first two levels comprise what can be called the "assimilation phase" (Shields, 1986), when the person acts to create moral balances that give preference to the needs and concerns of the self. This is not because the person is "selfish," but because she or he cannot comprehend with equal clarity and urgency the needs and desires of others. This situation is turned around during the "accommodation phase," Levels 3 and 4. People reasoning at these levels generally give to the moral exchange more than they receive. Finally, at the "equilibration phase," the person gives equal recognition to all parties' interests.

Secondary Moral Structures

The main structure that defines each moral level is the form of moral balance that the person seeks. Equally important, however, are what Haan called *secondary moral structures*, or substructures. The substructures may best be conceptualized as moral sensitivities and psychological skills that are needed to maintain flexible, responsive, and open moral dialogues and balances. The moral levels, with descriptions of the primary and secondary structures, are described in Table 4.3.

From Action to Thought and Back Again

To ask whether moral reasoning leads to parallel moral action turns Haan's theory upside down. Haan began her work with an investigation of moral action from which she abstracted the concepts that structure her theory. But she, too, recognized that gaps between a person's moral competencies and moral performance are not infrequent.

To help explain discrepancies between competencies and action, Haan placed her moral theory in the broader model of psychological functioning mentioned earlier (Haan, 1977b). This model highlights both structures and ego processes. In short, she theorized that for action to reflect a person's moral capabilities, the person must remain coping in her or his ego processing. Sometimes, however, psychological accuracy is abandoned for the sake of maintaining a coherent and positive sense of self. Particularly under stress, coping may give way to defending, and the quality of moral action may deteriorate.

The role of acute stress in eliciting defensive ego processes is of special interest to sport psychologists because competition often is associated with high levels of stress. Perhaps when excessive emphasis is placed on performance outcome, the resultant stress may encourage temporary moral dysfunctions. This is a relatively unexplored area that is ripe for research.

Table 4.3   Haan's Levels of Moral Adequacy

Level 1	Level 2	Level 3	Level 4	Level 5
		Forms of Moral Balances		
Assimilation > Accommodation (Self-interest > Other interest)	Assimilation > Accommodation (Self-interest > Other interest)	Accommodation > Assimilation (Group > Self- or Other interest)	Accommodation > Assimilation (Group > Self- or Other interests)	Assimilation = Accommodation (equilibration of Self-, Other, Mutual interests)
Assimilation of experiences to self-interest. No sustained view of others' interests; no view of mutual interest.	Accommodation to others' interests when forced. Differentiates others' interests from self but no view of mutual interests.	Assimilation of self-interests to others' interests as the common interest. Differentiates others' interests from self but mutuality is harmony.	Accommodation of self-interests to common interests. Assimilation of common interests to self-interest (self is object among objects).	Assimilation of self-, other and mutual interests. Self-, other, and mutual interests differentiated and coordinated.
		Primary Structure: The Moral Balance		
Vacillates between compliance with others/ thwarting others. Balance occurs when self is indifferent to situations, unequal exchanges of good and bad; momentary compromises.	Trade to get what self wants; sometimes others must get what they want. Balances of coexistence (equal exchange of good and bad in kind and amount).	Emphasis on exchanges is based on sustaining good faith (and excluding bad). Self-interest thought to be identical with others' interests.	Systematized, structured exchanges based on understanding that all persons can fall from grace. Thus balances are conscious compromises made by all people including the self (common interests protect the self-interest).	Integration of self-interests with other and mutual interests to achieve mutual, personally and situationally specific balances. (Balances are preferably based on mutual interests or if necessary, compromises or the lesser of two evils.)

(continued)

Table 4.3 *(continued)*

Level 1	Level 2	Level 3	Level 4	Level 5
A versus B	Prudential compromises by both A and B.	A compromises to "good" Bs; bad Bs rejected.	A and B = AB common	A = B
Secondary Structure: Self as a Moral Being and Object				
I have unqualified rights to secure my own good.	I have a right to secure my own good as others do.	I am a moral being and demonstrate that by my goodness. Thus I have a right to good treatment as do other people.	All persons fall from grace. Thus I subscribe to the common regulation to promote my own interests as well as others'. (Some private self-interests are not subject to negotiation.)	I have human vulnerability, weaknesses and strengths as a moral agent but I have responsibility to myself, others, and our mutual interest to require that others treat me as a moral object. If I don't, the moral balance will be upset.
Secondary Structure: Others as Moral Beings and Objects				
Others are objects who compel or thwart self or who can be compelled by self.	Others are subjects who want their own "good" as I want my own "good."	Most others are morally good; those who act badly to me are exceptions or are "strange," incomprehensible or outside my moral obligation.	Others (and myself) can be culpable. Thus, we must all agree to common regulation to protect our interests. Does not see that the common interest is not synonymous with the mutual interest.	Others also have strengths and weaknesses as moral agents that are variously manifest. I must require others to collaborate in achieving and sustaining moral balances. I need sometimes to forgive others for their

				impositions, given the complexity of situations and the individuality of others and myself.
Secondary Structure: Taking Chances on Others' Good Faith				
Self waits momentarily for others to demonstrate their good faith.	Takes blind chances on others' good faith; can't understand others' defaults as connected with own defaults.	Most people have or should have good faith; negotiates with those of good faith; shuns persons of bad faith as outside one's purview.	To gamble that others negotiate in good faith is foolhardy; the common practice protects all from bad faith and determines the limits of the chances that must be taken for moral balance to be achieved.	Gambles on good faith; instances of bad faith need to be handled in terms of one's moral consideration for one's self, other's individuality, the circumstances, and the self's own occasional transgressions.
Secondary Structure: Righting Wrongs Self Commits (Guilt)				
No idea self can do wrong; others cause self's wrongs.	Self can make a mistake (in the sense of taking more than others will allow).	Self intends no wrong but can make mistakes for which self is not responsible.	Self can commit wrongs, irrespective of intent. Self confesses and must "pay for" wrongs before one can be readmitted to the moral exchange.	Given the complexity of life, self can commit wrongs; reparations reestablish moral balance.
Redress: blame projected.	Redress: avoid further difficulty with other.	Redress: apologies to make it up and restore harmony, or withdrawal from relationship.	Redress: debt must be cancelled by repayment.	Redress: wrong cannot be undone but can be repaired, forgiven, or explained.

(continued)

Table 4.3 (continued)

Level 1	Level 2	Level 3	Level 4	Level 5
Overall Justification for Balance at Each Level				
Others force me/I force them.	Others get what they want so I deserve to get what I want.	I try to be good so I deserve to receive good from others.	I commit myself to the common structured exchange, so I deserve the same considerations and privileges as others receive from common practices.	I am a moral agent among other moral agents; thus I am responsible to others, myself, and to our mutual interests; we are a part of each other's existences.
Reason for Transitions Between Levels				
Increased capability of person to fend for self and awareness that others' desires and interpersonal exchange exists; negotiation is possible and necessary.	Growing awareness of the self's isolation from others if others' interests are not taken into account.	Basic assumption of self and others' goodness becomes insupportable in the face of countering evidence that others act with bad faith on occasion.	Admission of self's culpability; recognition of the insufficiency of common practice to resolve moral dilemmas in sufficient depth for self's and others' needs and rights.	

Reprinted by permission of New York University Press from *On Moral Grounds: The Search for Practical Morality*, by Norma Haan, Elaine Aerts, and Bruce Cooper, in collaboration with Kendall J. Bryant. Copyright © 1985, New York University.

Summary

In this chapter we summarized major theories that reflect a constructivist perspective on moral development. There is little doubt that Kohlberg's monumental work has been the most significant and influential, but several other theorists have contributed significantly to our understanding of human morality. In particular, the work of Gilligan and Haan provides insights into the moral life that are neglected in the Kohlberg formulation. In the next part, we begin a process of integration.

Part II
Understanding
Moral Action

In the previous part we summarized the main theoretical perspectives informing the psychological study of morality. In Part II we suggest ways of bringing these perspectives into relationship. Despite different organizing principles the theories are not as mutually exclusive as their proponents sometimes suggest. To some extent their differences simply reflect different entry points, methodologies, and questions. Those interested in understanding moral development and action need not commit themselves exclusively to one viewpoint.

We will use Haan's model as a beginning point for approaching the task of integration. Haan (1991) acknowledged the significance of Bandura's contributions, and the various self-regulatory mechanisms that Bandura details are no doubt important processes in moral action. In particular, Bandura's descriptions of moral agency and self-efficacy are critical contributions to the moral literature. But when Bandura (1991) discusses the mechanisms by which moral control is activated or disengaged, his description reads like an abbreviation of Haan's more elaborated model of coping and defending. Clearly, important conceptual conflicts—such as their quite different perspectives on ego, self, and cognition—prevent a simple synthesis of the two approaches, but it is equally clear that each theory addresses certain weaknesses in the other.

Haan's model also shares common features with Hoffman's empathy-based model of morality. Hoffman, like Haan, believes that affect plays a central role in moral functioning, and he offers a helpful scheme for organizing different forms of cognitive–affective interactions (Hoffman, 1986). Haan (1991) suggests that the cognitions of morality are usually "hot" cognitions, a significant term that Hoffman also uses to discuss the affectively charged nature of moral reasoning. From Haan's perspective, emotionally charged language communicates more immediate, compelling, and accurate moral information than does the more detached language of purely cognitive discussions of moral disagreements. Haan's blending of cognition and affect has been criticized because it undermines her ability to describe clearly the structural competencies underlying moral functioning (Blasi, 1983a), but just such an integration of cognition and affect is needed to understand the practical morality of everyday life.

Hoffman's sophisticated discussion of the development of empathy and the processes through which empathy is translated into moral motivation surpasses Haan's more superficial treatment of these themes. Haan's view of empathy is restrained by her inclusion of it in the coping processes, where it is more akin to role taking than Hoffman's conceptualization of empathy.

Haan wrote considerably (but inconsistently) about the relation between her theory and Kohlberg's (Haan, 1978; Haan et al., 1985). She vacillated between rejecting Kohlberg's theory outright and seeing the two models as reflecting different dimensions of moral life. We believe the two models are not intrinsically opposed. They address fundamentally different questions. Kohlberg asked, Faced with explicit moral conflicts, how do people optimally reason about them? and Haan asked, Faced with the practical task of coordinating needs and interests, how do people construct agreements they can live with?

Gilligan's theory makes three central claims, all congruent with Haan's conceptualization: Justice is not coextensive with morality; relationships involve subtle, ill-defined responsibilities to care, attend, and be responsive; and moral life is sometimes ambiguous, with no clearly "right" solution (which, incidentally, does not mean that there are no clearly "wrong" solutions). But Gilligan substantively expands Haan's discussion of the origins of moral sentiments through her sensitive description of the two childhood experiences of attachment and inequality. Gilligan does not, however, adequately describe what constitutes moral maturity and competent moral functioning (Walker, 1991). Haan's levels of interactional morality provide just such a description.

We have offered these brief reflections on points of convergence among various theories not to claim that we are at the threshold of a grand, comprehensive moral theory. We could also detail mutually contradictory presuppositions in the theories as well, but we want to enable you to use multiple vantage points to reflect on moral issues in sport and physical activity contexts, and we believe this is best done when points of convergence can be identified.

Perhaps moral development might be conceptualized as a three-track process: development of moral reasoning, development of such affective capacities as empathy and sympathy, and development of interactional moral skills. In rough approximations, we take Kohlberg's theory to reflect the development of moral reasoning, the theories of Gilligan and Hoffman to describe the development of moral affect, and the theory of Haan to describe the development of interactional moral skills (though none of the theories can be pigeonholed quite so neatly). Although the three tracks can be named for purposes of analysis, they are interactive, both in their development and in every concrete moral situation.

In this part we move from moral development to moral action. Chapter 5 presents a model of moral action that can be used to coordinate research findings from diverse perspectives. Each of the remaining chapters in Part II addresses research related to processes identified in the model.

Chapter 5
Toward an Integrated Model of Moral Action

Probably the most critical question for psychologists interested in moral phenomena pertains to the source of moral behavior. In moral accounting action is the bottom line. In this chapter we introduce a model designed to organize the major influences on moral action. The next several chapters elaborate on different components of this model, surveying theoretical and empirical work that sheds light on its component processes, particularly as they relate to sport and physical activity. But before summarizing the model, we need to mention two problems related to the study of moral action.

First, the study of morality necessitates investigating people's intentions, but these are not directly observable. A basketball coach who puts the second string in after the first string builds a commanding lead may be motivated by a desire to display good sportspersonship, a desire to not risk injury to the top players, or perhaps even a desire to humiliate the opponents. But an observer has no direct access to the coach's motivation.

To avoid complications arising from their lack of direct access to people's subjective experience, many investigators focus on "prosocial" rather than "moral" behavior. Though definitions vary somewhat (Eisenberg, 1982), most researchers concur that *prosocial behavior* is intentional behavior that benefits another. No specific motive for benefiting the other, however, is specified in the definition. Thus, a person may engage in prosocial behavior for altruistic, egoistic, or other reasons. In this and following chapters, we use the term *prosocial behavior* when referring to research that leaves the intention of the actor ambiguous. In contrast, we limit the term *moral behavior* to those instances in which researchers were interested both in behavior and its underlying motive or meaning.

A second problem associated with moral action research is the complexity one encounters in moving from an analysis of moral utterances in response to stylized, hypothetical stories to moral action in the real world. The causal factors responsible for moral behavior are multiple and varied, and they interact in complex ways. Some organizational tool is required to gain a handle on this complexity. The various factors involved in moral action must be divided into theoretically coherent clusters, and these clusters must be organized into a model that suggests how the factors might interrelate empirically. Introducing such a model is the main task of this chapter.

Rest's Model of Moral Action

James Rest (1983, 1984, 1986, 1994) elaborates an approach to model building that we have found useful. He begins with a straightforward question: "What do we have to suppose went on in the head of a person who acts morally in some situation?" (1984, p. 25). In answer, Rest suggests that at least four major processes are implicated in every moral action; deficiencies in any process can result in a failure to behave morally. In brief, a person must interpret the situation and the action possibilities, form a moral judgment about what should be done, choose a value (moral or nonmoral) to seek through action, and carry out the intended act. These four processes, summarized in Table 5.1, define Rest's four-process model for understanding moral behavior.

Rest's model is useful for at least three reasons. First, it renders the complexity of moral behavior more manageable by organizing moral constructs and research into meaningful components. Second, rather than dividing cognition and affect, it enables the investigator to consider cognitive–affective interactions within and among component processes. Finally, and perhaps most important, the model is built on a descriptive analysis of the necessary processes that flow into moral action. The description, however, is rooted in everyday language so that it remains as theory-independent as possible. As a result, scholars can use the model to coordinate insights from different research traditions without requiring that integrated approaches have no incompatible assumptions. The hope is that one can swim in an eclectic pool without drifting into theoretically shallow waters.

To clarify and illustrate the four processes, let's reflect on a hypothetical situation. Suppose Kate is playing a game of marbles with Tameron. Kate has

Table 5.1   Rest's Four-Component Model of Moral Action

Process 1

Question addressed: How does the person interpret the situation?

Major function: To interpret the situation in terms of how one's actions affect the welfare of others.

Cognitive-affective interactions: Drawing inferences about how the other will be affected and feeling empathy, disgust, and so on, for the other.

Situational factors influencing component: Ambiguity of people's needs, intentions, and actions; familiarity with the situation; amount of time available; degree of personal danger and susceptibility to pressure; sheer number of elements involved and the saliency of crucial cues; complexity of cause-and-effect links; preconceptions and prior expectations.

Process 2

Question addressed: How does the person define the moral course of action?

Major function: To formulate what a moral course of action would be.

Cognitive-affective interactions: Both abstract-logical and attitudinal-valuing aspects are involved in constructing moral meaning; moral ideals are composed of both cognitive and affective elements.

Situational factors influencing component: Factors affecting the application of particular social norms or moral ideals; delegation of responsibility to someone else; prior conditions or agreements; the particular combination of moral issues involved; preempting one's sense of fairness by prior commitments to some ideology or code.

Process 3

Question addressed: How does the person choose which valued outcome to pursue?

Major function: To select from among competing value outcomes or ideals the one to act on.

Cognitive-affective interactions: Calculation of relative utilities of various goals; mood influencing outlook; defensive distortion of perception.

Situational factors influencing component: Factors that activate motives other than moral motives; factors that influence estimates of costs and benefits; factors that influence subjective estimates of the probability of certain occurrences; factors that affect self-esteem and willingness to risk oneself; defensively reinterpreting the situation by blaming the victim, denying need or deservingness.

Process 4

Question addressed: How does the person implement the intention?

Major function: To execute and implement what one intends to do.

Cognitive-affective interactions: Task persistence as affected by cognitive transformation of the goal.

Situational factors influencing component: Factors that physically prevent one from carrying out a moral plan of action; factors that distract, fatigue, or disgust a person; cognitive transformations of a goal; timing difficulties in managing more than one plan at a time.

Adapted from "The Major Components of Morality" by J.R. Rest. In *Morality, Moral Behavior, and Moral Development* (pp. 356-629) by W. Kurtines and J. Gewirtz (Eds.), 1984, New York: Wiley.

just shot her "cat's eye" at Tameron's "clearie" and missed. Her marble eventually comes to rest off the sidewalk and in the grass some distance from the action. Knowing that Tameron is younger and more naive about neighborhood marble rules, Kate quickly invents a little verse that she considers reciting to advantage herself:

Marble in the grass,
My turn is in the trash;
Touch my toes, touch my face,
Back to the starting place,
Dash, dash, dash!

Perhaps, Kate muses, she could pick up her marble (after completing the gyrations described in her verse), run back to her original place, and take her shot over again—all with Tameron observing quizzically but contently. Now let's step back to the beginning of the episode and peek into Kate's brain as she moves toward a moral action.

Imagine that Kate has just completed her errant shot and is assessing the situation. She is involved in Process I. Kate wonders just how naive Tameron really is. If she recites her chant will it advantage her significantly? Would such an action hurt Tameron's feelings? How likely is it that another child playing nearby will notice and reveal her deception? In brief, Rest's first process reflects a recognition that moral action builds on a particular understanding or interpretation of a given situation. Implicit in that interpretation are the actor's views of the alternatives that might be taken and the anticipated consequences of those actions for the actor and for the others involved.

Having decided that she could probably get away with it, Kate next tries to decide whether the action she is considering would really be OK. Is this what she *should* do? Is it right to take advantage of Tameron's innocence? On the other hand, is it right to deny her own creativity? Is it her responsibility or her opponent's to monitor her rule compliance? Just what is a fair game? Process II of Rest's model involves considering "what is right" in a given situation. But moral options are never selected in a vacuum, and this is indicated by Rest's third process.

Kate has decided from a purely moral standpoint that she should refrain from her contemplated action. But it's just a game, she reasons, and it would be fun to do it. Furthermore, she knows that the outcome of the game is more important to her than to Tameron. But, on the other hand, if she did it, she would feel crummy inside. And if Tameron figured out what she had done, Tameron's feelings could be hurt. Kate is weighing what is really most important to her in this situation. The moral values elevated in Process II compete with a host of nonmoral values for priority. In the universe of real choices, moral values are but a few stars in a sky full of attractive options. Finally, Kate reaches a decision. She chooses in Process III to refrain from using her made-up verse because her moral values outweigh the nonmoral ones.

But then, on impulse, Kate slips up. With a grin, she recites the verse, picks up her marble, and trots back to her original position. Process IV of Rest's model reflects the fact that even after a moral action has been decided on, its successful completion requires a number of personal skills. Such constructs as ego strength or self-regulation skills refer to the colloquial "having the strength of one's convictions."

We hope that this example helped you better understand the four processes of Rest's model of morality. But even if we were successful in that effort, our illustration has several misleading features. First, we have presented the processes as if they occurred in an orderly temporal sequence. In reality, they may be experienced in varying order, and often more than one can be operative simultaneously. No doubt there are feedback and feedforward loops in sociomoral processing; partially completed aspects of one process influence how another process is being handled, and so on (Rest, 1983, 1984). Sociomoral processing often includes detours, dead ends, and conceptual and emotional gyrations that cannot be represented in a simple model. Nonetheless, there is a kind of logical progression among the processes so that it makes sense—for purposes of analysis—to divide the processes leading to moral action in the manner described.

In addition, we have described the processes as if they were primarily conscious ruminations. This is probably the exception rather than the rule. A considerable amount of sociomoral processing occurs outside awareness and is not as explicit as our illustration suggests.

Finally, our illustration emphasizes cognitive processing. Rest, however, envisions that each process exhibits both cognitive and affective dimensions, together with cognitive–affective interactions. Indeed, many moral situations may ignite more emotional heat than rational light. Rest assumes, as we do, that moral action is guided by moral reasoning that is infused with and partially motivated by such feelings as empathy, sympathy, pride, and guilt.

A 12-Component Model of Moral Action

Rest's model of moral action provides a highly useful tool for exploring moral action. We believe, however, that the model could be made more useful by elaborting a tripartite description of influences that impact each of Rest's processes. The three main sources of influence that we believe should be integrated systematically into a model of moral functioning are contextual factors, personal competencies, and ego-processing variables. Obviously a substratum of genetic and biological competencies and predispositions are also relevant, but we do not elaborate on them here.

Contextual Factors

The environment certainly plays a central role in eliciting and sustaining various forms of behavior, including moral behavior. As social learning and social cognitive theorists have documented at length, behavior conforms, at least in part, to environmental influences. Moreover, there is often an ecology to behavior that situates it appropriately within an environment (Barker, 1968). For example, when people enter stadium bleachers, they sit. Such behavior is not determined by desire for reward or fear of punishment; it is simply viewed as contextually "fitting."

Contexts are infinitely complex. In our model, we focus only on those aspects of the environment that consistently and significantly influence moral action in physical activity contexts. Let us summarize these.

The contextual influences most relevant to Process I—interpreting the situation—are the *goal structure* and the degree of ambiguity present. By goal structure, we are referring to the cooperative/competitive structuring of the environment.

Process II involves arriving at a judgment about "the moral thing to do." We suggest that the most significant contextual influence on this process is the *moral atmosphere*, the prevailing moral norms that are recognized in a group.

Selecting among competing values is at the heart of Process III. Related to the issue of value choice are what we call the "domain cues" present in the context. Environments are not uniform in terms of the competencies and motives they activate. Some contexts may tend to activate only a person's moral capacities and motives, but these are rare. More often the environment will activate simultaneously a person's moral, social-conventional, and prudential reasoning, to name just three "domains" of reasoning. Understanding how contexts provide cues that elicit different forms of processing and activate different motives is crucial for investigating Process III.

Contexts also vary widely in how power is distributed and exercised. Such variations clearly impact the impediments that may be encountered in carrying out one's decision to act in a particular manner, the process central to Process IV. Power structures play a major role in determining, for example, how one's gender, ethnicity, class, and social status influence one's ability, perceived and real, to carry out an intended action.

Two additional comments about the contextual influences deserve mention before we move to personal competencies. First, we do not claim a one-to-one correspondence between the features of the environment we have outlined and the associated process. Clearly, each contextual influence can affect each of the four processes of the model. The moral atmosphere, for example, will influence the process of choice as well as judgment. Still, we believe we have arranged the contextual factors in a logical and coherent fashion that should facilitate the investigation of how these factors influence moral action.

Second, we must emphasize that contexts are interpreted. Kelley and Thibant (1978) make this point in their differentiation of the *given matrix* and the *effective matrix*. The given matrix refers to the objective conditions of the external situation. These conditions are transformed through various mental processes into the final subjective image of the situation, the effective matrix. The individual acts in relation to the effective rather than the given matrix. For this reason we sometimes discuss relevant personal variables under the heading of context when these personal variables clearly mediate how a person perceives the contextual factors identified.

Personal Competency Influences

We adhere to the main tenets of the structural developmental approach and believe that an articulation of the cognitive and affective competencies that make moral action possible is essential to fully understanding morality. A description of a person's relevant competencies provides a window into how that person might behave when he or she lives up to full potential. Sometimes these competencies can be described in structural terms. Structural competencies, however, are theoretical abstractions that can be studied and understood only through an analysis of specific contents. For example, knowing a person's moral stage is useful in understanding moral action only as that stage is manifested through particular moral beliefs, attitudes, and values (aspects of moral "content"). Consequently, under this heading we sometimes include both a description of the relevant structural competencies and their associated contents.

Role-taking and perspective-taking abilities are the structural competencies that we believe most clearly underlie Process I, interpreting the context. The associated content pertains to whose perspective is taken and what information is gleaned.

Moral reasoning stage is the structural competence underlying the second process, with moral beliefs, attitudes, and values the complement. The processing of moral contents through a person's moral stage yields two types of judgments that influence the production of moral action: deontic judgments and responsibility judgments. Deontic judgments reflect a person's belief about what is right in the given context, whereas responsibility judgments reflect whether a person believes that she or he is obligated to act on that belief.

The self-structure—the person's organized perceptions and evaluations of the self—is a dynamic psychological organization that influences Process III. Two critical dimensions of the self-structure particularly important to the theme of moral motivation—the dominant theme of Process III—are motivational orientation and the moral self. Motivational orientation refers to whether one is oriented primarily to demonstrating competence relative to others or relative to one's own performance. The moral self refers to the moral qualities that one uses to define oneself.

People who can anticipate problems, creatively design solutions, negotiate differences, and rectify interpersonal errors are more likely to succeed in carrying out their moral intentions than others who are weak in these skills. The social-cognitive capacities that most clearly underlie these diverse skills are psychological autonomy and social problem-solving skills.

Ego-Processing Influences

We have used Haan's (1977b) model of ego processing to articulate the third track of influences related to each process of moral action. Ego processes mediate and coordinate among intrapsychic structures and between the intrapsychic world and the environment. Psychological structures such as moral stages are theoretical abstractions, and in their actual psychological functioning they are dependent on the elicitation, use, and manipulation of various kinds of information. Ego processes are invoked for these tasks.

The distinction between personal competencies and ego processes is the distinction between what defines a person's optimal capacity for moral action and what mediates that capacity in actual performance. Stated differently, if moral action is less than optimal, it may be because the person is immature (i.e., a developmental deficiency in a relevant personal competency) or because the person situationally defaulted (i.e., a deficiency in ego processing). Ego processes help us understand why people sometimes fulfill their potential and other times do not. In an elaborate series of moral investigations, Haan and her colleagues demonstrated convincingly that ego processes are significant mediators of moral action (Haan et al., 1985; also Bartek, Krebs, & Taylor, 1993). In fact, people's ego processing was of greater influence than their stage of reasoning (as assessed in hypothetical interviews), the situational context, or the group's structure.

Haan's taxonomy of ego processes identifies 10 generic functions, each reflecting a process, function, or regulation that is required for constructive-integrative psychological activity. Thus, for example, the generic function of "discrimination" is involved when the individual must separate idea from feeling, idea from idea, or feeling from feeling. Haan organizes the 10 generic functions into four categories, depending on the type of mental activity implicated: intraceptive, cognitive, affective impulse regulating, and attention focusing. Table 5.2 summarizes the 10 generic functions.

Generic ego functions are theoretical abstractions, labels used for collections of concrete processes. When a psychological task is performed that requires the use of a generic function, what is elicited is one of three possible modes of generic function expression—coping, defending, or fragmenting. That is, a person will exhibit a coping, defending, or fragmenting form of the generic function. Each of the 10 generic functions can be further specified by distinguishing its alternate modes of expression.

The three modes of coping, defending, and fragmenting are distinguished from each other by a set of formal properties. Most importantly, coping processes are flexible, purposive, and responsive to reality. Coping processes involve accurate handling of information or affect. In contrast, defending processes are rigid, distorting, and pushed from the psychological past. Fragmenting processes move further down the path of distortion into realms of fantasy. Although everybody fragments occasionally, fragmentation as a concept is most useful in studying severe psychological disturbance and will not be pursued further here. Table 5.3 presents the complete taxonomy of coping and defending ego processes.

The coping and defending processes reflect a hierarchical order of utility. Coping processes are most useful in maintaining open, clear, and flexible interchange, both intrapsychically and in interaction with others and the environment. People will use coping processes when they can. When someone's sense of self is threatened,

Table 5.2   Haan's Model of Ego Processing (Generic Processes)

Reflexive-intraceptive functions
 1. **Delayed response**: ability to hold up decisions, to time-bind tension due to personal or situational complexities or lack of clarity
 2. **Sensitivity**: apprehending often unexpressed feelings or thoughts of others
 3. **Time reversion**: replaying or recapturing experiences, feelings, attitudes, ideas of the past

Cognitive functions
 4. **Discrimination**: separating idea from feeling, idea from idea, and feeling from feeling by using cognitive functioning
 5. **Detachment**: letting one's mind "roam freely"; speculating and analyzing without a sense of forbiddance
 6. **Means-end symbolization**: relating causal connections; anticipating outcomes or analyzing alternative choices

Affective impulse–regulating functions
 7. **Diversion**: modifying or redirecting the expression, the aim, or the situation of one's affect
 8. **Transformation**: modulating, transforming, or reversing an affect
 9. **Restraint**: withholding the immediate expression of affect

Attention-focusing function
 10. **Selective awareness**: focusing attention

Note. Adapted from *Coping and Defending: Processes of Self-Environment Organization* (pp. 300-307) by N. Haan, 1977, New York: Academic Press. Copyright 1977 by Academic Press. Adapted by permission.

however, coping can be too painful or disturbing. Defending processes are used when necessary to maintain a positive, coherent sense of self. Stressful situations often result in the use of defensive ego processes. In actuality, people often use some combination of coping and defending processes in complex situations.

People have a repertoire of preferred coping and defending strategies. Some rely more heavily on the use of particular ego processes. And what ego processes are invoked depends heavily on the contextual demands. When faced with challenging situations, people tend to move up (or down) a hierarchy of preferred or situationally elicited processes to resolve the problem. With regard to moral problems, people will tend to function close to their optimal moral capacity if they remain coping, but moral defaults frequently accompany the slip into defensive processing.

In our model of moral action, we place the *intraceptive functions* under Process I. These processes reflect people's assimilatory engagement with their own thoughts, feelings, and intuitions in response to what is happening both internally and in the environment. Two of the intraceptive coping processes are particularly relevant to moral action: empathy and the ability to tolerate ambiguity.

The *cognitive functions* are associated with Process II. Clearly, the coping processes of objectivity, intellectuality, and logical analysis are essential to the

Table 5.3   Taxonomy of Ego Processes

	Modes	
Generic functions	Coping	Defending
Reflexive-intraceptive functions		
1. Delayed response	Tolerance of ambiguity	Doubt
2. Sensitivity	Empathy	Projection
3. Time reversion	Regression-ego	Regression
Cognitive functions		
4. Discrimination	Objectivity	Isolation
5. Detachment	Intellectuality	Intellectualizing
6. Means-ends symbolization	Logical analysis	Rationalization
Affective impulse–regulating functions		
7. Diversion	Sublimation	Displacement
8. Transformation	Substitution	Reaction formation
9. Restraint	Suppression	Repression
Attention-focusing function		
10. Selective awareness	Concentration	Denial

Note. Adapted from *Coping and Defending: Processes of Self-Environment Organization* (p. 35) by N. Haan, 1977, New York: Academic Press. Copyright 1977 by Academic Press. Adapted by permission.

formation of moral judgments. Similarly, the defending processes of isolation, intellectualizing, and rationalization can derail moral action at this critical juncture of the moral action process.

The *affective impulse–regulating functions* are associated in our model with Process III. These ego functions are particularly useful when different motive forces need to be coordinated, as is the case with Process III. The coping processes of sublimation, substitution, and suppression are certainly vital if conflicting emotional needs seek expression. Similarly, the defending processes of displacement, reaction formation, and repression are likely to result in poor coordination among activated motives.

Finally, the attention-focusing function of selective awareness is featured in Process IV. When people use the coping process of concentration, they can set aside disturbing or attractive feelings or thoughts to focus on the task at hand. Such ability is needed to follow-through on an action choice.

Summary

In this chapter we have outlined a 12-component model of moral action. Before a moral action can occur, the moral agent must

1. interpret the situation,
2. decide on a course of moral action,
3. choose to act on the moral value or a competing nonmoral one, and
4. move from intended action to completed action.

Each of the four processes is influenced by contextual factors, personal competencies, and ego-processing variables. The model, complete with exemplars of each component, is depicted in Table 5.4.

We elaborate the 12-component model of moral action in the coming four chapters. Each chapter discusses the three sets of influences as they relate to the process under consideration. Wherever possible, we report research related to physical activity contexts. Before we move to our discussion of Process I, however, two additional remarks are necessary. The first pertains to the intended scope of the model. Does the model apply to all moral behavior? The answer is a qualified yes. If by moral action we mean, as we generally do, action that is motivated by moral reasons and affects, then the answer is yes. But many quasi-moral actions are performed habitually or automatically with little processing (Langer, Blank, & Chanowitz, 1978; Piliavin, Dovidio, Gaertner, & Clark, 1981). Particularly when the behavior is of little cost to the actor and the act required is simple and straightforward, the action may be performed more-or-less automatically (Eisenberg & Shell, 1985). Many sport behaviors may fit this pattern because of the habituated, overlearned nature of much sport conduct. We prefer to label such behavior prosocial (or antisocial) rather than moral, however, to maintain the important theoretical distinction between action guided by moral motivations and simply intentional positive (or negative) action.

A second point regards our criteria for selecting key constructs to discuss in conjunction with each process. Because we cannot in a few short chapters discuss all the constructs potentially relevant to each of the four processes, we used three major selection criteria. First, we were interested primarily in elucidating major constructs related to moral action. We review literature related to empathy but not to countertransference, for example, even though an argument could be made that countertransference is relevant in some moral situations.

Second, we tried to draw from literature that is not radically discrepant theoretically from the main perspective offered throughout this book. We have not, for example, tried to integrate literature from sociobiologists because the underlying assumptions of most researchers in that field diverge so significantly from our focal viewpoint. Still, we have drawn from a wide range of literature (and may well be guilty of overintegration—see Blasi, 1983a, for a warning on this).

Our last major criterion was that the literature be relevant to an analysis of moral action in physical activity contexts. We believe that the psychological processes that underlie moral behavior in sport differ little from those that underlie moral action in other areas of life. Nonetheless, sport presents some unique features that need to be incorporated into the model. For example, in our discussion of the personal competencies that are engaged in Process II we will discuss "game reasoning." The construct of game reasoning may have less relevance to other moral settings, especially noncompetitive contexts. With those comments in mind, we turn to a detailed consideration of Process I—interpreting the situation.

Table 5.4   12-Component Model of Moral Action

Influences	Processes			
	1. Interpretation	2. Judgment	3. Choice	4. Implementation
A. Contextual	Goal structure; situational ambiguity	Moral atmosphere	Domain cues	Power structure
B. Personal competencies	Role taking; perspective taking	Moral reasoning	Self-structure	Autonomy and social problem-solving skills
C. Ego processing	Intraceptive processes	Cognitive ego processes	Affective impulse–regulating processes	Attention-focusing processes

Chapter 6
Interpreting the Situation

In the last chapter we summarized a 12-component model of moral action. Drawing from Rest (1983, 1984), we identified four interrelated processes that feed into moral behavior: interpreting the situation, forming a moral judgment, selecting an action choice, and implementing one's choice. In addition, we identified three sources of influence impacting each process: contextual, personal competency, and ego processing. In this chapter, we probe more deeply into the influences on interpreting the situation.

Narváez (1993) suggests that Process I can be subdivided into moral perception and moral interpretation. The process begins with a preconscious coming to awareness that a moral issue is at hand or is surfacing. From that point, the person begins a sequence of mental processes that lead to comprehending who and what is involved in the situation. Process I terminates with the identification of the potential implications of different courses of action that one might take. If moral action is to follow, Process I will activate moral sensitivities to the interests of self and other, sensitivities that are both cognitive and affective.

The manner in which someone perceives and interprets a situation is influenced by the degree and nature of situational ambiguity and the goal structure (contextual variables), the person's role-taking and perspective-taking capabilities (competency variables), and the person's ambiguity tolerance and empathy (ego-processing variables).

Contextual Influences

Several characteristics of a situation will influence how a person is likely to process it. Among the most important situational influences on moral action are the degree of ambiguity present and the context's goal structure.

Situational Ambiguity

Interpreting situations is not always easy, particularly with regard to moral qualities. Often one must interpret from ambiguous clues the meaning of several people's behavior, inferring their needs or desires and imagining how one's own actions might affect them both immediately and in the future. An athletic administrator who needs to make important policy decisions about sport programs, for example, inevitably faces great ambiguity because the impact of her choices is mediated through complex social structures and involves unpredictable chains of events.

The importance of ambiguity has been demonstrated experimentally. In general, the greater the ambiguity, the less likely is prosocial behavior (Bear, 1989; Staub, 1978). Environmental factors influence the level of ambiguity, including saliency of cues, the number of people involved, familiarity with the people and issues, and so on. In the context of sport, at least three sources of ambiguity stand out—time pressures, rules and norms, and the unobservable nature of motives.

In the fast pace of sport, athletes rarely have time to think through complex situational cues, and correspondingly they tend to act on only the most salient information. Furthermore, coaches may discourage athletes from reflecting on ambiguous cues. When a coach instructs her team, "Don't think, just do what I say" or says, "The opponent who is limping is the weak link," her athletes may fail to see the moral ambiguities present.

Another source of ambiguity in sport arises from its rule-governed nature. Sport action is governed by rules, but their application is often difficult and imprecise. An official, for example, must decide whether a pitch is a strike or a ball, whether a volleyball player's hand has crossed the midline, whether a particular physical contact in basketball constitutes a foul, and so on. Errors are frequent, but they often are difficult to determine with clarity. The resultant ambiguity creates a void into which athletes and spectators pour their attributions, many rife with moral implications. "The ref is against us" is probably one of the most common. Adding to the ambiguity is the fact that players develop informal norms that also guide behavior, and, like the formal rules, these are rife with ambiguity.

The inaccessible nature of motives also creates ambiguity. Because players' motives are typically unstated, and sometimes deliberately disguised for strategic purposes, the intentions of others are often unclear. For example, forceful physical contact during a contact sport may reflect aggression, assertion, or accidental collision, but the recipient may not know which. Clearly, if a player believes he or a teammate was deliberately hurt, he will respond differently than if he believes the contact was unintentional.

Situational ambiguity affects moral action by influencing the perception of the moral meanings latent in the situation. When perceptions of moral meaning are confused, distorted, or unclear, decisions about rights and responsibilities may be tentative or based on erroneous assumptions. Furthermore, ambiguity can encourage perceptions that lead to moral transgressions. The considerable ambiguity related to rules and rule enforcement, informal norms, and others' motives—all happening in the pressure cooker of time stress—easily fosters instances of perceived injustice where a player or fan believes that she or he has been unfairly disadvantaged. Perceived injustice is a main contributor to aggression and violence in sport, on the part of both athletes and spectators (Mark, Bryant, & Lehman, 1983; Smith, 1976).

No one has made a systematic empirical investigation of the relationship between moral behavior and amount or kind of ambiguity in a sport setting. It might reasonably be hypothesized that as ambiguity increases so might the prevalence of moral defaults. Such a hypothesis is supported indirectly by the finding that sports using equipment that can be viewed as either a sport implement or a weapon are prone to violence (Coakley, 1990; Mark et al., 1983). In such sports, the equipment itself is ambiguous in terms of intended use.

We have placed our discussion of situational ambiguity under the heading of contextual influences. In reality, however, situational ambiguity—like all other contextual mediators of action—is a product of both intrinsic features of the environment and characteristics of the interpreter, characteristics that may change developmentally. As children mature, they become more able to interpret accurately others' internal dynamics. For example, one study compared the ability of preschoolers and third graders to identify correctly the source of a child's distress (Pearl, 1985). Two videotapes were observed. In one video a child tries to open a cookie jar, can't, says ''Rats!'' and becomes distressed. The second tape is similar, but the expletive is deleted, making the cause of the child's agitation less explicit. The older children could accurately determine the nature of the problem in both tapes, but the preschoolers needed the ''Rats!'' as a cue.

Even individuals at similar developmental levels differ widely in their sensitivity to the needs and interests of others. The moral qualities of a situation may be ambiguous to some simply because they are less sensitive than others to moral cues. Schwartz (1977), for example, found wide differences in people's tendency to be aware of the possible consequences of their behavior for the welfare of others. This may account for a somewhat odd finding in a study involving male athletes. Marczynski (1989) found that a moral discussion program did not advance athletes' moral judgment ability but that participants' social behavior was improved nonetheless, perhaps as a consequence of an enhanced ability to recognize a moral situation.

Goal Structure

Another contextual influence particularly relevant to our theme is goal structure. Whether behavior occurs in a context that is competitive, noncompetitive, cooperative, or ambiguous is very important. Competition tends to both reduce the frequency of prosocial behavior and increase antisocial behavior (Barnett & Bryan, 1974; Berkowitz, 1973; Berndt, 1981; Bryan, 1977; Deutsch, 1985; Gelfand & Hartmann, 1978; Kleiber & Roberts, 1981; McGuire & Thomas, 1975; Rausch, 1965; Staub & Norenberg, 1981). In contrast, cooperative experiences enhance prosocial behavior (Aronson, Bridgeman, & Geffner, 1978; Debellefeuille, 1990) and decrease antisocial behavior (Sherif & Sherif, 1969).

David and Roger Johnson and their colleagues have extensively reviewed the literature on competition and cooperation (Johnson & Johnson, 1983; Johnson & Johnson, 1989; Johnson, Johnson, & Maruyama, 1983; Johnson, Maruyama, Johnson, Nelson, & Skon, 1981). Among the most important of their conclusions are the following:

1. Cooperation is more effective than competition in promoting achievement and productivity.
2. There is more positive interaction across ethnic lines among students in cooperative learning situations than in competitive ones.
3. Cooperative experiences promote greater cognitive and affective perspective taking than competitive ones.
4. Cooperative experiences promote higher levels of self-esteem than competitive ones.

Terry Orlick (1981b), in a study with mixed results, demonstrated the potential of cooperative experiences to enhance sharing behavior in physical activity contexts. Participants were 5-year-old children ($N = 71$) from two different schools in Canada. Each school had one experimental and one control group. Children in the two experimental groups played cooperative games for 18 weeks, while those in the control groups played traditional games for an equivalent period. Sharing behavior was assessed by asking children to share candy with children in another class. Conflicting results were found: Among children in the cooperative games programs, those in one school were significantly more willing to share, whereas those in the other school showed no change. Children in the traditional games program in one school were significantly less willing to share, but no difference was found for the other school. These inconsistent results may be attributed to the single measure of sharing or possibly to different instructional styles or curricula.

Another interesting study using cooperative games was conducted by Steven Grineski (1989a, 1989b). Studying 3- and 4-year-olds ($N = 13$), some developmentally delayed, he designed a games curriculum to promote affective, psychomotor, and cognitive development. Over the course of 3 weeks, children participated in 36 half-hour sessions of either cooperative games or gross motor play activities. A behavioral checklist was used to record positive and negative physical contact, verbal interactions, and goal-related cooperative behavior during posttest free play. Results indicated that the cooperative games, compared to the gross motor play, resulted in higher rates of positive physical contact, especially for the developmentally delayed children; higher rates of goal-related cooperative behavior; and decreasing instances of negative physical contact and negative verbal interactions. However, the generalizability of the results is limited, due to both the small sample size and the narrow age range.

Unfortunately, the bulk of the competition/cooperation literature does not clearly indicate the mechanisms through which competition is hypothesized to constrain moral behavior. Two hypotheses seem reasonable. First, competitive contexts may focus participants' attention on the self, decreasing sensitivity to the needs and interests of others, particularly opponents (Staub, 1978). This hypothesis rests on the idea that competitive contexts decrease prosocial behavior through reducing state empathy. A second mechanism through which experience in competitive contexts may impede prosocial behavior is by influencing participants' attributions of others' motives. For example, extensive competitive experience may encourage participants to attribute competitive orientations to others. Kelley and Stahleski (1970) found that those individuals who believed people in general are competitive rather than cooperative behaved more competitively in a game with an ambiguous goal structure.

Intergroup Competition

Both of these explanations can shed light on the effects of competition in individual terms. Competition, however, is often between groups. Muzafer and Carolyn Sherif were among the first to investigate intergroup behavior in a natural environment. Beginning in the 1950s, they conducted a series of field studies with summer boys camps that placed groups in competitive or cooperative contexts. Probably the most famous was conducted in Robbers' Cave State Park in Oklahoma (Sherif & Sherif, 1969). During the first phase of the experiment, lasting 3 days, the 12-year-old boys got acquainted and began to form friendship groups. For the following 4 days, the boys were divided into two groups, each having its own clubhouse and activities. Group cohesion was built by such things as developing group names (the Eagles and the Rattlers) and embellishing shirts and caps with distinctive group insignia. In the third phase, competition between groups was introduced. For 5 days, the groups competed for prizes in games like soccer and softball. As the days progressed, initial playful and sportspersonlike behaviors began to evaporate. For example, the customary after-the-game cheer ''2-4-6-8, who do we appreciate?'' turned into a derisive chant—''2-4-6-8, who do we appreci-hate?" By the end of the 5 days, hostility between groups was open and heated. In the final phase of the experiment, the Sherifs introduced "superordinate goals" to encourage a cooperative orientation. Tasks were introduced that required the groups to work together to achieve common benefits. By the time the campers left for home, the Rattlers and the Eagles had abandoned their antagonisms, and friendships had begun to form across group lines.

Diab (1970) attempted to replicate the Sherif's experiments and was rewarded for the effort with a trip to the hospital for exhaustion (Rabbie, 1982)! Diab had been highly successful in arousing intergroup hostility through competition. In fact, the experiment was abruptly terminated when police evacuated the camp after several boys were involved in knifing members of the other group.

The line of investigation begun by the Sherifs (Sherif, Harvey, White, Hood, & Sherif, 1961; Sherif & Sherif, 1969) and Diab (1970) and later elaborated in a series of investigations by Jacob Rabbie (1982) of the Netherlands clearly demonstrates that such morally relevant attitudes and behaviors as hostility and aggression can spring more from a contextual goal structure than from such intrapersonal factors as authoritarian personalities, low moral maturity, inability to empathize, and the like.

One way that competition may facilitate aggression is by shaping the perception of group differences. Even without competition, people tend to exaggerate differences between members of different groups and minimize differences among members of the same group (Secord, 1959; Tajfel, 1957). Competition furthers this "augmentation effect," leading participants to exaggerate differences in values and norms between the competing groups (Deutsch, 1985). The exaggeration of intergroup differences often has negative consequences. Erikson (1969) observed that people tend to define as less human those people who differ from "us" in terms of appearance, norms, cultures, and so on. Consistent with this perspective, Johnson and Johnson (1983) found that competitive experiences between individuals with disabilities and people without disabilities interfered with the promotion of perspective-taking ability between the two.

Competition: A Multifaceted Phenomenon

Competition of course does not always result in knifings, fights, or other acts of aggression. Competition is not a singular phenomena but a multifaceted process that is structured differently and experienced differently under varying circumstances. The question is under what conditions competition impedes prosocial behavior or facilitates antisocial behavior.

To illustrate, Pepitone and Kleiner (1957) studied the effect of game outcome and perceived threat on the social behavior of boys (ages 7 to 13) in a summer camp setting. Behavioral observations were recorded during preliminary and play-off games. After the preliminary games, half of the teams that won were told they would probably win the play-off game (high-status, low-threat condition) and half were told they would probably lose (high-status, high-threat condition). The high- and low-threat conditions were also administered to the teams that lost the preliminary games (low-status teams). It was found that the high-status, low-threat team members expressed more hostility toward their opponents than the high-status, high-threat team members. As for the teams that lost in the preliminary games, the players who were told they would probably lose again engaged in significantly less rough play toward their opponents and displayed more sharing and cooperation among their teammates than did the low-status teams who were told they would probably win the play-offs.

One problem with the literature on cooperation and competition is that the concepts are often treated as if they exist in a simple bipolar relationship—if a situation is competitive it cannot also be cooperative, and vice versa. The division of goal structures into two categories—competitive and cooperative—is inadequately differentiated. Within competitive goal structures, for example, rewards can be individual- or group-based; they can be based on effort or product or chance; one person's gain can be independent of or contingent on, either positively or negatively, the gain of another, and so on.

In most sports, the goal structure is zero-sum. The interests of competitors are mutually exclusive in the sense that the successful attainment of victory by one party necessarily implies the defeat of the other. But sport competition is also cooperative when viewed from another perspective (D.L. Gill, 1986; Nelson & Cody, 1979). Competition can be viewed as a process whereby competitors seek to enhance their own performance and enjoyment through meeting the challenge posed by a worthy competitor. From such a perspective, competition is a form of cooperation, not antithetical to it. The word *competition* itself literally means "to strive with," not against.

We would hypothesize that when competitors view competition and cooperation as opposites, they magnify the negative effects of competition. Competition and cooperation will be viewed as mutually exclusive when the competitor defines the value of competition exclusively in terms of outcome, winning or losing. But regarding competition as a process through which competitors mutually facilitate each other's best performance nestles it within cooperation. Such a view is unlikely to result in the kind of serious moral defaults that were common among the groups Sherif and Diab studied.

Competitive Orientation

Like all contextual features, goal structures are interpreted. It is clear that our personal orientations toward competition and cooperation are learned. This is evident, for example, in the finding that competitiveness is mediated both by gender and by the interaction of age and quality of relationship. In general, boys seem to be more competitive than girls (Sharin & Moely, 1976), and younger children are more competitive with friends than nonfriends, whereas the reverse is true by early adolescence (Berndt, 1982).

There also are clear cultural differences in the extent to which competitive orientations are endorsed. Millard Madsen and his colleagues (Madsen, 1967, 1971; Madsen & Shapiro, 1970; Madsen & Yi, 1975) have found significant cultural and subcultural differences in tendencies to become competitive in situations where such an orientation is dysfunctional: Children reared in traditional rural subcultures cooperate more readily than do children reared in modern urban societies. Nelson and Kegan (1972) also discuss cross-cultural differences in competitive orientations, concluding that American children are often irrationally competitive; they explain these cultural differences in competitiveness in terms of differential child-rearing practices.

Coakley (1990) has suggested that competitive orientations reflect inherent values in the economic structure, pointing out that capitalist countries typically define success in terms of competitive outcomes, whereas socialist countries prize cooperative activity more highly. Pepitone (1980) has provided evidence that children reared in competitive cultures like those of the United States and Canada often insist on defining success in terms of establishing superiority over others even when greater personal rewards are available through cooperation.

Native American culture is predominantly cooperative in its emphasis, and most Native Americans who have maintained their cultural heritage share a cooperative orientation (Allison, 1979; Allison & Luschen, 1979; Benedict, 1961; Duda, 1981). Maria Allison (1979) has investigated how this cooperative orientation influences Native American experience of sport. She found that adolescent Navajo athletes were more likely than Anglos to use sport to reaffirm their relationships, to prioritize group solidarity over winning, and to prefer individual standards of evaluation to competitive ones. In addition, the Navajo youth were ill at ease with intimidation and were particularly uncomfortable using their bodies as instruments of domination.

To what extent competitive/cooperative orientations influence other processes related to moral behavior is not clear. One study suggests that those with a cooperative orientation are more likely to score high on affective perspective taking (Johnson, 1975). Another study found that highly competitive 6- to 7-year-old boys (but not girls) were less empathic than their less competitive peers (Barnett, Matthews, & Howard, 1979). No relationship between cooperative orientation and empathy, though, was found for 4-year-old boys (Levine & Hoffman, 1975). But both studies need to be viewed with caution because competition is not a well-developed concept before about age 10 (Roberts, 1980).

Personal Competency Influences

To accurately interpret moral situations, a person must be able to infer from relevant cues how the situation appears to others (role taking) and how multiple views are related and coordinated (perspective taking). For example, a pitcher who considers hurling a fastball at the head of a batter must be able to anticipate how the batter would feel and how the action would be viewed by others, including teammates, coaches, officials, opponents, and fans. The pitcher must coordinate all these pieces of information to anticipate the likely outcomes of various behavioral options. Role taking and perspective taking are the psychological constructs that depict the underlying social cognitive capacities necessary to successfully interpret a moral situation.

Role Taking

Role taking is really a collective name for at least three separate though interrelated processes (Kurdek, 1978; Shantz, 1975; Staub, 1979). *Perceptual role taking* refers to the ability to understand that others have visual fields different from one's own and to comprehend the nature of the differences. More important from the perspective of moral action are skills in *cognitive and affective role taking*, defined respectively as the ability to understand that others have different cognitions or affects and the ability to comprehend the nature of the differences. Even affective role taking is essentially cognitive, because it refers to the task of understanding or intuiting another's affective state. The intercorrelations among role-taking tasks are generally low to moderate (Kurdek, 1978; Shantz, 1975).

Not all models of role taking are developmental in nature, though there is considerable evidence that role-taking ability improves rather dramatically from infancy through adolescence (Ausubel, 1952; Feffer & Gourevitch, 1960; Flavell, Fry, Wright, & Jarvis, 1968; Kurdek, 1977; Selman, 1980; Shantz, 1983). The Piagetian concept of egocentrism is often used to interpret why young children have difficulty understanding the internal psychological states of others. Egocentrism, as the name implies, means that the child is unable to get beyond the limitations of his or her own immediate experience. The infant or toddler does not realize that others have different psychological experiences from those of the self. However, with both general cognitive development and specific interactional experiences, "decentration" takes place, and the limitations of the child's egocentrism are gradually dissolved.

Social Perspective Taking

Selman's (1976, 1980) elaborate description of the development of social perspective-taking ability has been used extensively by moral development theorists (e.g., Enright, Lapsley, & Olson, 1986; Keller & Edelstein, 1991; Kohlberg, 1976; Walker, 1980). Kohlberg (1984), for example, believed that a particular stage of social perspective taking is *necessary but insufficient* for obtaining a parallel stage of moral development, though he vacillated on the nature of social perspective taking (Keller & Edelstein, 1991).

Selman defines social perspective taking as how the individual differentiates her or his perspective from other perspectives and relates these to one another. In Selman's five-level model (see Table 6.1), each advance represents a shift, qualitative in nature, in the child's understanding of persons and of the relationship between the points of view of self and others.

Table 6.1   Selman's Five Levels of Social Perspective Taking

Level 0—Undifferentiated and egocentric perspective taking (about ages 3–6): The child can distinguish the physical self from other selves but not the social perspectives (thoughts, feelings) of other and self. The child can correctly label the manifest feelings of another but does not comprehend psychological cause-and-effect relations. The child assumes that another person interprets social reality in the same way he or she does and has difficulty distinguishing another's intentional and unintentional acts.

Level 1—Differentiated and subjective perspective taking (about ages 5–9): The youngster now recognizes that each person has a unique covert psychological life. This advance is based on the differentiation between physical and psychological characteristics of persons. The child can appreciate the distinction between intentional and unintentional acts. The main limitation of this level is that social perspectives are not yet able to be coordinated. The child's experience is still the model for understanding others' perspectives. Thus, if playing marbles makes the self happy, it will also appeal to the self's playmates.

Level 2—Self-reflective and reciprocal perspective taking (about ages 7–12): The youth is now able to step mentally outside himself or herself and take a second-person perspective on her or his own thoughts and action. At the same time, the youth realizes that others can be self-reflective as well. These advances enable the youth to differentiate between the self-presentation of another and the inner, truer reality of the other. The youth is also aware that each person is conscious of the other's perspective and that this awareness influences self and other's view of each other. This level of social perspective taking is prerequisite for youngsters' understanding of competition.

Level 3—Third-person and mutual perspective taking (about ages 10–15): Persons are now seen as holding organized attitudes and values that have continuity across time, as opposed to randomly changeable assortments of mental states as was true in the previous level. The critical conceptual advance is toward the ability to take a true third-person perspective, to step outside not only one's own immediate perspective, but outside the self as a totality. The budding adolescent can now view himself or herself both as subject and object. Interactions with others can now be seen from the perspective of a "generalized other" outside the interaction.

Level 4—Societal-symbolic perspective taking (about age 12 to adult): The adolescent now recognizes that there are limits to the understanding that both self and others have of themselves and of each other, and that actions may arise from motives not understood by the actor. People are now seen as complex, multifaceted, and potentially internally contradictory agents. In addition, there emerges at Level 4 a new idea of personality as an historically evolved complex of traits, beliefs, values, and attitudes. In terms of the coordination of perspectives, the adolescent is now able to perceive how relations can be coordinated within systems that rely on a generalized other perspective, such as legal, conventional, and moral systems.

Note. Adapted from Selman, 1980.

Selman derived his model in part from an analysis of responses to moral dilemmas. In addition, Selman used a series of board games as one method for analyzing and assessing perspective taking. For example, in one specially designed game, Decoy and Defender, two players compete on a 36-square checkerboard. Each player lines six tokens across the six back spaces of the board, which is defined as the goal line. Two of the six tokens are designated with special markers as flag carriers; the other four are defenders. The player to whom the tokens belong can see which two are flag carriers, but the opponent cannot tell the difference between token types. The object of the game is to get a flag carrier to the opponent's goal line. Players alternate moves and are allowed to move one token one space per turn. The basic defensive move is the freeze. A freeze occurs when a player moves a token into a square already occupied by an opponent's piece. When a freeze is made, the two frozen pieces are removed from play, but neither player is told what types of tokens (flag carriers or defenders) have been eliminated. Each player is limited to two freezes. Successful Decoy and Defender play requires significant social perspective-taking skill, because it is a game in which the winning player deceives the opponent with respect to the self's strategizing and at the same time is not deceived by the opponent's strategy.

Selman maintains that his depiction of social perspective-taking development fits the criteria for a universal, invariant stage sequence. That is, the stages are organized hierarchically, with each stage more encompassing and advanced than the previous stage; in addition, each higher stage represents a structural reorganization of the preceding stage based on a new operational principle.

If role taking and perspective taking are key constructs supporting Process I of the moral action model, then we should expect to find empirical support for a positive relation between these abilities and measures of prosocial behavior. Because the two constructs overlap and have not always been clearly distinguished in the literature, we discuss them together. In a meta-analysis of a large number of studies relating role taking (or perspective taking, or both) to prosocial behavior, Underwood and Moore (1982) found a positive and significant relationship between the two. The relationship between role taking and prosocial behavior is strongest when multiple measures of role taking and prosocial behavior are employed as indices (Elder, 1983; Kurdek, 1978).

As we mentioned earlier, role taking is not a single process. Staub (1978), after reviewing the literature, suggests that affective role taking is more relevant to prosocial action than other kinds. Perhaps future research on the relationship between moral variables and these different aspects of social cognition will be more precise in operational definitions.

Sport, Role Taking, and Perspective Taking

The relationship between sport participation and role taking or perspective taking is relatively unexplored. On a theoretical level, we might anticipate that sport experiences promote social perspective-taking ability. Sport interactions, particularly in team sports, are predicated on an ability to coordinate actions, and such coordinations in turn require an ability to comprehend the game through multiple frames of reference. For example, to play shortstop effectively, Julie needs to be able to anticipate what each teammate is likely to do in any number of fielding situations. That involves complex coordinations of different perspectives on the game. Most sports also involve a strategy component that pulls on the participants' abilities to anticipate the behavior of the opponent. Successful employment of game strategy quickly spirals up the perspective-taking ladder.

It is no accident that George Herbert Mead, a pioneer in the area of social perspective taking, used play, games, and sport to illustrate what is involved in the development of perspective-taking ability (Mead, 1934). In fact, he labeled the first stage of this ability the "play stage" and the next the "game stage." Games and sports are miniature social systems that provide the growing child with experiences of social rules and roles that need to be coordinated.

Coakley (1984) built on both Mead and Selman to provide guidelines for children's participation in team sports and counteractive individual sports. He concluded that an emphasis on rules, structured relationships, and both offensive and defensive strategy should be introduced gradually to children between the ages of 8 and 12. Coakley is primarily concerned with keeping sport experience within the social cognitive capacities of children, but his recommendation to introduce role-taking and perspective-taking challenges gradually also seems to imply that sport may be a good medium for developing these social cognitive capacities. Martens (1976) stated that hypothesis explicitly. Unfortunately, there is no empirical validation for the reasonable hypothesis that sport is a good medium to develop perspective-taking ability. Should future research substantiate the potential of sport, or some sports, to promote role-taking or perspective-taking ability, the development of these capacities may be one mechanism through which sport experience might enhance moral development and promote moral action.

Despite the potential that sport may have for promoting social perspective-taking skills, it also appears that competition generally impedes role taking. For example, Tjosvold, Johnson, and Johnson (1984) placed undergraduate students in dyads and assigned them a negotiation task. Some dyads were structured cooperatively, some competitively. In the competitively structured dyads, participants were less accurate in understanding each other's perspectives.

Role taking and perspective taking are critical moral abilities. But moral motivation is only weakly activated by perspective taking alone. Perspective taking needs to be complemented by coping ego functions before Process I can be concluded successfully.

Ego-Processing Influences

In our 12-component model of moral action, we placed the reflexive-intraceptive ego functions with Process I. These ego functions reflect the person's assimilatory engagement with situationally aroused thoughts, feelings, and intuitions. Two coping processes are particularly important to appropriate moral functioning during Process I: tolerance of ambiguity and empathy.

Tolerance of Ambiguity

People who have coping hierarchies that emphasize tolerance of ambiguity can cope with cognitive and affective complexity without the need to come to premature resolution. They are capable of qualified judgment. Perhaps most important, they can be "of two minds," recognizing the complexity of social life.

The person able to cope with sport's numerous ambiguities is more likely to fulfill her or his moral potential than someone with little tolerance for ambiguity. The player must be able to accept the inevitable ambiguity of rules and norms, for example, without translating that ambiguity into "anything goes if you can get away with it." Similarly, in sport, where opponents are both players and people, the person who can tolerate ambiguity will less readily reduce his or her opponents to objects, depersonalizing competitors in the quest for victory.

Empathy

Empathy is another coping process in the intraceptive category. If role taking and perspective taking enable one to become aware of another's need, empathy often figures in transforming simple role taking into a source of moral motivation. Empathic arousal is critical to Process I because it engages the person in the context, motivates further moral processing, and ultimately provides a check on the more cognitive forms of guidance to moral action. Though Haan defines empathy similarly to cognitive and affective role taking, we will take the liberty to expand her definition in the direction of Hoffman's conceptualization (see chapter 3).

Terminology is of particular importance in discussions of empathy. Researchers use the word in quite diverse, sometimes imprecise, and occasionally contradictory ways (Eisenberg & Strayer, 1987). As a result, studies purporting to investigate empathy may be about entirely different psychological phenomena. Following Hoffman, we conceptualize empathy as a process of affective attunement—through empathy, the person comes to have an emotion similar to that of the other. Though it is possible to experience a wide diversity of emotions through empathy, most research has focused on empathic distress. With empathic distress, one comes to vicariously experience the pain of another. But empathic distress needs to be carefully distinguished from two similar affects: sympathic distress and personal distress (cf. Eisenberg, 1986; Eisenberg & Mussen, 1989; Eisenberg & Strayer, 1987; Strayer & Eisenberg, 1987).

Sympathic distress can be defined as "the heightened awareness of the suffering of another person as something to be alleviated" (Wispe, 1986, p. 318). Like empathic distress, sympathic distress is an emotional response to another's state or condition, but the affective relation between the self and the other person is different in the two emotions. With *empathic distress*, the two people experience similar emotions; in contrast, sympathic distress involves a feeling of concern or sorrow for the other.

Empathic distress also needs to be distinguished from *personal distress*, a distinction that Hoffman generally does not make. When a person perceives that another is in pain or need, the perceiver may experience anxiety, worry, or other negative affective states that are not parallel to the emotions being experienced by the other. Such affects focus one's attention inward and may lead a person to act out of self-regard more than other-regard, even if the outward behavior is prosocial. Thus, a person may help someone in distress to alleviate her or his own distress (Batson & Coke, 1981; Batson, Fultz, & Schoenrade, 1987). Unfortunately, because personal distress is associated with the same types of contexts that elicit empathy or sympathy and may lead to behaviors that are prosocial, the three emotions are often confused in the literature (Eisenberg & Strayer, 1987).

Empathy and Prosocial Behavior

If empathy is a critical component of Process I, then it should be empirically associated with prosocial behavior. In fact, there is strong and ample evidence—both direct and indirect—to support the link between empathy and prosocial behavior (Eisenberg, 1986). Still, the results—especially with children—are equivocal (Eisenberg & Miller, 1987). In fact, in a meta-analysis conducted on a number of relevant studies, most done with children, Underwood and Moore (1982) found no significant relationship between empathy and various measures of prosocial behavior. Two methodological problems, however, may account for most of the discrepancies in the findings. First, as we just pointed out, empathy often has not been distinguished from sympathy and personal distress. In studies where these emotions have been distinguished, the links between empathy or sympathy and prosocial behavior are robust (Eisenberg, 1986; Eisenberg, Fabes, Miller, & Fultz, 1989).

The other methodological problem concerns the way empathy is measured (Eisenberg, 1986; Eisenberg & Miller, 1987; Eisenberg & Mussen, 1989). In studies of children, empathy has often been assessed through the use of picture story techniques. Children are exposed to stories, pictures, or both containing clues about another's affective state or situation; after viewing them the children are asked to report on their own feelings. They are scored as empathic if they report experiencing emotions similar to the ones depicted in the stimulus material. Such techniques, however, are highly problematic: They may be too brief to elicit empathy, and children may try to give the response that they believe is desired by the experimenter (Eisenberg & Lennon, 1983; Hoffman, 1982). Further, such techniques are attempts to measure "trait" empathy—enduring empathic skills—though it may be "state" empathy (situationally aroused empathy) that is most clearly associated with prosocial behavior (Eisenberg & Miller,

1987). When physiological measures are used in conjunction with psychological measures of empathy, the link between empathy and prosocial responding is strong even with quite young children (Eisenberg, Fabes, Miller, & Shell, 1990; Radke-Yarrow & Zahn-Waxler, 1984; Radke-Yarrow et al., 1983).

Sport and Empathy

We know very little about the relationship between sport experience and empathy (or sympathy). It might be hypothesized, however, that sport experience may decrease empathy for others. Empathizing with opponents may be counterproductive to the goal of winning, and empathizing even with teammates may detract from focused concentration on personal performance. Furthermore, many coaches deliberately discourage concern for opponents. As part of the "psyching up" process, opponents are sometimes dehumanized and turned into targets for the expression of negative affect.

Such a conclusion receives partial support from a study of 1,381 Finnish girls and boys, aged 8 to 16, who played baseball. Kalliopuska (1987) found that the athletes, who had attended three national training camps, became less sensitive (one component of empathy) the more years they spent in Finnish baseball training. No change in overall empathy level was revealed, however. This was true for both genders, though Kalliopuska reported significantly higher scores for girls than boys in sensitivity and overall empathy.

If sport experience discourages empathy, the decline is most likely a consequence of the competitive element in sport. Given the importance of empathy and sympathy in moral action, it is unfortunate that the sparse literature available indicates that competitive contexts inhibit the development or elicitation of these affects (Barnett, 1979; Kalliopuska, 1987).

When we talk about the impact of competition on empathy, two interpenetrating issues are at stake—one contextual, one personal. The contextual issue pertains to the goal structure of the situation. Does a competitive reward structure lead to a decrease in empathy? The personal issue pertains to the extent to which an individual embraces a competitive orientation. Does a more competitive orientation discourage empathy?

In one interesting study that brings the two issues together, 6- and 7-year-old children ($N = 84$) were tested for trait competitiveness (competitive orientation) and trait empathy while preparing to participate in either a competitive or noncompetitive game (Barnett, Matthews, & Howard, 1979). The researchers found that among boys (but not girls), competitive orientation was associated with lower empathy. They also found no relationship between empathy and preparing to participate in either a competitive or noncompetitive game. These results may indicate that, at least for boys, the personal dimension of competitiveness more than the contextual goal structure is associated with reduced empathy. The results, however, need to be viewed with caution for several reasons. First, children at this age have only a rudimentary understanding of the competitive process and may not have developed very stable orientations. Second, the measure of empathy was given before the actual participation in the competitive or noncompetitive game. Finally, it was found that boys' trait competitiveness was related to their trait empathy, but the competitive context was not related to trait empathy. Because participation in a competitive context is typically of short duration, it may be that the nature of the goal structure impacts state empathy more than trait empathy, and vice versa for competitive orientation.

The inhibition of empathy and sympathy characteristic of modern sport may not be necessary. Though the concept is empirically untested, it seems reasonable to believe that if competition is understood as one form of cooperative activity, empathy could find a significant place in competition. For example, if in playing racquetball one player discovers that she is significantly more skilled than her opponent, her empathic skills might signal the need to redefine the game to re-create the conditions for a genuine contest.

Finally, it is also worth noting that some forms of noncompetitive physical activity may encourage the development of empathy. For example, Kalliopuska (1989) found that junior ballet dancers were more empathic than controls. Perhaps dancers are encouraged to attune to emotional expressiveness in a way that sport participants generally are not.

Summary

In this chapter we reviewed the major influences on how a person interprets the moral meaning of a situation. Situational ambiguity and the goal structure were identified as key contextual influences, and role taking and perspective taking as central personal competencies. Finally, the coping processes of tolerance of ambiguity and empathy were identified as central to effective moral functioning in Process I. Of course, none of these variables operates in a vacuum. Each influences and interpenetrates the others. In chapter 7 we turn to the second major process in the model—forming a moral ideal.

Chapter 7
Constructing a Moral Ideal

In the last chapter we reviewed influences related to the process of interpreting a moral situation (Process I). The unique contribution of Process II is the generation of a moral ideal, the construction of a moral judgment about the right thing to do. This ideal represents a moral synthesis in which situationally relevant information is coordinated with a person's general moral perspective. Process II essentially supplies the moral meaning to which the ultimate action is referenced.

Several important research traditions are relevant to Process II. In keeping with our 12-component model, the same three headings frame this discussion: contextual, personal competency, and ego-processing influences.

Contextual Influences

Moral reasoning does not occur in a social vacuum. Humans are social beings, and individuality is always in relation to community. Sometimes the relations are harmonious, and personal identity is in comfortable continuity with communal expectations. Other times one must forge aspects of personal identity in creative tension with one's communities. In neither case is moral reasoning isolated from the social context.

Most of Kohlberg's early work was committed to identifying the sequential patterns of moral reasoning that people use in their journey toward maturity. But as Kohlberg developed his educational theory, he shifted his focus from individual stages and stage promotion to an emphasis on "moral community" and community development. Kohlberg and his colleagues developed an approach for conceptualizing and assessing the "moral atmosphere" of a community that we have found useful. We will use that construct as the organizing principle for discussing contextual influences on Process II of our moral action model.

The Moral Atmosphere

The quality of the moral context was first given serious attention in the field of education. Jackson (1968) coined the term *the hidden curriculum* to denote the moral influence of "the crowds, the praise and the power" in the school setting. Soon, however, the concept of moral atmosphere was investigated in other contexts.

The term *moral atmosphere* is imprecise, and one of Kohlberg's contributions was to give it greater clarity and operational definition. As Kohlberg began to work in schools to develop "just communities," he gained new appreciation for what Durkheim (1925/1961) had argued, namely, that groups have moral norms that are sui generis, or in a class of their own. Group moral norms are not reducible to the sum of the individuals' moral perspectives, nor can group morality be adequately characterized by simply transferring onto the collective the same conceptual framework used to understand the individual. Groups develop their own culture out of the synergistic interactions of the group's members.

To clarify the moral atmosphere of schools, Kohlberg and his colleagues identified two major units of analysis—the collective norm and the institutional value. Both constructs provide theoretical insights into the nature of group life, and focal points for educational interventions designed to create "just communities." In brief, just-community interventions were designed to develop democratic schools with a justice-based decision-making structure, strong collective prosocial norms, and an earnest sense of community belonging and valuing (Power, Higgins, & Kohlberg, 1989).

Collective Norms

A collective norm is "a complex of specific behavioral expectations that share a common value" (Power et al., 1989, p. 115). For example, a collective norm of cooperation may be behaviorally broken down to mean that one should assist another when asked; that one should seek assistance when help is needed; that one should offer to help even when no explicit request is made, and so on. The various behavioral expectations are unified by their adherence to the norm of cooperation; it is belief in cooperation that provides the rationale, justification, and grounds for the specific behavioral expectations.

To describe his educational aims, Kohlberg identified a number of parameters that characterize how collective norms may evolve. He labeled these developments as changes in the phase, degree of collectiveness, and moral stage of norms. The term *phases* refers to the process of norm acquisition. Norms are initially proposed; then they may be accepted as a group ideal but with little anticipation of actual behavioral conformity. With further progress, behavioral conformity may become expected. Finally, the group may come to accept the responsibility of norm enforcement.

Kohlberg also described a 15-step sequence in the full empowerment of collective norms. He referred to these as their *degree of collectiveness*. In brief, the sequence moves from norms initially being held only by individuals, with little sense of group identity. Next, people may see the norms as characterizing the group, but only because of authority expectations. Then norms may become ''aggregate norms,'' operative for subgroups but not the group in its entirety. Finally, norms become truly collective.

Collective moral norms may also be characterized by their *moral stages*. It is important to emphasize again that collective norms are unique; the stage of a collective norm is not equivalent to the average of individuals' moral stages. In general, as group life progresses, improvements will be noted in the stage of collective morality.

To illustrate how the collective norm theory might shed insight into sport culture, let's consider the potential norm of fair play. First, with regard to phase it might be reasonable to argue that in most organized sport settings fair play is either accepted as an ideal with little expectation of actual, voluntary behavioral conformity (Phases 2 and 3), or it may be expected (Phases 4 and 5). In organized sport, there is seldom a need for the group to accept responsibility for norm enforcement (Phases 6 and 7) because that task is typically transferred to officials. Interestingly, it is in the informal games of children where the highest phases are most likely to operate.

With regard to the degree of collectiveness, fair play may exist anywhere along the 15-step continuum, but it is probably most often in the range of authority norm (Degrees 6 and 7) or aggregate norm (Degrees 8 and 9). Players may adhere to a fair play norm because their coach consistently advocates it, or because some of their teammates firmly believe that fair play is essential if the contest is to have any meaning. Finally, a sport group may evolve an understanding of fair play consistent with almost any moral stage, though in most organized sport programs the higher stages are rarely seen. The heavy emphasis on competitive outcome in contemporary sport practices mitigates against a high moral stage conceptualization of fair play.

Institutional Value

In addition to wanting to promote collective norms of high phases, degrees, and stages, Kohlberg was concerned with the institutional value of moral atmosphere.

The institutional value is analyzed along two dimensions. The first pertains to how the members feel bonded to the group. For example, one person may profess loyalty to a group because it has instrumental value for him. On the other hand, another individual may see the group as intrinsically valuable, regardless of any specific benefit she may obtain from group membership. Altogether, five levels of institutional value were identified (Power et al., 1989).

In addition to levels of institutional value, the stage of community can be determined by assessing the moral stage of the shared understanding of community. For example, a Stage 2 understanding of community is people who "get along." A Stage 3 understanding is people who have developed trust and care.

Moral Atmosphere and Moral Action

The distinction between content and structure made by structural developmentalists may be useful in conceptualizing how moral atmosphere influences moral action. Moral atmosphere probably influences the content more than the structure of moral reasoning. For example, if Nathan, a young lacrosse player, thinks that most of his teammates believe winning is more important than playing fair, that will not alter how he structurally conceptualizes fairness, but it may influence his belief about how integral those conceptualizations are to the sport of lacrosse.

An interesting study by Moriarty and McCabe (1977), designed and conducted within a social learning framework, may be interpreted as demonstrating how modeling can provide informational cues about collective moral norms. In a study of participants in youth baseball, lacrosse, and ice hockey, 259 children were put in one of three groups: One group watched a series of antisocial videos of their sport, another group watched prosocial videos, and the control group watched neutral videos. The results indicated that, except for the baseball players, the prosocial videos positively influenced the subsequent display of prosocial behavior. No consistent impact of watching antisocial videos was found. The authors interpret the prosocial findings as a reaffirmation of the potency of modeling. But one might ask further how—through what psychological mechanisms—the modeling had its influence. From our perspective, modeling provides context-specific information about expected behavior. In this study, the prosocial videos may have offered the young players information about the operative collective norms of their particular sports. One reason the antisocial videos had no consistent impact may have been that the youngsters were already aware of antisocial norms in their sports.

In addition to influencing the content of a person's moral perspective, the moral atmosphere may affect the organization of thought itself. In fact, Kohlberg and his associates found that when people reason about their everyday moral conflicts, their stage of reasoning is significantly influenced by the moral atmosphere (Higgins, Power, & Kohlberg, 1984). However, it is interesting to note that efforts to promote moral stage growth through just-community interventions shared about the same measure of success as earlier efforts using moral discussion groups (Power et al., 1989). Further, because schools that employed the just-community approach typically included moral discussion groups in the just-community apparatus, what positive development did occur in individual stage growth might be attributable to the discussion groups and not to changes in moral atmosphere. The failure of "just communities" to more effectively promote stage growth may indicate that the moral atmosphere makes its most potent contribution to moral action through influencing the content of a person's moral thinking. The effort to enhance the moral atmosphere of a Pop Warner football team, for example, may stimulate little growth in individual players' moral reasoning competency, but it may reduce the amount of cheating or aggressive play exhibited by team members through affecting operative beliefs, attitudes, and values.

The Moral Atmosphere of Sport

Play, games, and sport have often been described as "set apart" from everyday life. This claim might be interpreted naively to mean that sport is disconnected from, uninfluenced by, or irrelevant to the broader culture. Of course, such is not the case. Sport presents and re-presents culturally defined relations between people and the norms and values that guide those relations.

Despite the interpenetration of sport and society, there is an element of truth to the perspective that sport is set apart. Sport is a world-within-a-world that is separated from daily life through clear spatial and temporal boundaries. Sport occurs in its own unique space, with clear demarcations of in-bounds and out-of-bounds. Similar temporal demarcations separate "sport" time from "other" time. Unlike everyday life, activity in sport—consisting of body movements that often have little functional utility outside of sport—is directed toward ends that are purely symbolic (e.g., getting a ball through a hoop, carrying a ball across a line).

The separateness of sport may have implications for the moral atmosphere that characterizes sport experience. A fundamental imperative of human social life is to continually attend to the moral quality of interactions (Haan et al., 1985). Sport, however, represents what Ennis (1976) has termed an "institution of release." It is a zone of experience characterized by such intrinsic rewards as enjoyment, fun, pleasure, and satisfaction. One aspect of the enjoyment of sport may be that it provides a temporary relaxation of the need to constantly monitor the moral exchange.

We have postulated that sport involves a "bracketed morality" that legitimizes a temporary, nonserious suspension of the usual moral obligation to equally consider the needs and desires of all persons (Bredemeier & Shields, 1986a, 1986b; Shields & Bredemeier, 1986). Several formal features of the sport context may create and legitimate the "brackets" that separate sport morality from everyday life. First, spatial and temporal markers make the delimited character of sport salient, emphasizing its short term and nonserious character. Competitors who lose a contest return unscathed to their normal lives at the conclusion. And in many formal sport settings, decision-making power and moral responsibility are concentrated in the roles of coaches and officials. Investing these roles with regulatory obligations provides institutionalized sanction for a limited transference of player accountability and provides concurrent protection for participants against serious moral defaults. Finally, the need for players to engage in moral dialogue and negotiation is reduced considerably by carefully structured rules, both formal and informal, which provide several moral functions:

- They guarantee initial conditions of fairness.
- They both restrict and make explicit the legitimate means to achieve the desired goal (winning), which provides all participants with equal information and eliminates the need to negotiate legitimate from illegitimate strategies.
- They provide equal protection from harm.
- They resolve the issue of retributive justice by designating appropriate penalties for rule violations.

Given these moral services, it is not surprising that much sport activity can occur without the exchange of a single word among participants.

If our analysis is correct, certain formal properties of sport allow the moral atmosphere to be characterized by a greater degree of personal freedom, of moral latitude, than the moral atmosphere of most other spheres of life. Thus, common norms against egocentrism are largely suspended in sport.

We must hasten to say that all sport experience is of course not cut from one cloth. The formal properties of sport that allow the moral atmosphere to be characterized by a degree of moral release are only some of the influences shaping particular sport environments. The specific procedures and practices of any given sport are also influential, as are the informal norms shaped through history and experience. Significant individuals, such as coaches, can also shape the moral atmosphere in accord with their own philosophies. Players, coaches, and others involved in a particular sport setting have great latitude to develop collective norms of varying phases, degrees, and stages. As a result, the moral atmospheres in various sport settings may be quite distinct. The moral atmosphere common in collegiate football, for example, may differ markedly from that of equestrian clubs, and the prevailing atmosphere of one team may differ from another. And certainly as one moves up and down the competitive ladder, from informal backyard sports up to professional competition, the prevailing norms are likely to diverge.

Variation in sport moral atmosphere is illustrated by Gary Alan Fine's (1987) creative study of youth baseball. Over a 3-year period, Fine collected data on 10- to 12-year-old boys on 10 teams in five different youth baseball leagues. He found that boys on each team developed their own collective system of meanings and interpretations that guided their interpersonal activity and moral exchange. Over the course of a season, through such processes as the development of in-group jokes, special nicknames, unique slang, and distinctive modes of teasing, each team acquired its own more-or-less coherent system of shared meanings and behavioral norms. Labelling the shared system of meanings and norms an *idioculture*, Fine observed that as the moral language of adults, containing idealized moral rules and codes, was filtered through the idioculture, it was not accepted at face value. The idealized moral norms were transformed or reinterpreted to fit the more immediate needs of the youth, such as the need to establish masculine identity. Fine's (1987) fascinating study illustrates how moral atmospheres were constructed and how they operated among a group of preadolescent, middleclass, European American boys playing baseball in the eastern United States. Analyses of moral atmospheres in different sports with different population groups would, no doubt, identify points of commonality and divergence from those reported by Fine.

In short, moral atmosphere is a product of both formal and informal influences on the sport environment. We will have more to say about the impact of sport moral atmospheres on moral reasoning in the next section, where we deal with the personal competencies that influence the outcome of Process II.

Personal Competency Influences

Moral reasoning is the structural competency most directly undergirding Process II. Moral reasoning, in our view, can be analyzed at two levels: content and structure. In chapter 4 we summarized the theories of Kohlberg, Gilligan, and Haan, theories designed to describe structural competencies that underlie moral action. In this section, we extend the discussion of moral reasoning in five ways. First, we briefly review the evidence that a person's moral reasoning stage influences her or his moral behavior. Second, we review studies of moral reasoning conducted in physical activity settings. Third, we summarize research suggesting that games and sport may elicit a modified form of moral reasoning. Fourth, we discuss the problem of moral bias as it relates to moral reasoning and affect. Finally, we reflect on the role of beliefs, attitudes, and values (that is, moral content) in moral reasoning, concluding with a discussion of the relationship between sport participation and sport-specific value hierarchies.

Moral Reasoning and Moral Action

In 1980, Augusto Blasi published a classic review of the literature that relates moral reasoning stage to moral action. After surveying studies relating moral development to such issues as delinquency, sociopathy, teachers' ratings of children's moral behavior, and direct behavioral measures of items like cheating, honesty, and altruism, Blasi concluded that moral reasoning was indeed an important contributor to moral behavior. Although different renditions of the Kohlberg scoring system were used in different studies, most reported statistically significant relationships between moral reasoning and the selected index of moral behavior. For example, in studies of delinquents and sociopaths, 70% to 80% were rated as preconventional in their moral reasoning maturity. Other reviews of the moral reasoning and moral action literature have reached similar conclusions (Mwamwenda, 1992; Smetana, 1990; Thoma, Rest, & Barnett, 1986). Throughout the literature, however, the correlations between reasoning and action are generally low to moderate, suggesting that moral reasoning capability is an important contributor to moral action, but it is not the only or even necessarily the main one.

The theories of Gilligan and Haan have not been used as extensively as Kohlberg's model, and studies using these frameworks were not included in the reviews just cited. Because the theories of both Gilligan and Haan were developed by analyzing how people dealt with real moral problems and, in Haan's case, by direct study of moral action, these theories may correlate more closely with moral action. With regard to her theory, Haan offers tentative evidence to that effect (Haan et al., 1985). But additional research clearly is needed on the relationship between hypothetical reasoning (which is, in fact, a placid form of moral action) and action in real-life contexts.

Moral Reasoning and Sport

Morality has not been an important theme in sport psychology research until quite recently. The first investigation using a structural developmental model was conducted by Jantz (1975), who modified Piaget's clinical interview to see if American children's reasoning about basketball rules would conform to the same developmental trajectory as that described by Piaget. Jantz's findings supported Piaget's depiction of moral development as a shift from an original heteronomous stage to an autonomous stage.

In another early study, Horrocks (1979) had upper elementary school teachers assess their students on selected prosocial play behaviors and related these to the students' stages of moral development, perceptions of sportsmanship, and participation in youth sports. He found significant positive correlations between prosocial play behaviors, on the one hand, and moral reasoning and perceptions of sportsmanship, on the other. No significant correlation between participation in youth sports and prosocial play behaviors, however, was found.

Elizabeth Hall was the first to use Kohlberg's stage theory of moral development in an empirical study of intercollegiate sport (Hall, 1981). She investigated the moral reasoning stages of 65 male and female basketball players using both Kohlberg's standard moral dilemmas and dilemmas written to reflect a sport context. Hall found that the athletes generally scored lower in their stage of moral reasoning than college norms reported by Kohlberg; that female athletes scored higher than male athletes; that athletes' reasoning about sport-specific dilemmas reflected higher stage properties than their reasoning about standard dilemmas; and that length of sport involvement was unrelated to moral reasoning stage.

Crown and Hetherington (1989) examined the relationship between moral orientation and sport reasoning and found, contrary to predictions based on Gilligan's theory, that women and men were equally likely to use justice and care reasoning when reflecting on a hypothetical intercollegiate sport dilemma. Women, however, tended to characterize the dilemma as involving moral considerations and men did not. These results must be viewed with caution; participants were selected for the study because they were enrolled in an introductory college course, not because they had any sport knowledge or experience. Recently, Fisher (1993), using Gilligan's model, investigated the moral orientations of 10 professional female bodybuilders. She found that all study participants responded to two personally experienced moral dilemmas using both justice and care reasoning, but five of the participants could be classified as predominantly justice-oriented and five of them as care-oriented.

Since the mid-1980s we have been studying moral development and sport involvement. In our first investigation (Bredemeier & Shields, 1984a), we used Rest's Defining Issues Test (DIT), which is based on a slightly modified depiction of Kohlberg's stages, to see how the moral reasoning of 46 female and male collegiate basketball players related to their tendencies to aggress. To help you better understand the results of our study, we'll summarize the scoring properties of the DIT.

The Defining Issues Test provides a profile of the extent to which a respondent endorses reasoning at each of six levels: Stages 2, 3, 4, 5A, 5B, and 6. In addition, an overall "P" score reflects the percentage of reasoning at the postconventional level (5A, 5B, and 6 combined); the P score is the index of moral reasoning development. Our study revealed that both male and female athletes were below reported college norms on their P score. Females scored significantly higher than males. In contrast, Rest reports very few gender differences in studies using the DIT.

We hypothesized that high usage of either Stage 2 or Stage 4 would correlate positively with an index of athletic aggression. The egocentric and instrumental reasoning characteristic of Stage 2 can readily be adapted to support the instrumental use of aggression, and the belief among many basketball players that aggression is normative within the system of their sport makes aggression appear reasonable within a Stage 4 perspective. Conversely, we hypothesized that high usage of either Stage 3 or the postconventional stages would be inversely related to aggression scores. The naively prosocial, other-oriented nature of Stage 3 reasoning is generally inconsistent with aggression, as is a principled orientation that demands fairness for all. The results fulfilled our predictions: Stages 2 and 4 were positively associated with aggression scores, and there was an inverse relationship between athletic aggression and Stages 3, 5B, and 6, though the patterns were not equally strong for males and females. The reasoning–aggression relationship was significant for males at Stage 3 and for females at Stages 5B and 6.

In a more elaborate study, we used Haan's model of moral development to test the reasoning maturity of male and female basketball players and nonathletes in high school and college (Bredemeier & Shields, 1986a). Respondents reasoned about four hypothetical moral dilemmas, two set in everyday contexts and two in sport situations, yielding a "life" and a "sport" moral reasoning maturity score. Among the 50 college students, the nonathletes had significantly more mature moral reasoning than the basketball players, a finding that held for both sport and life dilemmas. Among the 50 high school students, however, no reasoning differences between athletes and nonathletes were found. Both college and high school females reasoned at a more mature level than males in response to sport dilemmas, and high school females also exhibited more mature reasoning in response to the life dilemmas.

In a related study, we added 20 swimmers to the college sample to determine whether the same athlete–nonathlete relationship would hold for college athletes other than basketball players (Bredemeier & Shields, 1986a). Swimmers' mean scores for life and sport moral reasoning were between those of the nonathletes and the basketball players. Life reasoning differences only approached significance, but basketball players' sport reasoning was less mature than that of both the swimmers and the nonathletes; sport reasoning for the swimmers and nonathletes did not differ significantly.

A number of questions are suggested by these findings. What are the critical mediating variables—the amount of physical contact in one's sport, the length of involvement, the competitive level, the type of interpersonal interaction? Are people with more mature reasoning less interested in, or purposefully "selected out" of, some college athletic programs? The cross-sectional methodology of these studies did not allow us to address these questions.

Differences in males' and females' sport reasoning raise similar issues. Given typical gender socialization and the traditional role of sport in that process, it is not surprising that males' moral reasoning may be more influenced by the egocentric aspects of competitive sport, but this area of research is at a beginning stage (Bredemeier, 1982, 1984).

Game Reasoning

One of the most intriguing findings of our study (1986a) was a significant divergence between life and sport moral reasoning. Hall (1981) found sport reasoning to reflect more sophisticated patterns of thought than was used about general social situations, but we found the reverse (Bredemeier, 1983; Bredemeier & Shields, 1984b, 1986b; also Frankl, 1989). The difference in findings may be explained in terms of the content of the sport dilemmas. In Hall's research, the dilemmas *pertained to* sport but did not involve athletic action *within* sport.

For example, Hall asked study participants to reason about whether a basketball coach should ask the timekeeper to delay starting the clock at critical moments that would benefit the home team. Another scenario probed whether an academically pressured athlete should ask the coach to exert influence to assure the athlete a good grade in a class. Such dilemmas reflect decisions at the edges of sport, not within the flow of sport itself. In contrast, we used dilemmas that tap into the action of sport. For example, we have asked study participants whether a football player should follow the instructions of a coach to try to injure an opponent. Hall's findings may reflect the issue of stimulus familiarity more than divergence in sport–life contextual reasoning. When people are familiar with the types of situations presented in a dilemma, they may more easily marshal their best reasoning (Davidson, Turiel, & Black, 1983).

The discrepancy we have found between life and sport moral reasoning may be one aspect of a larger phenomena. Huizinga (1955) has described play as a "stepping out of 'real life' into a temporary sphere of activity with a disposition all of its own" (p. 8). Several philosophers, anthropologists, sociologists, and psychologists have suggested that play, and by extension sport, exists in a unique sphere, framed apart from the rest of life, and that entry into that sphere involves cognitive, attitudinal, and value adjustments (Bateson, 1955; Corsaro, 1981; Giffin, 1982; Schmitz, 1976; Sutton-Smith, 1971). Handelman (1977), for example, has observed that entry into the play realm requires a "radical transformation in cognition and perception" (p. 186). Schmitz (1976) similarly has suggested that play transfers participants into a world with new forms of space, time, and behavior, "delivering its own values in and for itself" (p. 26). Referring to sport, Firth (1973) discusses how rituals and conventions serve to mark temporal boundaries and symbolize the reconstitution of people into players and players back into people.

If entry into sport involves a transformation of cognition and affect, then it is reasonable to hypothesize that moral reasoning undergoes some change in its underlying organization when one moves from general life into sport. The divergence in moral reasoning scores we have described partially supports this hypothesis. We have labeled the type of moral reasoning that occurs in sport "game reasoning."

In one multipronged investigation, we used Haan's model to explore sport–life moral reasoning and the way athletes reason about issues of athletic aggression (Bredemeier, 1985; Bredemeier & Shields, 1984a, 1986a, 1986b). One hundred high school and college basketball players and nonparticipants in interscholastic or intercollegiate sports—30 athletes and 20 nonathletes at each school level—participated. The sample included equal numbers of males and females. Each study participant was asked to reason about four moral dilemmas—two set in sport and two in everyday life. In addition, 20 high school and 20 college basketball players were randomly selected for second interviews, conducted immediately following a late-season game, in which they discussed their own aggressive basketball behavior and their perceptions of teammates' and opponents' athletic aggression.

To better understand the underlying structure of "game reasoning" we constructed life and sport moral reasoning profiles, which record the percentage of reasoning that occurred at each moral level during the moral dilemma interview. We compared life and sport reasoning profiles to reveal the changes in the organizing framework of moral reasoning about issues in these two types of contexts. Figure 7.1 depicts these changes graphically.

Statistical analyses supported what is evident from a cursory examination of Figure 7.1. Sport moral reasoning is much more egocentric (assimilative) than is life moral reasoning. Despite this, accommodative reasoning was dominant in both sport and life. In follow-up analyses, it was evident that athletes more than nonathletes changed their reasoning patterns from life to sport, especially male athletes.

The Moral Balance, Bracketed Morality, and Game Reasoning

We used Haan's model of interactional morality in investigating moral reasoning in general life and sport-specific contexts. The central concept in Haan's model is the moral balance, a situation-specific agreement that subjectively equalizes the parties in terms of rights, obligations, privileges, and the general give-and-take of the relationship.

In sport, moral balances are created under atypical conditions:

- There is an artificial, scarce goal—winning.
- Participants' game-relevant interests are in zero-sum opposition.
- The system of action depends on each individual or team pursuing its narrowly defined interest (players must "want to win" for sport to exist).
- The actions allowed have no meaning apart from the artificial context.
- At least in formal, organized sport, action is continually and externally monitored to insure conformity to an equalizing and protective rule structure.

In this highly artificial context, participants are partially freed from the usual demands of morality. As one basketball player in our study put it (Bredemeier & Shields, 1986b),

> In sports you can do what you want. In life it's more restricted. The pressure is different in sports and life. It's harder to make decisions in life because there are so many people to think about, different people to worry about. In sports you're free to think about yourself. (pp. 262-263)

We have called the moral exchange that occurs in sport *bracketed morality* (Bredemeier & Shields, 1986a, 1986b; Shields & Bredemeier, 1984). We use the term *bracketed* to connote two points. First, the moral exchange that occurs in sport is different from that of daily life, where mature moral action is marked by attention to relational equalization in terms of obligations and benefits. Sport, however, is characterized by a greater degree of personal freedom and a lessening of relational responsibility. Focus on self-interest is not only allowed in sport, it is presupposed. But not all action supportive of self-interest is morally appropriate, even in sport; that is the second point. Bracketed morality connotes a form of moral action that is nested within a broader, more encompassing morality—the

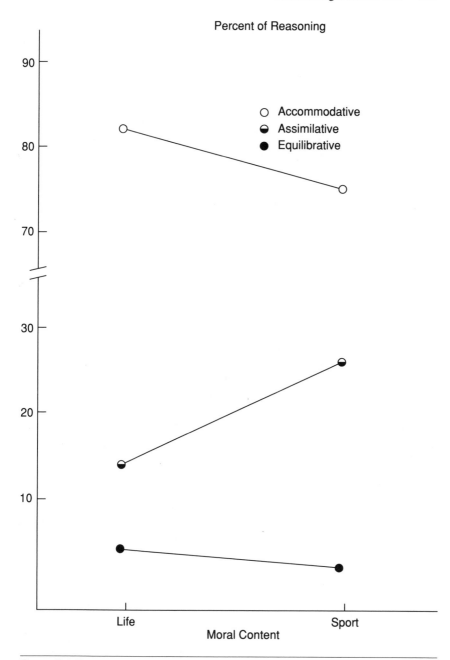

Figure 7.1 Percentage of moral reasoning at the assimilative, accommodative, and equilibrative levels in response to life and sport dilemmas.
From "Game Reasoning and Interactional Morality" by B.J. Bredemeier and D.L. Shields, 1986, *Journal of Genetic Psychology*, **147**, p. 270. Copyright 1986 by Heldref Publications. Reprinted by permission.

morality of everyday life. It is set apart, yet it remains connected to the basic presuppositions of morality. For example, the focus on self-interest presupposes the moral necessity of guaranteeing initial conditions of fairness, procedural safeguards that insure fair opportunity throughout the process of play, and reasonable protections of physical well-being.

We use the term *game reasoning* to refer to that form of moral reasoning that arises from and reflects the bracketed moral exchange. Asked to reflect on moral action in sport, most people use game reasoning. Often game reasoning seems to reflect a "legitimated regression" (Shields & Bredemeier, 1984) to a form of reasoning resembling more immature stages. But we also hypothesize that not all game reasoning is alike. We believe mature game reasoning places limits on the exercise of egocentric reasoning.

Game Reasoning and Moral Legitimacy

Our interviews led us to conclude that when people enter sport they tend to shift their moral perspective in the direction of egocentric reasoning. The transition in moral perspective from life to sport is attested to in numerous informal observations as well. Consider, for example, a comment by former heavyweight boxing champion Larry Holmes. Before he enters the ring, Holmes said, "I have to change, I have to leave the goodness out and bring all the bad in, like Dr. Jekyll and Mr. Hyde" (quoted in Bredemeier & Shields, 1985, p. 23). Ron Rivera of the Chicago Bears likewise described the personality transformation he undergoes when entering his sport. The off-field Ron, he said, is soft-spoken, considerate, and friendly. When asked to describe the on-field Ron, he replied, "He's totally opposite from me. . . . He's a madman. . . . No matter what happens, he hits people. He's a guy with no regard for the human body" (quoted in Bredemeier & Shields, 1985, p. 24). Rivera's comment is echoed continually by sport commentators who note perceived discrepancies between an on-field and an off-field athlete.

Many readers no doubt question the moral legitimacy of the reasoning transformations implied in these quotes. The moral issues that surface in connection with game reasoning present a host of philosophical questions beyond the scope of the present book. Our main point is that a shift in moral reasoning patterns does occur. Whether one believes that such a shift *should* occur will depend on philosophical presuppositions that we are not prepared to probe here.

From a psychologist's vantage point, however, it is worth noting that the form or structure of game reasoning itself suggests certain limitations to its applicability. Most importantly, as we have suggested elsewhere (Bredemeier & Shields, 1986a; Shields & Bredemeier, 1986), it would be internally contradictory to use game reasoning to legitimate any form of action that has game-transcending implications. Because game reasoning itself is premised on the nonserious and "set-aside" character of sport, actions that have implications beyond that realm must be justified (if they are to be justified) by norms of morality applicable in daily life. For example, it would not be legitimate to use the egocentric thrust of game reasoning to justify intentionally inflicting an injury that would persist after a game's conclusion. Actions with intended consequences that do not allow players to return to their pregame status cannot be justified by appeal to the unique qualities of sport.

The Holmes and Rivera quotes also illustrate that the transformation that often accompanies entry into sport is at least as much an affective change as a cognitive one. In fact, former President Ronald Reagan once said that in football "you can feel a clean hatred for your opponent. It is a clean hatred since it's only symbolic in a jersey" (quoted in Bredemeier & Shields, 1985, p. 23). Again, whether such an affective transformation is legitimate is not our point. We simply underscore the fact that it is a common experience in the world of competitive sport.

Game Reasoning: Future Research Directions

Many questions are yet unanswered about game reasoning. Perhaps most importantly, no systematic investigation of the development of game reasoning patterns has been conducted. We have found that life and sport reasoning patterns begin to diverge around ages 12 or 13 (Bredemeier, in press). But we know very little about development within game reasoning itself. It would be instructive to administer sport dilemmas to a cross-sectional sample and then follow the participants longitudinally. In this way we could determine whether there are age-related changes in game reasoning patterns that exhibit stagelike properties.

Several questions also remain about the coordination between game reasoning and life morality. Are these two forms of reasoning coordinated differently at different stages of development? How do athletes (and others) decide which takes precedence when there is a conflict between them? These are only a few of the questions that could be asked.

Another potential approach to game reasoning is reflected in the interesting work of Theresa Thorkildsen (1989). She suggests that when the fairness of social practices (as opposed to individual behavior) is considered, the implicit contracts or definitions of a situation need to be taken into account. She analyzed children's evaluations of the fairness of such practices as peer-assistance, contests to determine superiority, and testing: She found that the evaluations differed depending on whether the practices were embedded in an educational or sport setting. In light of these findings, researchers interested in game reasoning might want to probe people's moral thinking about sport practices (e.g., NCAA eligibility rules) as well as about individual behavior (e.g., cheating).

Another line of inquiry is how sport and game images are used metaphorically in other areas of life. The languages of politics and business, for example, are liberally sprinkled with sport metaphors. Political campaigns need a "game plan," executives search for "team players," international trade negotiators talk about an "even playing field," and so on. One purpose of such metaphor may be to recast politics or business in a sport mode for the very purpose of having actions evaluated with reference to the lenient moral norms of sport. Game reasoning may transmute relatively easily into other competitive contexts, but without the structural protections of sport (protections that guarantee conditions of fairness, a high level of rule compliance, swift compensation for defaults, and temporal boundaries that return players to their equalized status at the conclusion of the game) the legitimating conditions for its existence may rapidly evaporate. Can the "dirty tricks" of politics really be equated with sporting strategy? Can deception in advertising claim a parallel to deception in sport? Is the battlefield really just an extension of the playing field?

So far, we have suggested that game reasoning is responsive to the zero-sum, nonserious, set-aside structural qualities of sport. Game reasoning may be responsive not only to the formal properties of sport but also to the informal norms characterizing the moral atmosphere of a particular sporting environment. If this is the case, we may hypothesize that game reasoning is not inherently egocentric in form. It may involve a contextual adaptation of moral reasoning in the direction of the prevailing stage of the collective norms of the particular sport situation. For example, a coach who strongly believes in sport as a context for "cooperating through competition" may emphasize the values of fairness, inclusivity, and mutual support. Team members may be encouraged not only to help each other but also to maintain playing conditions that optimize the possibility for excellent performances by opponents as well as themselves and teammates. Under such conditions, high-stage norms may characterize the moral atmosphere. It may be that a relatively low-stage moral reasoner may actually advance in her reasoning when entering such a sport setting. Unfortunately, we have not found much evidence of this in the descriptive dimension of our research program, though it remains theoretically possible.

Moral Reasoning, Emotion, and Moral Bias

We have spent considerable time discussing the underlying structure of moral reasoning, particularly as it may reflect the unique context of sport. But a cognitive-structured description is inadequate in a model of moral action because actual moral reasoning is invariably infused with affect and governed as much by content as by structure.

Hoffman argues that moral action is motivated by and moral reasoning is rooted in affect, especially empathy. Similarly, Gilligan argues for care-based reasoning as a moral framework distinct from principle-based reasoning.

We believe that empathy-based and principle-based reasoning are complementary moral frameworks, each needing the other to protect against tendencies for bias (see Gilligan & Attanucci, 1988, for a similar position). Although one framework may predominate in some individuals, the mature moral agent simultaneously uses both cognitive and affective approaches to moral situations. Take, for example, a youth sport coach who must decide whether to play a particularly unskilled player in the final game of an important tournament. Let us suppose that the coach is a morally mature individual who empathizes with the unskilled youth, perhaps identifying with such feelings as the child's yearning to play, his anxiety about fulfilling his parents' expectations, and his fear that should he play he might mess up and become the target of ridicule. Trying to weigh these different, vicariously aroused affects, the coach may decide that the desire to play outweighs the unskilled youth's other concerns. The coach also may empathize with the other players' desires to win but conclude that their desires are not nearly so compelling.

But her decision-making process probably does not end there. The coach also may try to view the situation impartially from the perspective of each person involved, resolving various questions: Is it fair to deny my team the best chance of victory when the kids have worked so hard to win? How is our success strategy related to our beliefs about sportspersonship and the ideal nature of competition? Is it fair to make one player sit on the bench due to factors beyond his control? There is no necessary way in which the empathy-based and principle-based reasoning come together, so we will leave it to your imagination (and moral sensitivities!) to decide the outcome of this process.

This scenario illustrates how an individual might employ double-checks on her or his own affective and cognitive processes. Our depiction of moral maturity, however, has one important implication that will be offensive to strict adherents of the Kohlberg model. For Kohlberg, justice takes precedence over care, and moral decisions are ultimately resolvable through ideal role taking. In contrast, we maintain that there is no necessary and predetermined priority between justice and care. Can one legitimately be more concerned about one's own team members than members of another team? Perhaps. Must one always operate out of strict impartiality? We believe not. But we are not advocating complete moral relativism. A mature empathy-based reasoning and a clear principle of impartial justice considerably narrow the options for action that might be considered moral, but the circle is not so narrowed in every situation as to allow only one alternative. We are arguing for a certain latitude of moral indeterminacy, and we suggest that this neither undermines the cognitive status of morality nor places on cognition a greater weight than it can bear.

Haan's model indicates yet another way that people's moral perspectives are checked against bias—they are subjected to dialogue among people who may be impacted by its outcome. Kohlberg, and to a lesser extent Gilligan and Hoffman, seems to theorize as if the moral agent is cut off from social interaction. Though Kohlberg, Gilligan, and Hoffman all discuss the concept of relationship, they describe the decision-making process as if it were purely intrasubjective. Haan's work reminds us that a great deal of daily moral decision making occurs through a process of intersubjective negotiation. The relevant moral skills are not only ones of intrapsychic capacities but also of interpersonal moral communication and exchange.

Mature moral reasoning involves a series of double-checks and integrations drawing from one's full range of moral competencies. But the outcome invariably reflects one's commitments to particular moral contents, as well as structural capacities.

Moral Beliefs, Attitudes, and Values

Process II ends with a moral judgment about what ought to be done in the situation at hand. The construction of a situation-specific moral ideal involves an integration of perceived situational factors with the preexisting contents of one's moral perspective—the specific beliefs, attitudes, and values that one advocates. Most early moral research, such as the Hartshorne and May studies reviewed in chapter 2, sought to reveal a direct link between moral beliefs and moral action, but it was generally unsuccessful. Moral content needs to be viewed in light of the organizing structure of thought, but that does not make moral content irrelevant.

The underlying moral structure (whether described in the terms of Kohlberg, Haan, or others) provides grammarlike rules that influence how perceived situational factors are integrated with the content of one's moral perspective. There is no straightforward, direct relationship between moral structures and the content of specific moral decisions. The same moral structure can support diverse beliefs, attitudes, and values, as well as multiple action choices. This is illustrated, for example, in a study by Case, Greer, and Lacourse (1987), who found no significant relationships between people's moral reasoning maturity and their attitudes toward "unacceptable" spectator behavior in sport. Similarly, Solomon (1993) found no relationship between moral reasoning level and children's legitimacy judgments about gender stratification in sport. On the other hand, though moral structures do not determine specific contents or choices, a person's level of moral reasoning may predispose him or her to certain judgments (Candee, 1976; Kohlberg & Candee, 1984). For example, our research demonstrates that athletes' and children's moral reasoning levels correlate with their judgments about the legitimacy of intentionally inflicting injury in a sport context (Bredemeier, 1985; Bredemeier, Weiss, Shields, & Cooper, 1986, 1987).

The precise mechanisms that mediate moral structures and moral contents are not well understood. No doubt, affect plays a significant role in this. For example, when a person experiences empathy for another, the aroused affect may activate moral concepts and precepts, and these in turn are given organizational structure in accord with the underlying stage of reasoning. Of course, as we indicated before, there is a reciprocal interactive relationship among cognitive structure and affective competencies. A person's stage of reasoning may influence when and how affects like empathy are experienced.

Value Hierarchies

Value hierarchies, which tend to be both cognitive and affective organizations, would seem to lie at an intermediate level between structure and content, so they may provide a particularly useful entry point in the study of moral content. Like moral structures, value hierarchies exhibit an organizational pattern that cuts across diverse contexts, they are generally stable (evolving slowly in the process of development), and they predispose a person to notice particular cues in a situation, organize information in a particular way, and reflect on action choices using somewhat constant criteria. Unlike moral structures, however, value hierarchies resemble content in that they are highly variable across cultures and time, do not develop in an invariant sequence, and are not reducible to a relative few stable structural patterns.

One of the researchers most influential in the study of the relation between value hierarchies and prosocial behavior is Ervin Staub (1978, 1979, 1986). Staub subsumes moral values into what he labels "personal goals," preferences developed in the socialization process that encourage a valuing of certain outcomes or end states and an aversion to others. Underlying moral personal goals are prosocial value hierarchies, which Staub divides into two general types: duty- or justice-based and empathy-based. In addition to moral personal goals, individuals have other personal goals related to such things as material gain, social approval, professional achievement, and the like. In a concrete situation, several personal goals may be activated. The hierarchical relations among the goals will partially determine which goals are acted on. Staub (1974) has demonstrated that people who highly prioritize prosocial value orientations exhibit more helping behavior when they encounter someone in an emergency situation than do those with less commitment to prosocial values.

Value Hierarchies in Sport

A variety of studies have been conducted in the sport setting on what has come to be called the professionalization of values (or attitudes). In this line of research, investigators study the relative priority that people give to playing well, playing fairly, and winning (and, sometimes, having fun) in their view of sport. The hierarhical ordering that a person gives to these values has been labeled *game orientation* (Knoppers, 1985).

The professionalization literature received its impetus from a seminal study by Harry Webb. Webb's (1969) methodology was simple. He asked 1,200 children the following question: What do you think is most important in playing a game: to play as well as you can, to beat the other player or team, or to play the game fairly?

According to Webb (1969), a regular sequence of priorities emerges that is related to age, gender, religion, and socioeconomic status. Most importantly, Webb found that children initially have a *play orientation* in which fairness is of greatest concern, game outcome least. But as experience in sport increases, the play orientation eventually gives way to a *professional orientation* in which the values are reversed: Outcome is stressed most, fairness least.

A number of variables have been linked to the professionalization of values. Consistent with Webb (1969), several researchers have found that age is a significant predictor of game orientation, with the professional orientation increasingly embraced with advancing age (Blair, 1985; Card, 1981; Maloney & Petrie, 1972). Webb believed that children learn to adapt to the value preferences of the adult world. But Knoppers (1985) has suggested that it may be the experience of formalized athletic programs in the high school that makes the difference.

In addition to age, two other variables have often been reported to correlate significantly with game orientation: athletic status (Card, 1981; Knoppers, Schuiteman, & Love, 1988; Loy, Birrell, & Rose, 1976; Maloney & Petrie, 1972; Mantel & Vander Velden, 1974; Nicholson, 1979; Nixon, 1980; Snyder & Spreitzer, 1979b; Theberge, Curtis, & Brown, 1982) and gender (Blair, 1985; Card, 1981; Kidd & Woodman, 1975; Knoppers et al., 1988; Maloney & Petrie, 1972; McElroy & Kirkendall, 1980; Loy et al., 1976; Nixon, 1980; Petrie, 1971a, 1971b; Sage, 1980; Snyder & Spreitzer, 1979b; Theberge et al., 1982; Webb, 1969). In general, athletes and males progress further or more rapidly toward a professional value hierarchy than nonathletes and females. In addition, within the athletic population, more-elite athletes tend to exhibit a more professional orientation than less-elite competitors (Knoppers et al., 1988).

But exceptions to the athletic status and gender associations have also been found. For example, not all types of sport involvement appear to be associated with a professionalization of values. Participants in intramurals have been found to have less of a professional orientation (Loy et al., 1976; Maloney & Petrie, 1972) than their counterparts in athletics, especially women intramural participants (Loy et al., 1976). An exception to the general findings about gender occurs when the subjects are drawn from elite athletics; male and female elite sport participants equally endorse the professional orientation (Knoppers et al., 1988; Theberge et al., 1982).

The meaning of the professionalization literature is not entirely clear. Webb (1969) characterized a professional game orientation as consistent with workplace values and suggested that involvement in sports socialized youth into the economic sphere. Because Webb believed that females were less inclined to seek fulfillment in the occupational world, he proposed they would be less inclined to adopt the professional orientation in sport.

Webb's interpretation rests on the assumption that sport is a socializing influence that intrinsically promotes a professional orientation. But professionalization studies have relied on correlation techniques, making it impossible to determine cause-and-effect relationships. It certainly is possible that only those individuals who have professional value orientations, or are already predisposed to their development, choose to participate in sport, stay in sport, or get selected for sport (Theberge et al., 1982). It may also be that it is not sport per se but the value orientation of sport coaches that is most influential, a hypothesis that has received some support (Albinson, 1973).

In a review of the professionalization literature, Knoppers (1985) offers several insightful critiques. She points out that the rank ordering technique used in the Webb scale determines only each value's relative importance; such a procedure fails to reflect the magnitude of importance of each value. For example, a person who does not embrace any of the identified values very much may nonetheless order them identically to someone who is heavily invested in one or more of the values. More importantly, the Webb scale assumes a unitary variable underlying the trio of values bounded by the play and professional orientations at opposite ends of a continuum. It may be, however, that the "play" and "professional" value orientations are independent. A person may highly value both winning and playing fair.

Knoppers (1985) also points out that gender differences and athletic status differences may reflect different meanings attached to the same stimulus variables. For example, when an athlete is asked what is most important in a "game," the meaning matrix the athlete uses may reflect experience in highly structured, organized, competitive games. A nonathlete responding to the same question may have in mind more informal games. A female athlete may respond to yet a third conceptualization of "game." Similarly, people at different ages may attach quite different meanings to the same words. Finally, those who think about structured, competitive sports when asked about their value priorities in games may stress winning because they believe that fairness can be presumed to exist. Fairness may need more focused attention in the context of informal games, and therefore it may be ranked higher by those who interpret "game" in this way.

A study by Knoppers, Schuiteman, and Love (1986) addressed several of the problems in the Webb scale. Rather than leaving the meaning of game ambiguous, the investigators presented two specific scenarios: an informal sport game among friends (labeled the recreational scenario) and the state high school basketball championship (labeled the competitive scenario). In addition, rather than have respondents rank the values of fairness, fun, playing well, and winning, they had their subjects rate the importance of each on a 7-point Likert scale. The purpose of the study was to explore the dimensionality, situation specificity, and magnitude of game orientation in teenagers across the independent variables of gender, athletic status, and ethnicity. The main findings were the following:

- Game orientation is not a unitary construct; in no instance were high scores in one orientation accompanied by low scores in the other, indicating that the play and professional orientations are not opposite ends of a single continuum.
- All subgroups responded differently to the two game contexts, indicating that game orientation is situation-specific.
- Game orientation was mediated to some extent by ethnicity but not by gender or athletic status. Interestingly, the African American and European American samples were similar to each other in their responses, and Hispanics dissimilar.

More work clearly needs to be done in this area. The study by Knoppers, Schuiteman, and Love (1986) provides a helpful model, but it leaves important questions unanswered. Like Hartshorne and May, they demonstrated that response is situation-specific, but it may well be that beneath the apparent diversity is a coherent pattern yet to be clearly identified. Replacing the rank-order technique of the Webb scale with a Likert scale resolves some problems and creates others. People may give identical ratings to two or more values, but this does not give any indication of what they would do when those values directly conflict. The rank-order technique is better for that. A more inductive, open-ended approach would also be useful. For example, it might be helpful to have participants identify, define, then prioritize the values that are most important to them.

Let us conclude this section by noting that some of the findings of the professionalization literature can be interpreted in light of what was said earlier about game reasoning. We have suggested that sport may reflect an "institution of release" in which moral concerns can be set aside temporarily and within limited bounds. This is particularly true when officials are on hand. Under such conditions, players are freed to concentrate on winning. Those sport settings most conducive to facilitating "moral release" may also facilitate a professional orientation toward sport. Athletes with more experience in these settings may come to habitually define winning as the most important value, not because they genuinely believe that it is more important than fairness, but because fairness is presupposed.

Ego-Processing Influences

Cognitive processes are particularly important in constructing a moral ideal. For this reason, we have identified the cognitive ego functions, comprised of three pairs of coping and defending processes, as particularly relevant to Process II of our moral action model. Objectivity, intellectuality, and logical analysis are the relevant coping processes. The same generic functions reflected in these coping processes are distorted into defending processes when a person resorts to isolation, intellectualizing, or rationalization.

The cognitive coping processes enable people to accurately connect their moral constructs with situation-relevant moral cues. In moral reasoning these processes enable people to think clearly and coordinate their ideas and feelings. In the context of moral dialogue, these processes facilitate the communication of clear and precise moral information, enhancing the possibility of achieving a mutually satisfying resolution.

In Haan's extensive study of moral action in simulation games, avoiding defensive isolation was a particularly significant contributor to moral action (Haan et al., 1985). When people resorted to isolation they defensively separated their cognitions from their affects. This points to the centrality in moral action of integrating ideas and emotions. Our discussion of the importance of recognizing and integrating both empathy-based reasoning and cognitive-based reasoning points to the same general conclusion.

Intellectualizing also strongly tended to thwart moral action (Haan et al., 1985). Bandura (1991) also highlights intellectualizing and rationalization in his discussion of mechanisms by which moral self-regulation is disengaged. Clearly, people are able to distort their cognitions about morality to serve their own interests.

Assuming people remain coping, they will be able to logically connect their ideas, reason coherently, integrate their affective and cognitive responses to the situation, and arrive at a moral ideal that reflects their optimal cognitive-affective capacities. But situations are multidimensional; they elicit various forms of processing, moral reasoning being only one among many. They may activate different and sometimes contradictory motives. In the next chapter, we explore the multidimensionality of contexts and probe how moral values relate to nonmoral ones.

Summary

In this chapter we have examined the major influences that affect Process II—the construction of a moral judgment and the generation of a situation-specific moral ideal. The moral atmosphere, identified as a key contextual variable influencing the formation of a moral judgment, was elaborated in terms of collective norms and the institutional value. Moral reasoning both in daily life and sport contexts was identified as the key personal competency variable. Finally, we discussed the contribution of the cognitive ego functions to the formation of a situation-specific moral ideal.

In the next chapter we examine Process III of our model of moral action—selecting a value alternative.

Chapter 8
Deciding on a Course of Action

In the last two chapters we reviewed the processes of interpreting a moral situation and identifying a situation-specific moral ideal. In Process I, an individual's moral sensitivities are activated, and she imaginatively constructs possibilities for alternative action. In Process II, the individual weighs different moral values and arrives at a decision about a course of action believed to represent the best moral alternative. Once the situation has been interpreted and a moral course of action identified, a critical moment of choice looms. Process III of our model is centered on choice—whether to choose the moral course of action or an alternative.

The centrality of choice in Process III raises two issues. First, choice implies that the situation has elicited competing motivations. Sport, for example, allows for different goals such as mastery, victory, fun, and fair play. In this connection, we will review the theme of domain cues. Second, choice involves two interrelated themes associated with moral judgments: motivation and the self-structure. These are the central themes of the second section of this chapter. We will conclude with a discussion of affective impulse–regulating ego processes.

Contextual Influences

What role do social contexts play in eliciting different and sometimes competing motivations and values? A key assumption is that social contexts are multifaceted and correspondingly engage different aspects of social cognition. Elliot Turiel and his colleagues have conducted an important research program that focuses on the relation between the multifaceted character of social environments and domains of social cognition (Smetana, 1981a; Turiel, 1983, 1989a, 1989b; Turiel & Davidson, 1986; Turiel, Killen, & Helwig, 1987; Turiel & Smetana, 1984; Turiel, Smetana, & Killen, 1991). In short, they claim that a parallel exists between how one organizes an understanding of the environment and the structural qualities of the environment itself. For sport psychologists, this is an important theme because of the unique social organization of ''games.''

It is a fact both intuitively obvious and well documented that behavior is influenced by social context. But contextual stimuli do not mechanically or directly determine behavior. Contexts are interpreted, and it is the interpreted stimuli that influence behavior. In turn, interpretation is not arbitrary; contexts partly determine interpretation. When a basketball coach draws Xs and Os on a chalkboard during half-time, these contextual stimuli are likely to elicit patterns of strategic reasoning organized around concepts of games. Similarly, some social stimuli are likely to elicit moral cognitions—or even a particular moral orientation like justice or care—whereas other situations may ''pull'' for a different form of social cognitive processing.

The concept of context–person *interaction* has been a consistent theme of structural developmental theorists. Most theorists concentrate on the ''person'' side of the interaction, but Turiel has focused on the organization of the environment as well as the person's cognitive structures (Turiel, 1977, 1978a, 1978b, 1983). He is especially interested in the social environment and different domains of social interaction. Drawing from such sociologists as Max Weber (1922/1947), Turiel differentiates social actions that are conventional from those that are moral. Let us illustrate.

Eyal is watching a film in school, sitting next to a friend. When they see a particularly upsetting scene, the friend turns toward Eyal and launches a right fist into his unsuspecting cheek, knocking him over. Turiel maintains that there are some social actions that have immediate and obvious consequences for the welfare of others. Experience with contexts where welfare consequences are salient, or where fairness is clearly at issue, are major contextual sources for the development and elicitation of concepts of morality.

Sorren also is watching the film with a friend. When the upsetting scene comes on the screen, the friend—in violation of a school rule—gets up and leaves the room without permission. In this situation, as in the previous example, something ''wrong'' was done by the friend. But the transgression is different; it is wrong only because of the social rules in place. Without the classroom context and the school rule, there is nothing wrong with what Sorren's friend did. Experiences of this sort lead to a different organization of social knowledge, what Turiel calls concepts of social convention.

The Environment and Domains of Reasoning

Turiel (1983) has divided social cognition into three main categories according to the types of social experience that are at their root. He writes,

> It is proposed that the child's structuring of the social world revolves around three general categories. These are (1) concepts of persons or psychological systems (the psychological domain), (2) concepts of systems of social relations and organizations (the societal domain)—of which convention is but one component, and (3) prescriptive judgments of justice, rights, and welfare (the moral domain). (p. 4)

Turiel is arguing that the child is a budding psychologist, sociologist, and moral philosopher and that these areas of social cognition form distinct, largely independent domains of thought. Each domain of social cognition arises from interaction with different types or dimensions of contexts. Because each domain reflects experience with different environmental qualities, each social cognitive domain has a qualitatively unique pattern of development.

The thrust of Turiel's argument may become clearer when it is contrasted with the position of Kohlberg. Like Turiel, Kohlberg maintained that personal, conventional, and moral concerns are distinct. But Kohlberg believed that the distinctions among them evolve slowly within a singular process of sociomoral development. According to Kohlberg, morality is initially confused with self-interest. Typically, sometime in late childhood, self-interest is differentiated from moral concerns, but morality then becomes confused with convention during adolescence. Only at the postconventional level are morality, convention, and self-interest separated and "correctly" prioritized.

In contrast, Turiel has maintained that even young children can distinguish personal, conventional, and moral aspects of their social environment. Developmental progression, according to Turiel, occurs within each of the three, more or less independent, domains of social cognition as children interact with multidimensional environments.

Criterion Judgments and Domain Cues

Turiel has proposed the concept of criterion judgments to describe how people distinguish one type of experience from another. *Criterion judgments* are social-cognitive constructs that people tacitly employ to distinguish different types of social-environmental experiences. Morality is one domain of social cognition, preconsciously distinguished from others by a set of criterion judgments. Let's return to our school film example. It doesn't matter whether Eyal is watching a film in Berkeley, Reykjavik, the Australian bush, or rural Tanzania, observers of his friend's physical act will view it as a *moral* offense because of its intrinsic relationship to welfare concerns. Cultural independence is one criterion judgment by which people distinguish the moral domain. A similar concept is rule independence. It is morally irrelevant whether there was an explicit rule against what the friend did. It was wrong regardless. Furthermore, the friend's action (hitting) is wrong whatever the context: watching a film, playing tag, walking down the street, or eating at a restaurant. In short, Turiel suggests that an action is judged as within the moral domain if it involves welfare concerns or fairness and judgments about it are

- imperative (a person should or should not do it),
- noncontingent (the correctness of the action is not based on rules),
- unalterable (a "wrong" action cannot be made "right" by social consensus), and
- universalizable (the action is "right" or "wrong" irrespective of cultural context).

The second school film example also involved a transgression (leaving the room), but it was a social violation belonging to an entirely different class of social interactions. Correspondingly, Turiel has posited that a distinct set of criterion judgments within all people's tacit social knowledge enables them to place the second violation in a different framework. In short, an act is viewed as conventional if it does not directly affect welfare or fairness concerns and judgments about it are

- contingent (the act is right or wrong based on rules, authority dictates, or roles),
- alterable (the correctness of the act can be changed by social consensus), and
- relative (different cultures can take different positions on the legitimacy of the act).

Turiel has placed less emphasis on the "personal" domain, but it has been explored by some of his colleagues, who suggest that actions deemed inappropriate for social regulation belong to this domain of social cognition (Nucci, 1981; Smetana, 1981b). For example, choice of hobbies should be a personal matter, not something regulated by moral or conventional norms.

In one illustrative study of criterion judgments, Nucci (1981) presented subjects who ranged in age from 7 to 19 with a series of "transgressions" and asked them to group the acts they would consider wrong regardless of the presence or absence of a rule. Acts like hitting, stealing, and athletes' throwing a game were viewed as wrong irrespective of rules. Acts like eating in class, talking without raising a hand, and eating with fingers were viewed as convention; they were wrong only if a rule prohibited them.

Criterion judgments are implicit or tacit forms of knowledge that people use to distinguish domains (moral, conventional, personal) of social experience. Criterion judgments are nondevelopmental, cutting across all ages except for the very young. They are responsive to *domain cues*, configurations of environmental stimuli that "pull" for a particular domain of social-cognitive processing. An act of hitting, for example, tends to activate moral processing. There is a close (but not perfect) correspondence between the intrinsic qualities of the social context (the presence or absence of various domain cues) and the domain or domains of social cognition used to reason about the context.

The domain of social cognition that is applied to an event will largely determine the categories of reasoning used to evaluate it. Such categories as rights, duties, fairness, and welfare will be used to reason about events that are interpreted as moral. In contrast, the categories of social organization and coordination, authority, and custom will be used to think about events seen as conventional. Turiel (1983) frequently refers to these as *justification categories*. Unlike the criterion judgments, the justification categories undergo regular, age-related changes in their structural organization.

Multifaceted Environments and Mixed Domain Reasoning

To understand the genesis of action, Turiel maintains, it is helpful to understand the domains of reasoning that are likely to be elicited by the structural properties of the environment. Turiel and Smetana (1984) write,

> Starting with the assumption that many behavioral situations are multidimensional, it is proposed that action is a product of the coordination of domains of social judgment. Behavioral situations are multidimensional in that more than one type of judgment is brought to bear on behavioral decisions. For example, social-behavioral decisions may include moral judgments of harm, rights and justice, and societal concepts (such as concepts of institutions, authority relations, customs, and social conventions). Therefore, the study of relations between social judgments and action requires analyses of the interrelations among domains of social judgments in interaction within the parameters of the situational context. (p. 261)

Some social situations are relatively simple and elicit only one form of reasoning. For example, deciding whether to call someone by a first or last name is a relatively simple social issue resolvable within a single domain of reasoning. Often, however, social situations are complex, containing domain cues of more than one type. Such contexts tend to elicit social cognitions from more than one domain of reasoning. Correspondingly, the individual may coordinate conclusions, subordinate one to the other, or focus on one, neglecting the other.

The Milgram "authority" experiments provide an example of a social context with multidimensional domain cues (Milgram, 1963, 1974; cf. Turiel, 1983, and Turiel & Smetana, 1984). As you may recall, in the classic Milgram paradigm the experimenter told subjects that they were participating in a learning experiment. The subject was placed at an instrument panel and told to administer shocks to a volunteer learner (who was actually a confederate of the experimenter) whenever the learner gave a wrong answer. The "learner" was in another room, so the subject could hear but not see him. To the dismay of social psychology students everywhere, 65% of the subjects, when ordered to do so, continued to increase the voltage and administer shocks, even when they believed a dangerous level had been reached.

Turiel pointed out that the Milgram experiments combine and place in conflict two domains of social cognition: morality and social-convention. The experimenter deliberately created a social environment that had all the trappings (i.e., domain cues) of a genuine, legitimate form of social organization—a social science experiment. From all appearances, the social system was under the competent direction of a credentialed scientist who wielded legitimate authority over the progress of the experiment. The subject's role in the social system was to follow the instructions of the experimenter. With the situation interpreted primarily as an "experiment," the social-conventional issues of conformity, authority, and hierarchy came to the fore.

At one and the same time, the situation could be viewed from a quite different and contrasting perspective. Because someone was ostensibly being hurt, there were moral domain cues in the context. From a moral point of view, it made sense to disobey the authority and refuse to administer dangerous shocks. Turiel's main point is that the problem contained in the Milgram experiment is not simply a moral problem, but a problem of coordinating different conclusions based on different domains of reasoning. Interestingly, Turiel notes, when the researcher modified the experimental design to emphasize the pain of the learner (and thus enhanced the salience of the moral domain cues) or when he decreased the authority's status (and thus minimized the salience of the social-conventional domain cues), most experimental subjects refused to obey instructions to increase the shock voltage.

Sport as a Multifaceted Environment

There are interesting parallels between the Milgram experiments and situations that sometimes arise in sport. Behavior in sport, like behavior in the Milgram experiments, occurs in a context that prominently features social-conventional domain cues. Conformity, authority, and hierarchy are salient and valued in many sport settings. Particularly as one moves up the competitive ladder, coaches and game officials—each serving a special systems function—are viewed as well-established and legitimate authorities whose dictates often are accepted with little question. However, sport also is permeated by moral domain cues. Sport actions sometimes involve putitng self or others at risk, and issues of fairness arise frequently. When an athlete is instructed by a coach to engage in potentially injurious behavior—whether legal or illegal from the standpoint of the rules—the player is in a multidimensional social environment where different domains of social cognition need to be coordinated.

More than most other social action, sport action occurs in a highly rule-governed environment. To effectively coordinate the domains of reasoning that may arise in sport, clarity about the nature, purpose, and limitations of game rules is essential. Game rules are one of the most prominent contextual features of sport settings; let's examine them more closely.

Game Rules

Turiel (1983) defined games and sports as neither strictly social-conventional nor strictly moral. Games have social-conventional and moral aspects, but they are not themselves encompassed by either. They are unique social contexts. Perhaps the clearest way to amplify this point is to examine the nature and significance of game rules. It is within the rule-bound game context that moral action in sport takes place, and game rules serve multiple functions.

There are many types of rules, and philosophers have proposed various rule categorizations for different purposes. Searle (1969), for example, differentiates "constitutive" from "regulative" rules. *Regulative rules* shape behavior that exists before or independent of the rules. Traffic laws that govern the proper driving of a car, for example, are regulative rules because driving a car can occur whether or not rules exist regulating it. On the other hand, *constitutive rules* create the behaviors they define. Without the rules of badminton, no game of badminton exists.

The formal rules of a game are constitutive rules; they define what it is to play that game. But game rules—or at least a subset of them—have functions besides defining the game. For our purposes, it will be helpful to distinguish how game rules function similarly to and differently from social-conventional and moral rules (Weston & Turiel, 1980).

Game rules, like social-conventional rules, regulate "arbitrary" behavior by imbuing it with social meaning. Raising one's hand is a relatively meaningless act until it is given meaning in a specific social system like the classroom. Similarly, tossing a ball through a hoop is meaningless until given meaning in a specific rule-defined game like basketball. Sport rules set up a miniature and temporary social system; they create a competitive achievement context. Because of the close parallels between game rules and social conventions, game rules often serve as domain cues eliciting social-conventional reasoning. Thus, athletes reasoning about sport issues may readily employ concepts of authority, rules and roles, hierarchy, social coordination, and the like. The analogy to social convention, however, is not perfect. Unlike game rules, social-conventional rules enhance social organization in the context of ongoing, purposeful, and necessary social systems. Social-conventional rules, though viewed as changeable, tend to be more enduring and resistant to modification than game rules.

Game rules also resemble moral rules. In fact, the similarity has resulted in some problematic research. In an earlier chapter, we noted that Piaget (1932/1965) used the game of marbles as one of his social contexts for studying morality. Similarly, several other researchers have used game rules as if they were directly analogous with moral rules (Burton, Allinsmith, & Maccoby, 1966; Burton, Maccoby, & Allinsmith, 1961; Grinder, 1961, 1962; Hartshorne & May, 1928; Sears, Rau, & Alpert, 1965). In Turiel's view (1983), the assumption is mistaken. The actions that moral rules are designed to proscribe—for example, stealing property, inflicting injury, breaking promises, telling lies—are nonarbitrary. The actions themselves are considered wrong (except when more pressing moral concerns take priority), regardless of the presence or absence of formal rules. Game rules, in contrast, transform actions with no intrinsic significance into socially meaningful behavior.

The relationship between game rules and moral rules is closest when we turn to the equalizing and protective functions of game rules. Constitutive rules define a game, but they also provide a set of conditions that are identical for all participants, thereby equalizing opportunity. The rules also often function to protect participants from high risk of injury. But the formal rules can promote these goals only to a limited degree. Weiblen (1972) suggests that it is the informal "spirit of the game" that is analogous to morality, not the formal rules themselves. Written rules are imperfect expressions of the unwritten rule to have a fair and noninjurious contest. When an athlete orients to the spirit of the game, he or she may reason about actions using concepts drawn from the moral domain—concepts of fairness, responsibility, welfare, and the like.

Contextual Influences—Summary

Sports are multidimensional social contexts. They contain many social-conventional domain cues, such as hierarchical organization, institutional roles and rules, and conventional modes of coordinated action. Such domain cues have a natural tendency to elicit social-conventional reasoning. Sport also has many moral domain cues, such as the presence of physical risk and the saliency of issues of fairness. These domain cues have a natural tendency to elicit moral reasoning. In addition, sport is an artificial arena set up as a competitive achievement context, and issues of personal interest are salient.

As a result of its multifaceted nature, sport often elicits different and sometimes competing modes of thought. For example, a basketball player in a situation where committing an intentional foul may advantage her team but risk minor injury to an opponent faces a multidimensional context. Moral, conventional, and personal and prudential concerns are all relevant. How she interprets, prioritizes, and integrates these concerns will largely determine the course of her subsequent action. To better understand how people may prioritize different concerns or values, we turn now to the topic of personal competencies.

Personal Competency Influences

In the last chapter we discussed the specifically moral competencies that undergird moral action. So far in this chapter we have emphasized that moral processing is likely to be only one form of social cognition applied to a context like sport. As this multidimensional processing occurs, different motivations may be activated. For example, moral motivations may compete with the desire to maintain order, status, or social harmony (social-conventional concerns) or the desire for personal mastery or victory (personal concerns).

One way to think about the relationship between the outcomes of Processes II and III is to focus on Kohlberg's distinction between deontic moral judgments (Process II) and responsibility judgments (Process III). Responsibility judgments can be influenced by motives that are moral and by a host of other motives as well. In this section, we first rehearse the place of responsibility judgments in Kohlberg's theory of moral action, then we discuss prosocial reasoning as a bridge between judgment types. We next discuss the broader issue of moral motivation. Finally, in the major portion of this section, we discuss the role of the self-structure in Process III. Under the construct of self-structure, we deal with motivational orientations and the moral self.

Responsibility Judgments

Recall that in Kohlberg's theory, responsibility judgments play an important intermediary role between deontic judgments and moral action. Deontic judgments are generated in Process II and reflect decisions about the right or moral good. In contrast, responsibility judgments relate the right to the self.

Imagine that Jose is competing in a rugby match, and he perceives that emotions are getting out of hand. The intensity of physical contact is spiraling upward to a dangerous level, and Jose believes that it would be best if everyone would calm down. But he does not think that he is the one who should take responsibility for calming people down. For Jose, there is a gap between his deontic judgment and his responsibility judgment. One reason that responsibility judgments do not invariably follow a deontic judgment is that most situations present a host of other values (what Kohlberg calls quasi-obligations) that can be the focus of attention and the object of choice. In the rugby example, friendship issues, authority structures, and competitive interests all may provide justifications for inaction.

Age may play a role in the degree to which appropriate responsibility judgments are made. Blasi (1984, reported in Blasi, 1989) conducted an intriguing investigation of responsibility judgments among young people. Children in three age brackets (averaging 6, 12, and 17) were presented with a series of moral stories and asked questions regarding their opinions about the obligations of the protagonists. The youngest children acknowledged that certain actions are morally good, but with few exceptions they consistently said that one does not have to do the right action if one does not want to. Most 12-year-olds, in contrast, argued that an obligation to act followed on the recognition that something was right. Finally, in many 17-year-olds there was a relaxation of the sense of obligation. The sense of responsibility was qualified in an effort to integrate other values that were subjectively important to the self. When these older adolescents did argue for consistency between judgment and responsibility, they did so on the basis of needing to be true to one's own beliefs and values. The construct of self-structure is key to understanding these adolescents' responses, and we will return to it shortly. First, however, we discuss prosocial reasoning as a bridge between judgment types; we then lay a foundation for our investigation of self-structure with a brief discussion of moral motivation.

Bridging Deontic and Responsibility Judgments: Prosocial Reasoning

One theorist who has researched a developmental model of moral reasoning that spans judgment types is Nancy Eisenberg (1976, 1982, 1986; Eisenberg, Cialdini, McCreath, & Shell, 1987; Eisenberg-Berg, 1979). Like Kohlberg, Eisenberg has used the dilemma format. Two differences between the approaches of Kohlberg and Eisenberg—one theoretical and one methodological—make the contributions of these theorists difficult to integrate but suggest their complementary nature.

First, Eisenberg is not a structural developmentalist, preferring to work in the social learning tradition. As a result, though she uses the dilemma format, she is not tied to a strict structuralist analysis of participants' responses. For example, her reconstruction of developmental "levels" freely combines cognitive and affective elements. From a theoretical standpoint, this can be problematic because affects are less amenable to developmental categorization, but her model is rich with suggestive material about cognitive-affective interactions.

Methodologically, Eisenberg (1976) modified the dilemma format because her concern is not "pure" moral reasoning but moral reasoning as it relates to multidimensional value conflicts. Unlike Kohlberg's dilemmas, designed to pit one moral value against another, Eisenberg's stories typically reflect choices between taking a prosocial action that comes at a personal cost and acting on self-interest. For example, one story is about a swimmer who was asked to help children with disabilities learn to swim so they could strengthen their legs; to do so, however, would require a major sacrifice of his own practice time.

Eisenberg and her colleagues found that there is a regular, age-related progression in the way people respond to dilemmas like the one just cited. Her depiction of the development of prosocial reasoning reflects a developmental trajectory not unlike Kohlberg's stages. But her characterizations of levels are less structural than Kohlberg's, bridging structure and content distinctions, cognitive and affective dimensions of reasoning, and deontic and responsibility judgments.

The close relation of prosocial reasoning to moral action makes Eisenberg's description useful. Because the dilemmas resemble the kinds of multifaceted moral conflicts present in everyday life, there is reason to believe that the reasoning–action relationship may be relatively robust. In fact, in a series of investigations researchers have demonstrated a positive relationship between prosocial reasoning and prosocial behavior (Eisenberg et al., 1987; Eisenberg & Shell, 1986; Eisenberg-Berg &

Hand, 1979; Weidman & Strayhorn, 1992). But Eisenberg's prosocial reasoning levels still do not tell us why a person might choose a prosocial alternative that comes at some cost to the self. To better understand such value decisions, we need to probe the theme of moral motivation.

Moral Motivation

Motivation is probably the thorniest issue in the field of moral psychology. In this subsection, we summarize some of the main approaches to the topic, examine cognitive and emotional components of moral motivation, and conclude by probing how cognitive and emotional motivations are rooted in enduring passions and commitments.

Theories of Moral Motivation

What motivates a person to select moral values over nonmoral ones? There is no single or simple answer to this question, and numerous theories of moral motivation have been offered as possible responses. Rest (1983, 1984) identifies eight. Six of these theories, described briefly here, have substantial empirical support and may be relevant to sport settings:

1. People behave morally because they fear their negative emotional reactions if they fail to conform to internalized standards (Aronfreed, 1968; Eysenck, 1976). Thus, a player may choose not to use illicit drugs because she knows that if she did, she would "really get down on herself."
2. Moral motivation is identical to all other forms of motivation; people are innately attracted to rewarding experiences and repelled by negative ones. What counts as "rewarding" is a combination of innate predispositions and social learning (Bandura, 1977). A tennis player, for example, may truthfully admit that his opponent's serve was inbounds because he views such honesty as more rewarding in the long run.
3. Appreciation for the central role of cooperation in human collectives leads to a desire to maintain systems that promote cooperation and mutual respect (Dewey, 1959; Piaget, 1932/1965). According to this view, a person may be motivated to follow the rules of sport because he realizes that to do otherwise is to undermine the very cooperation that makes sport possible.
4. Moral motivation stems from the person's commitment to an ideal that transcends the self, to a larger goal (Durkheim, 1925/1961; Erikson, 1958). A sportswoman's dedication to the ideal of the "good contest" can root this form of motivation.
5. Empathy is the motivation for morality (Hoffman, 1976, 1978). In sport, for example, a player may refrain from dangerous illegal behaviors because he is concerned about what may happen to the opponent.

6. Concern for a sense of personal integrity—a belief that one is a moral person—motivates behavior in conformity with one's highest moral ideals (Blasi, 1984; Damon, 1984; Haan, 1991). For example, an athlete may find her fundamental moral beliefs and values to be intrinsically worthy of pursuit and act with integrity because of her personal commitment to those beliefs and values.

These six theories reflect a diverse range of opinion about whether the underlying motivation for moral behavior is fundamentally cognitive, affective, or volitional. The theories are not mutually exclusive, and moral motivation may often reflect a confluence of two or more of these factors. Nonetheless, we suggest in this chapter that the personal-integrity theory is the most adequate of the six.

Cognitive Motivation

Let us first focus on the cognitive roots of moral motivation. Most of us, most of the time, believe that *reasons are motives*. When we behave in a particular way, we believe we can explain our behavior by referring to a rationale underlying it. There is a functional unity to the reasons and the behavior. But the specific relationship between cognition and motivation is complex and the subject of considerable controversy. To illustrate, we will employ a pair of stories similar to ones used by Blasi (1983b), transposed to a sport setting. Compare Story A with Story B.

STORY A

I want to play second base on the school softball team. I *think* that I will be able to get the assignment if I continuously harp on my desire to the coach. My teammate, however, *points out* that I will only anger the coach. She suggests that I flatter the coach instead, try to get in good with her, and then suggest that I would be good for that position. I *realize* that this is *true* and that my friend is *correct*. So I resort to flattery because I *know* that it will get me the position.

This story involves a number of cognitive processes that mediate action. Each italicized word or phrase indicates a cognitive operation. The reasoning is reality-oriented, and a number of correct inferences are drawn. But one cannot say that the perceptions of reality and truth are the motives for this hopeful athlete's actions. The cognitive processes simply serve a preexisting affective motive. This is the usual meaning of the word *cognitive* in social-"cognitive" learning theory. Compare this understanding of cognition with that in Story B.

STORY B

I want to play second base, and my friend suggests that I flatter the coach. But I believe it is not right to resort to dishonest means to get the position. If I were to flatter the coach, it would be insincere, and I am convinced that truthfulness in communication is very important. People, because they are people, should not be manipulated to get what someone desires. Also, a person, because she is a person, should not be dominated by her own selfish wants.

In Story B, the cognitive considerations modify the original motive itself. Motives are questioned, evaluated, and prioritized based on beliefs about what is right and true. Most importantly, what one believes about morality is itself motivating. This is what structural developmentalists mean by cognitive motivation, and it is the kind of motivation, we believe, that is most central to genuinely *moral* action.

We readily acknowledge that much of what is commonly labeled moral behavior resembles Story A more than Story B in terms of the relationship between cognition and motivation. People act prosocially to obtain rewards, often subtle rewards that go unnoticed as motives, such as social praise or self-esteem (Gelfand & Hartmann, 1982; Rushton, 1982). Reciprocally, ample empirical evidence suggests that as personal costs rise, prosocial behavior declines (Batson, O'Quin, Fultz, Vanderplus, & Isen, 1983; Eisenberg & Shell, 1985; Midlarsky & Midlarsky, 1973; Wagner & Wheeler, 1969).

Based on such observations, many "moral" theories promote the idea that cognition is an unwitting slave to affective motivations. For example, theories of prosocial behavior that center on cost-benefit analysis reflect this viewpoint (Batson & Coke, 1981; Piliavin et al., 1981, 1982; Pomazal & Jaccard, 1976). However, such models assume (but do not demonstrate) that moral ideas hold no motivating power in themselves. In contrast, we believe that people's behavior, particularly in situations of moral conflict, often is chosen to reflect what they believe to be right, not just personally useful. We would suggest that part of the definition of moral action is that it is motivated, at least in part, by one's belief in its rightness or virtue.

Affective Motivation

We have just argued for the motivational significance of moral-cognitive insight. But we also believe that empathy and its related affects clearly play a part in moral motivation. Moral motivation involves a fusion or close interaction between cognitive and emotional processing. In this connection, Hoffman's (1987) discussion of moral principles as "hot cognitions" is relevant. Here is a description of the development of "hot" moral principles:

When one experiences a moral conflict, one inevitably wonders what to do, considers alternative actions, and anticipates consequences for others. Such thoughts may not only bring to mind victims and potential victims, thus arousing empathic affects, but may also bring to mind the guidelines to action, including relevant moral principles. . . . The empathic affect and moral principles may be evoked independently, or empathic affect may be aroused first and then may prime the moral principles. Either way, the co-occurrence of a principle and empathic affect should produce a bond between them (or strengthen any existing bond). The result may be that the principle, even if learned initially in a "cool," didactic context . . . acquires an affective charge. . . . As a consequence of being coupled with empathic affect in moral encounters, a moral principle may be encoded and stored as an affectively charged representation—as a "hot" cognition or category. (p. 72)

We find this description of how moral cognitions can become emotionally charged helpful in understanding moral motivation. But in Hoffman's theory, moral behavior is thought to be motivated primarily by the desire to alleviate self-distress that comes from empathizing with the distress of others. Hoffman's model is basically a variant of tension-reduction theory. For these reasons, we find his theory incomplete.

Cognition, Emotion, and Motivation

Throughout the foregoing discussions we have oversimplified the connection between motivation on the one hand and cognition and emotion on the other. Neither cognitions nor emotions are in themselves directly motivating. A person can have moral insight or empathy for someone without experiencing any compelling motivation to act. Both cognitions and emotions are motivating only to the extent that people are *committed* to their vision of truth, right, or good. In this connection, it is helpful to distinguish between two types of affects (see Blasi, 1990b, for a similar distinction). Emotions—empathy, sadness, joy, exhilaration, and fear, for example—are one type of affect. The emotions are relatively transient and malleable. Other affects—passions—are more enduring and directly motivational. Love and captivation to an ideal, as well as basic needs and drives, are passions that directly motivate behavior. They are more deep-seated in personality than the emotions. When morality is connected to the passions of a person's life, its cognitive and emotional content is experienced as compelling. If morality is an important and salient component in the self-structure, then moral cognitions and emotions are likely to be highly motivating.

The Self-Structure

Even relatively simple situations can be processed through multiple frames of reference, and various values may come into conflict. The extent to which moral values are likely to be given priority is a function, in part, of the person's *self-structure*, the psychological conceptual system through which people apprehend their identity and value. Though the self-structure is highly complex, we reduce it for our purposes into two main themes: motivational orientations and the moral self.

The Self-Structure and Motivational Orientations

A person's self-structure can be conceptually divided into two primary components: how one views oneself as a person in relation with other people, and how one views one's core identity. The theme of motivational orientation draws more on the first of these divisions, though by no means does it exhaust this component. The theme of the moral self more naturally relates to the second component.

Nicholls's influential work on achievement motivation (1983, 1989, 1992) focuses on how the individual constructs the value of achievement activities. Fundamentally, different motivational (or goal) orientations involve differing understandings of the self in relation. For some, motivation arises from a comparative stance toward others. For others, motivation is self-referenced. For example, in academic settings some students are motivated primarily by the challenge to perform well relative to others, whereas other students are motivated by the challenge to exceed their own previous performance. An *ego orientation* is one in which a person is motivated to display competence in relation to others, seeking to demonstrate superiority at the task at hand. In contrast, a *task orientation* is characterized by a concern for self-referenced personal achievement.

Nicholls (1989) maintains that "different motivational orientations are not just different types of wants or goals. They involve different world views" (p. 102). He maintains that a person's goal orientation (task or ego) will correspond with a set of attitudes, beliefs, and values that are congruent with the trajectory of achievement calibration that the goal orientation defines. A person with a high ego orientation calibrates achievement through referencing self against others, and this approach to defining success is likely to correlate, Nicholls suggests, with a relative lack of concern for moral issues like justice or fairness. A person with a high task orientation, on the other hand, defines success in terms that are self-referenced and is likely to emphasize such values as fairness and cooperation.

A study by Joan Duda (1989b) examined the relationship between goal orientation in sport and beliefs about the purposes of sport participation among high school athletes. Her main findings revealed a positive association between athletes' task orientation and their view that sport should teach people such values as trying hard, cooperation, obedience to rules, and being good citizens. In contrast, athletes who were predominantly ego-oriented tended to believe that sport should increase one's social status and show people how to survive in a competitive world.

It makes sense that one's goal orientation would be associated with one's view of the relative importance of moral values in an achievement context. As Nicholls writes (1989), "A preoccupation with winning (beating others) may well be accompanied by a lack of concern about justice . . . and fairness" (p. 133). Duda empirically investigated this logical connection and found, indeed, a strong relationship between goal orientation and behaviors perceived as legitimate in the pursuit of victory (Duda, Olson, & Templin, 1991). Athletes who were more task-oriented endorsed less cheating behavior and expressed greater approval of "sportsmanlike" actions; high ego orientation scores related to higher approval ratings of intentionally injurious behavior, a finding replicated with a sample of high school and college football players (Huston & Duda, 1992).

Dawn Stephens (1993) extended Duda's investigation of motivational orientations and moral behavior factors. Stephens administered a test battery to 214 female soccer players, ages 10 to 14, that included a sport-specific achievement orientation scale, a measure of participants' perceptions of their coaches' motivational orientation, a sportspersonship inventory, and a self-report measure assessing participants' temptation to violate moral norms during a sport contest (lie to an official, hurt an opponent, or break one of the rules). Stephens found that players who described themselves as experiencing high temptation to play unfairly differed significantly from those experiencing low temptation (Stephens & Bredemeier, 1992). Specifically, players who were more tempted were more ego- than task-oriented and perceived their coaches as being more ego- than task-oriented. Also, high temptation was associated with greater approval of behaviors designed to obtain an unfair advantage over an opponent, belief that more teammates would play unfairly in the same situation, and longer involvement with the current team. Stephens's work points to the need to directly study the relationships among moral atmosphere variables (e.g., perceptions of coaches' goal orientation, and beliefs about the likelihood of teammates' engaging in unfair sport practices), moral reasoning level, motivational achievement orientation, and sport behavior.

The Self-Structure and the Moral Self

Just as individuals form conceptual systems pertaining to physical objects, other persons, social organization, and morality, so they develop concepts of the self. The conceptual system through which we understand and interpret ourselves is highly complex. It varies from person to person in terms of its sophistication, saliency, degree of coherence, and valence. To simplify our discussion of how moral motivation is embedded in the self-structure, we now address the concept of the moral self and its place in one's self-understanding. Our thesis can be stated simply: The more one defines oneself in moral categories, the more committed one becomes to living morally, and the more likely it is that moral action will cohere with moral judgment.

The organized totality of concepts and constructs that an individual uses to interpret the self can be called self-understanding. Included in people's self-understandings are their interpretations of various aspects of self, such as one's physical, psychological, social, and moral characteristics, and so on. But what dimensions of the self are at the core of self-understanding appear to vary developmentally and individually.

William Damon (1984) argues that during some periods of development the conceptual systems comprising self-understanding and morality operate as two distinct psychological structures, with little direct bearing on one another. At other times, he claims, there is more integration and reciprocal influence between the two. This has tremendous significance for Process III because moral ideals that belong to a conceptual system that is peripheral to one's self-understanding are not likely to carry much motivational weight.

Damon (1984) reports on a series of investigations in which he asked children a number of self-definitional questions, such as What kind of person are you? or How would you describe yourself? In addition, he probed children's descriptions of their own self-interest—what was important to them. He found that children of all ages had self-understandings that reflected some appreciation for their physical, active, social, and psychological aspects. However, regular changes in the saliency and sophistication of these different areas of focus accompany children's development. Two developmental trends are especially relevant to our discussion of Process III. First, as children develop they tend toward integrating and systematizing their self-conceptions. With maturity the physical self and the psychological self, for example, become less dualized. In addition, though children have some awareness of the various dimensions of themselves throughout development, the domain that children use to define their core identity changes in a consistent developmental progression. Young children focus their self-definitions on the physical dimension. The active, social, and psychological dimensions of self are, in turn, favored respectively as children mature.

The major focus for self-definition has important implications for moral action. Damon (1984) contends that because the self is construed first physically (''I'm big'') and then in terms of one's activities (''I'm athletic'') during childhood, children's moral cognitions are only minimally integrated into their concepts of self. One consequence of the split between the peripheral ''moral self'' and the central ''physical or active self'' is that children often view their self-interests in opposition to the demands of morality. This may help to explain the inconsistencies so common in children's moral thought and action. Children may know what is right, but moral concerns are not critical to how they define who they are or what they want for themselves; consequently, their moral knowledge lacks the motivational force necessary to propel moral action. In contrast, the moral and self systems become increasingly coordinated in adolescence, when self-understanding is construed primarily in social and psychological terms. The psychological focus allows young adults to define themselves morally and to become aware of how self and moral interests are related. We might anticipate that as adolescents move toward moral definitions of self, there will be an increasing tendency to choose moral values over nonmoral ones when there is a conflict among values (see Damon, 1977, and Gerson & Damon, 1978 for support of this thesis).

Damon's view of self-understanding is compatible with Blasi's interpretation of how personal identity mediates the relationship between moral knowledge and practical moral decisions. For Blasi (1983a, 1983b, 1984, 1985, 1988, 1989), most psychological theories are deficient because they lack an adequate construct of the self-as-subject. Blasi views the self-as-subject as the integrating center of personality; it is the sense of self-agency wherein a person owns her actions, feelings, and thoughts as self-expressions. Blasi refers to the person's interior, integrating self-as-subject as identity.

The role of morality in one's identity, Blasi claims, is a function of both development (Damon, 1984) and individual differences. Individual differences include how important being moral is to a person's identity and which moral aspects are emphasized in one's moral identity. For example, one person may see compassion as essential to his identity, while another sees fairness and justice as central to hers. Interestingly, there may be a relationship between the saliency of morality in one's self-definition and the content of one's moral perspective. In a study of female professional bodybuilders, Fisher (1993) reports that those women who described their "bodybuilding self" as the most important part of their identity tended to be justice-oriented, whereas those who prioritized either gender or morality in their self-definition were care-oriented. Unfortunately, the small sample (N = 10), the specialized population, and questions about the reliability of Gilligan's moral orientation measure make these results difficult to generalize.

For Blasi, moral identity is the key source of moral motivation. One's sense of personal moral integrity—that is, one's view of oneself as a moral person who both believes in and acts on particular moral constructs—provides the motivational dynamic to choose moral over nonmoral values. Blasi appeals to Erikson's notion of fidelity, the basic virtue that Erikson considers inherently tied to the development of identity, and suggests that the connection between moral identity and moral functioning is expressed by a perceived obligation to act with consistency, according to one's judgment of what is right.

When the moral self is at the core of self-structure, moral cognitions and emotions will be experienced as compelling. Self-evaluative emotions will play critical roles in guiding moral action (Bandura, 1991). In contrast to emotions like empathy or sympathy, where the affects are rooted in perceptions of the other, self-evaluative emotions arise from the relation one perceives between one's own behavior and moral standards. Such emotions presuppose cognitive moral standards and necessarily depend on cognition. Pride and guilt are probably the quintessential self-evaulative emotions. Thus, when John, whose self-definition is structured largely in moral terms, completes a moral act, he feels pride and elevated self-esteem. Anticipation of such feelings augments his moral motivation. Correspondingly, the anticipation of guilt feelings for moral deviation serves as a motive to act morally.

Personal Competencies—Summary

The task of Process III is to arrive at a responsibility judgment that is congruent with one's deontic judgment and to decide to act on one's responsibility. The personal competencies undergirding Process III have been described in terms of prosocial reasoning and, most importantly, the self-structure. The self-structure is likely to undergird moral action when one has developed a task motivational orientation and when the moral self has a central place in one's identity. Even if the relevant competencies are in place, however, moral action can deviate from personal capacities, especially when one is under stress. Ego-processing skills are required if moral action is to remain consistent with optimal capacities.

Ego-Processing Influences

In Haan's theory of moral action, a person continually uses ego processes in the course of interpreting, coordinating, and acting on intrapersonal and situational information. In our discussion of the third major process of moral action, we highlight the affective impulse–regulating ego functions. These functions are particularly useful when different affectively charged motives need to be coordinated, as is the case with Process III.

The affective impulse–regulating ego functions comprise the following three pairs of coping and defending expressions:

	Expression	
Generic function	**Coping**	**Defending**
Affective diversion	Sublimation	Displacement
Affective transformation	Substitution	Reaction formation
Affective restraint	Suppression	Repression

We will discuss first the coping alternative of each pair, then the defending alternative.

Coping Processes

The coping processes of sublimation, substitution, and suppression are certainly vital when conflicting emotional needs seek expression. *Sublimation* occurs when a person finds satisfying and socially acceptable means to express strong affects that may be problematic if expressed in their unmodulated form. Disappointment following a close sporting loss can be stated frankly and emphatically, for example, but without acrimony.

Substitution, sometimes referred to as a "good reaction formation" (Haan, 1977b), occurs when a person transforms, tempers, or domesticates negative affects flexibly and appropriately. For instance, an athlete feeling hostile toward an opponent may, in a self-aware and flexible way, choose to act civilly toward that opponent even in the midst of competitive stress.

Finally, *suppression* refers to the coping process by which a person holds the expression of an affect in abeyance until it can be expressed in the proper place and time and with the appropriate persons. A coach who is angry with a player, for example, may wait for a private time to discuss the issue.

Defending Processes

The potential impact of the affective impulse–regulating ego functions is probably the most evident when we examine the defending alternatives.

Displacement occurs when someone temporarily and unsuccessfully attempts to control problematic affects or impulses through redirection. For example, an athlete frustrated by a game loss may express anger at a roommate who had nothing to do with the sport situation that created the frustration. Displacement is relevant to Process III because moral affects like empathy, sympathy, guilt, and indignation may be displaced from their appropriate context and thereby neutralized as effective moral motivators. In research on moral action, displacement has proven to be one of the most frequent contributors to dysfunctional moral action (Haan et al., 1985).

Reaction formations occur when impulses or affects are disguised in their opposites. Some behavior that appears to be prosocial, for example, may in fact be the result of reaction formations. A person who is "excessively" kind or altruistic may be so as a defensive response to hostile impulses. An example might be the rugby player who graciously helps to his feet the opponent whom that player had just smashed to the turf. Again, reaction formation may distort moral action by creating rigid adherence to social norms and values in a way that does not allow flexible response to realistic needs and desires of self and other.

Repression occurs when a person unconsciously or purposefully forgets. Memories with affective elements that are threatening or unpleasant may not be consciously recalled. Perhaps an athlete was molested by her father as a young child but has repressed the memory. She may still "act out" angers, resentments, or fears on the playing field when situations remind her, without her awareness, of her earlier experience. Like the other two defense mechanisms, repression may lead to value choices based on distorted information.

Whether a person remains coping or defending results from a complex set of personal and situational circumstances and stresses, but mood states often indicate the prevalence of coping or defending. Although negative mood does not necessarily imply that a person is resorting to defending processes, defense is more prevalent at such times. We will close this chapter with a brief consideration of the impact of mood states on moral action.

Mood States

Moods play an important role in how people decide to weigh competing values. In general, people are more likely to choose to act on their moral perceptions when in a positive mood state (Bryant, 1983; Cialdini, Baumann, & Kenrick, 1981; Isen, 1970; Rosenhan, Salovey, Karylowski, & Hargis, 1981; Shaffer, 1986; see Staub, 1978, for a review). For example, in the Bryant study, two groups of boys played a competitive game against other children and won. One group was led to believe that their victory was due to skill, the other group to chance. The group that believed their victory was due to skill experienced more positive affect and subsequently shared more of their prize coupons with peers than did boys in the other group.

The impact of negative mood states, however, is more complex. Sometimes negative mood may inhibit prosocial activity (Barden, Garber, Leiman, Ford, & Masters, 1985; Barnett, Howard, Melton, & Dino, 1982). On the other hand, negative mood may also, at least under some conditions, augment the tendency to act prosocially, especially among adults (Carlson & Miller, 1987; Cialdini, Darby, & Vincent, 1973; Cunningham, Steinberg, & Grev, 1980; Kidd & Berkowitz, 1976).

One parsimonious explanation for the influence of mood states on prosocial behavior is offered by Cialdini, Kendrick, and Baumann (1982), who argue that the impact of a given mood state depends on the functional significance of the potential prosocial action to the actor. In short, when one is in a good mood prosocial acts may be simply a passive concomitant to the mood, or one may engage in prosocial acts to deliberately sustain the positive affects. On the other hand, prosocial behavior may serve an instrumental function to reverse a negative mood state. It may help one to break out of a bad mood to help another. If this interpretation is correct, prosocial acts conducted in a negative mood state may depend highly on the perceived psychological reward structure. Other explanations are also possible. For example, negative moods may increase helpfulness when attention is directed toward the misfortunes of others, but decrease helpfulness, or not affect it, when one's attention is focused inward (see Carlson & Miller, 1987, for a review of literature on helpfulness and attentional focus).

Summary

After an individual interprets a moral situation and identifies a situation-specific moral ideal, the task of deciding on a course of action comes to bear. Contextual influences on Process III include the distinct domains of social interaction involved. Game interactions may elicit conventional, moral, and personal values, norms, and motivations. Game rules, for example, are complex phenomena that may draw social cognitions from different domains of reasoning. How individuals prioritize conflicting value choices depends, in part, on such personal variables as their motivational orientation and moral self-definition. Finally, affective impulse-regulating ego functions are activated in the process of choosing among competing action choices. In the next chapter, we conclude this unit with an examination of Process IV—implementing action.

Chapter 9
Implementing Action

At the conclusion of Process III the individual has decided on a course of action, but it is an intention, not yet a completed act. Process IV encompasses the factors necessary to translate intention into behavior. This process of implementation may involve such activities as figuring out the specific behavioral sequences needed to accomplish one's aims, working through unanticipated difficulties, managing fatigue and frustration, and resisting distractions. Depending on the nature of the situation, these processes may be relatively brief and insignificant or quite protracted and influential.

We noted at the outset of discussing the 12-component model of moral action that each of the four major processes could be isolated for purposes of analysis only. In actuality, the processes are interactive, overlapping, and interdependent. Nowhere is this more evident than in Process IV. Clearly, as a person is engaged in moral action all components of the model are implicated. Correspondingly, throughout this chapter we mention influences that analytically belong to other model processes. We hope this will underscore the interpenetration of the processes without leading to confusion.

Perhaps the most influential contextual variables impacting Process IV pertain to the power relationships. How power is distributed or exercised can facilitate or impede the expression of intended moral action. After discussing power issues, we probe self-regulation and social problem-solving skills. Finally, we discuss ego processing, particularly the attention-focusing function. We conclude the chapter with a brief discussion of interactions among components of our model and limitations of the model.

Contextual Influences

Deutsch (1985) maintains that power distribution is one of the core variables that define the quality of human relations. Unequal power characterizes all forms of social hierarchy. The power between coach and player or teacher and student, for example, is clearly unequal. In building a model of moral action, moral behavior that occurs in hierarchical structures cannot be abstracted from those contexts and adequately understood in isolation.

The relative power among different parties in a moral context may reflect simple social stratification and division of roles. Most, if not all, complex social practices and organizations—sport included—are characterized by social hierarchy. But power differentials may also reflect the workings of prejudice, discrimination, and exploitation.

Power dynamics are particularly important to consider when analyzing moral action that occurs between the genders, among racial and ethnic groups, among people with different sexual orientations, and the like. It is important that the moral agent be understood as situated in a power structure that is determined, in part, by the agent's social identity markers, such as gender, race, class, sexual orientation, and physical capabilities. Developmental psychology too frequently has ignored these dimensions of the social context within which action occurs.

In numerous obvious and subtle ways, the sport world reflects, perpetuates, and further shapes the power differentials among human groups whose differences have acquired social meaning. Social stratifications are prevalent in sport and other physical activity contexts. Beginning with the play and games of little children and continuing through professional sports, physical activity participants learn about, reinforce, and modify the power differentials that characterize life in our culture. Though racial and ethnic stratification is not as extreme as it once was, it is important to point out that opportunities for racial minorities in professional sports expanded only in response to the needs and desires of those at the top of the economic stratification ladder (Sage, 1990). To this day, many professional and college sports do not have many minority participants. Not surprisingly, these sports (including bowling, golf, skiing, and tennis) tend to be linked to upper-class sponsorship. Even when racial and ethnic groups are well represented, stereotyping appears to influence team position assignments (Coakley, 1993). The gates leading to coaching and sport administrative positions also appear to be less than fully open to minorities, and people of color remain underrepresented (Sage, 1990). Although sport opportunities for females have increased tremendously since the passage of Title IX in 1972 (apart from the professional ranks), women have lost significant ground in leadership positions like coaching and administration, despite no lack of qualified candidates (Acosta & Carpenter, 1992; Anderson & Gill, 1983; Knoppers, 1988; Sage, 1990). Given the pervasiveness of racism, sexism, and other forms of group discrimination in physical activity contexts, moral action in these settings must continually take account of power dynamics.

Domination has no place in moral negotiation, and the use of power to compel or leverage a particular outcome is morally illegitimate (Haan et al., 1985). Of course, such uses of power are commonplace despite their moral illegitimacy. Correspondingly, when subordinated group members interact with dominant group members, their moral action inevitably involves finding vehicles to claim increased social status, resources, and opportunities. When subordinate groups find themselves victims of the misuse of power, they may resort to protests and covert strategies for achieving balance. Studies of "prosocial" behavior may misconstrue such actions, because the actions may not conform to the usual meaning of altruism or cooperation.

Power and Competition

In this chapter we primarily address how power shapes moral response and facilitates or inhibits intended action. Before we move on, however, it is useful to note that how one is situated in a power structure also influences one's cognitive, motivational, and moral orientation (Deutsch, 1985). The combined influence of power hierarchy and goal structure on moral orientation is particularly significant to the themes of this book. Milton Deutsch has studied moral orientations as influenced by context; Table 9.1 summarizes his conclusions about the combined effect of goal and power structures.

The table should not be read in a deterministic fashion. People respond to contextual variables differently, and the moral orientations in the matrix suggest probable, though not necessary, relationships among the variables. This point will again be highlighted when we discuss research on power relations and moral action.

Power Relations and Moral Action

The relationship between power dynamics and moral action has been most thoroughly studied by Norma Haan and her colleagues (Haan et al., 1985). Haan explored the issue of power and moral action in a sophisticated and complex investigation of friendship groups in simulation games. One of the issues under study was the impact of group leadership dynamics. Haan recognized that cohesive groups are more than the sum of their members' individual characteristics. As group life develops, individuals take on different group tasks, with some becoming

Table 9.1   Moral Orientation as Influenced by the Goal and Power Structures

	Unequal power contexts	Equal power contexts
Competitive contexts	• Moral orientations are likely to support exploitive relationships. • The more powerful party is likely to develop a sense of moral superiority; the less powerful party may internalize negative self-images and develop a "victim" morality.	• Moral orientations are likely to emphasize equal opportunity but have little concern for equal outcomes.
Cooperative contexts	• The more powerful party is likely to develop a moral orientation that accepts responsibility to employ power to benefit the less powerful. • The less powerful party is likely to develop a moral orientation focused on appreciation of and deference to the more powerful party.	• Moral orientations that emphasize egalitarian values are likely to develop.

Note. Adapted from Deutsch, 1985.

leaders, others peacemakers, others humorists, still others emotional watchdogs, and the like. As Haan notes (Haan et al., 1985, p. 108), "In many ways, friendship groups are microcosms of society."

Not all friendship groups are alike. They vary in demographic characteristics and power distribution. Haan's study involved 15 groups of friends, each with 4 women and 4 men, drawn from a population of undergraduate students. To describe the groups' power relationships, Haan had each participant rate every other member of their group on 11 characteristics using a 5-point scale. Of particular importance were the scores on three characteristics: dominant, fair, and leader. A group was designated as *dominated* if a single member had a score of 4 or more—averaged from friends' evaluations—on "dominant." A group was designated as *led* if a single member had a score of 4 or more on "leader" combined with an above-average score on "fair." Nine friendship groups qualified as dominated and six as led.

Five friendship groups participated in a sequence of weekly moral discussions similar to ones promoted by Kohlberg. The other 10 participated in a series of simulation games over 5 weeks. The simulations ranged from the relatively innocuous Humanus to the highly stressful Starpower. Based on a complex set of analyses, the following conclusions were reached (Haan et al., 1985):

• Before participating in the research the members of led groups, compared to the members of dominated groups, gave their friends higher evaluations on three characteristics: knowing right from wrong, understanding others' points of view, and being able to handle themselves in a conflict (p. 117).

• Members of led groups were consistently more engaged with the moral problems than members of dominated groups and more analytic toward their own group process (p. 117).

• During the moral experiences, the led groups were consistently more integrated, more egalitarian in their operation, and more open to the staff leader; dominated groups were more perturbed, disjointed, and inconsistent in their functioning (p. 119, 126).

• Clear differences were observed in the extent to which members adopted various group roles. Proportionately fewer conformists and more social-emotional leaders were found in led than in dominated groups; more members of dominated groups were antagonists and isolates (p. 121).

• Differences in ego processing were also observed; members of led groups coped more and defended less than members of dominated groups. Specifically, members of led groups obtained higher scores for objectivity, logical analysis, and empathy (all coping processes) and lower scores for two defenses: isolation and denial (p. 138).

• Differences in ego strategies within groups were also observed. Perhaps due to their unproblematic operations, members of the led groups had individuated ego strategies, and thus no significant differences were found between the ego processes of leaders and the led. But this was not at all the case in the dominated groups. Haan observed that

> [the dominated groups'] more stressed and polarized confrontations produced a substantial difference in ego strategies between the dominators and the dominated in each session. . . . The nine dominators seemed to enjoy themselves, they were more playfully coping (ego regression) during four sessions, but also defensively displaced their negative, angry emotions onto their friends in all five sessions. Faced with that behavior, the dominated coped in all five sessions by tolerating the ambiguity of their position and by recognizing, but suppressing, their feelings. But in all five sessions they also became defensively self-righteous as is shown by their higher scores for the process of reaction formation. Also they were defensive, doubting in four sessions and regressive in two sessions. Altogether the dominated seemed to have tolerated the dominators' treatment by controlling their feelings and quietly regarding themselves morally superior. (pp. 173-174)

• During postintervention evaluation sessions, members of led groups discussed their experiences without cynicism, generally felt satisfied, and reported that they had learned from the experiences. In contrast, members of dominated groups were cynical, seemed disgruntled, and did not feel that they had benefited from participation (p. 124).

• The quality of moral action during the simulations was assessed using both Kohlberg's "cognitive" model and Haan's "interactional" one. Haan et al. (1985) reported, "The egalitarian structure of the led groups facilitated cognitive moral action in three sessions, while the atmosphere of the dominated group had a deleterious effect on cognitive moral action that became especially strong for males by the last session" (p. 156). The group structure had fewer statistically significant effects on interactional moral scores, but the pattern was similar.

• Interestingly, the conditions that promoted moral dysfunction also promoted moral growth. Although members of led groups exhibited consistently higher levels of moral action, they were less stimulated in their development by the experience than were participants in dominated groups. Haan hypothesized that the "social disequilibrium" that characterized the functioning of dominated groups was conducive to growth (p. 252; see also Haan, 1985).

These, then, were the study's main findings pertaining to the impact of power structure in friendship groups. In short, led groups were more open and engaged, more coping, and more consistently moral than dominated groups. Still, members of dominated groups achieved more developmental gains from the experience.

Haan and her colleagues observed that their initial ideas about how led and dominated groups would function were generally supported but were too simplistic. As they reflected on their results, they refined their perspective both on the nature of led and dominated groups and on the extent of individuality within the groups. With regard to the nature of groups, they pointed out that their initial assumption that a free and open exchange of ideas would characterize led but not dominated groups was oversimplified (Haan et al., 1985). Sometimes, for example, what appeared to be the smooth communication of a "led" group was really a subtle coercion into "groupthink." Conversely, dominators in some groups were not so much stubbornly authoritarian as vibrant individuals who had attractive ideas.

The research team—in a manner reminiscent of Deutsch's hypothesis that competitive-unequal power contexts will facilitate a moral orientation of "victim" in the less powerful—had anticipated rather passive and morally disintegrating responses by members of dominated groups. In general, this was the case. But the researchers had not accounted for the moral reactions of rebellious "whistle-blowers" who stubbornly resisted the dominators and maintained high levels of moral functioning.

Before we leave the theme of power and leadership, let's review selected relevant research in the area of sport.

Sport Leadership and Moral Action

In chapter 8, we noted that Duda et al. (1991) found a connection between goal orientations and unsportspersonlike behavior. People high in ego and low in task orientation were more likely to endorse behaviors generally considered to be unsporting. Stephens (1993) extended those basic findings among early adolescent female soccer players, finding that players' self-described temptation to play unfairly was best predicted by their perceptions of their coaches' goal orientations and leadership styles and found that these made independent contributions to the players' moral decision-making process (Stephens, Bredemeier, Shields, & Ryan, 1992). Those girls with a coach they perceived as high in ego orientation and autocratic style were more likely to express a high temptation to play unfairly.

These findings suggest that the coach is in a powerful position to facilitate or impede prosocial behavior in sport. It is not clear from the study, however, whether the coaches' power was exercised through direct pressure, indirect influence through promotion of a particular moral atmosphere, or some other process. Further research is needed in this relatively unstudied area.

Leadership and power clearly play a role in athletic aggression as well. A study by Smith (1979), for example, indicated that 52% of hockey players between the ages of 18 and 21 perceive their coaches as high approvers of violent behavior. It is likely that coaches not only approve of violence but, given the strategic gains that it may secure, actively encourage it. Not surprisingly, then, Smith (1977) also found that the more coaches approve of violence, the more their players perform violent acts.

Sport organizations also exercise power, particularly through rule and enforcement structures. Such exercises of power have not always been positive. In the National Hockey League, for example, the structures actually make aggression beneficial to teams. Penalties are so light and enforced so irregularly that high levels of aggression become essential components in a success strategy. The result is that most teams hire ''enforcers'' whose sole job is to intimidate or hurt better skilled opponents.

Even the exercise of societal power through the court system has given license to athletic aggression. In 1975, Dave Forbes of the Boston Bruins butt-ended Henry Boucha of the Minnesota North Stars with his hockey stick. As Boucha fell to the ice, Forbes pounced on him, grabbed a handful of hair, and hammered his head against the ice. Forbes was charged with aggravated assault, but a jury found him innocent, accepting the argument that fights are normal occurrences in hockey and that participants therefore assume the risks. Despite a few notable exceptions, most court cases have been decided similarly.

Of course, power structures can facilitate prosocial as well as antisocial behavior. Coaches can encourage and reward prosocial actions on the part of players. Rules can discourage dangerous practices. Spectators and the media can exercise their power by what they endorse. Whether the power arrangements facilitate or impede moral action, however, people bring to the person–context interaction various competencies that can enable them to act on their moral vision.

Personal Competency Influences

Power dynamics clearly shape the nature and quality of moral behavior. Haan, for example, found that members of dominated groups are less likely to perform at their level of moral capacity than are members of nondominated groups (Haan et al., 1985). But, as Haan also found, personal characteristics and skills enable some people to resist domination and maintain moral integrity.

Two psychological constructs are particularly relevant to Process IV: self-regulation and social problem-solving skills. Self-regulation pertains to marshaling interior resources for persisting at difficult tasks; the concept of autonomy is particularly relevant here. Social problem-solving competencies pertain more to negotiating problems with others. Neither set of skills is intrinsically moral; the skills could support immoral intentions as well as moral ones. Assuming that a person has chosen to act on her or his moral vision, however, both sets of skills are useful in the face of obstacles, temptations, and distractions.

Self-Regulation Skills and Autonomy

Self-regulation skills incorporate those competencies related to monitoring and managing one's own psychology in action; they include such interrelated constructs as ego strength, ego resiliency, impulse control, and the ability to delay gratification. The literature relating self-regulation skills to moral action is sparse, but existing studies generally support a link between these skills and prosocial or moral behavior (Alterman, Druley, Connolly, & Bush, 1978; Block & Block, 1973; Grim, Kohlberg, & White, 1968; Lind, Sandberger, & Bargel, 1981; Long & Lerner, 1974; Mussen, Rutherford, Harris, & Keasey, 1970; Strayer & Roberts, 1989).

In one longitudinal study of preschool children, for example, both ego strength and ego resiliency (the ability to recover after stressful experiences) were positively correlated with prosocial behavior (Block & Block, 1973). Ego strength and altruism were also related in a study with preadolescents (Mussen et al., 1970). Finally, in a study of West Germans, ego strength and moral maturity were correlated (Lind et al., 1981). The evidence with regard to ego strength, however, is not unequivocal. Krebs (1967), in a study of cheating, found that the contribution of ego strength to moral action was mediated by moral judgment maturity: Those students high on both ego strength and moral stage rarely cheated, but those students high on ego strength and low on moral maturity actually cheated more than did students low on ego strength with similar stages of moral judgment. It would seem that ego strength itself is not a moral capacity but that it can support higher level moral functioning for those with sufficiently developed moral reasoning.

Research on the ability to delay gratification and impulse control supports including them in the model. In their study of preschool children, Block and Block (1973) found that children low in ability to delay gratification tended also to be low in generosity. Similarly, Long and Lerner (1974) found that fourth graders who were high on ability to delay gratification were more generous than peers low on that ability. Various measures of ego or impulse control have also been shown to contribute to honesty or teacher ratings of moral behavior, or both (Grim et al., 1968; Krebs, 1967; see Kohlberg, 1984).

Perhaps the concept that best subsumes and summarizes the self-regulation skills, as operative in moral contexts, is autonomy. According to Lindley (1986), "the underlying idea of the concept of autonomy is self-mastery" (p. 6). Autonomy encompasses an ability to define goals, to take responsibility for action, and to assert oneself, when needed, in order to not conform to social expectations or pressures counter to one's views. A player, for example, who is high in autonomy may refuse to obey a coach's instructions to take performance-enhancing drugs, commit an intentional foul, or join a fight. Not surprisingly, autonomy has been postulated by many as a central element mediating moral reasoning and moral behavior (Erikson, 1950, 1968; Hodge, 1988; Hogan, 1970, 1973; Kurtines, 1974, 1978; Meakin, 1982).

Though autonomy is a useful construct, its use must be tempered by an awareness of its limitations. Autonomy typically has been connected to processes central to male socialization (Gilligan, 1982). It reflects the fruition of the individuation and separation processes associated with early masculine development (Chodorow, 1978; Gilligan, 1982). Correspondingly, when autonomy has been incorporated into moral development theory, it typically has been seen as underlying the justice orientation featured in Kohlberg's (1984) work. But as Gilligan (1986) herself makes clear, autonomy is important to women as well as to men, to people who prefer a moral orientation based on care as well as to people who tend toward a justice orientation. The language of autonomy more naturally coheres with discourse about justice and fairness than with discourse about responsiveness and relationality, but the two perspectives are complementary, not contradictory. Both women and men develop, or can develop, a strong sense of autonomy as well as a sense of being embedded in a web of human interdependency.

If empathy, care, and responsiveness are typically "feminine" themes and autonomy and justice typically "masculine" ones (both questionable assertions), it may be that when moral action fails, it typically fails in different parts of the moral action process for men and women. Men, for example, may "act" decisively (Process IV) without adequate sensitivity (Process I) to the subtle moral nuances present. Women, alternately, may pick up on the moral dimensions of situations (Process I) but be stymied in their action (Process IV) as a result of strongly felt connections to those who may be hurt by even fair and just behavior. Obviously, this is overstereotyped, but it may reflect a kernel of truth.

Self-regulation skills are necessary to deal with internal obstacles to moral action, such as paralyzing fear, fatigue, or lack of confidence. In moral action contexts, people also must be able to negotiate interpersonal problems that may arise.

Social Problem-Solving Skills

Social problem-solving skills are important to carrying out moral action (e.g., Shure, 1980, 1982; Solomon et al., 1985). Though a number of specific such skills have been isolated (Shure, 1982; Spivack, Platt, & Shure, 1976), two in particular have received significant support: alternative solution and means–ends thinking. *Alternative solution thinking*—the ability to generate multiple solutions to an interpersonal conflict—has been demonstrated to have a positive relationship with low social withdrawal (Olson, Johnson, Parks, Barrett, & Belleau, 1983a) and positive peer interactions (Olson, Johnson, Parks, Barrett, & Belleau, 1983b) in 4- to 5-year-olds and with peer or teacher ratings of prosocial behavior (Shure, 1980). *Means–end thinking* refers to the ability to articulate the steps necessary to carry out a solution to an interpersonal problem and to the recognition that obstacles might interfere with goal completion and goal satisfaction may be delayed. Low means–end thinking has been related to psychiatric problems and acting out in adolescents and adults (Butler & Meichenbaum, 1981); conversely, high means–end thinking has been related to low aggression in girls (Marsh, Serafica, & Barenboim, 1981). Finally, means–end thinking has been related positively to a number of indexes of prosocial behavior (Marsh et al., 1981; Shure, 1980).

In Haan's model of interactional morality, there are two "secondary structures" that can be considered social problem-solving skills: the ability to take appropriate chances on another's good faith (differentiated trust) and the ability to find means to restore moral balance once a wrong has been committed by either the self or another. Haan identified five levels of adequacy that can define increasing skill in these areas. Let us begin first with extending differentiated trust.

Differentiated Trust

Moral relationships are based on an assumption that another will act in good faith. In sport contests, for example, there must be a tacit assumption that others will follow the rules if the contest is to sustain itself as fair. Sometimes the assumption of good faith is warranted, other times not. The challenge is to maintain a flexible ability to extend trust, neither naively assuming others are unambiguously good nor recoiling excessively from instances of bad faith.

Haan (Haan et al., 1985) posits that at the first level of adequacy, a person, let us call him Thor, will wait momentarily for others to demonstrate good faith. If convincing demonstrations are not immediately forthcoming, Thor will not trust the other person. At the next level, Thor extends trust blindly but haphazardly to those he favors. Soon he finds, however, that others fail to treat him favorably when he is so ego-bound. Correspondingly, at the third level, Thor extends trust widely and naively to all but those who are considered odd or outside his purview. Experiences of "bad faith," however, are inevitable, and at the fourth level Thor, having been disappointed numerous times, takes refuge in common practices that clearly define his obligations and delimit the risks he needs to take. Finally, at the most adequate level, Thor recognizes that he needs to gamble on good faith if human relations are to be full and satisfying. Thor recognizes that instances of bad faith need to be handled in terms of considerations of the self as a moral being, recognition of the complexity of motivations and circumstances, and a realistic appraisal of limitations on human agency.

Restoring Moral Balance

Invariably people commit moral injustices against one another, and moral balances are upset. Someone may cheat in a sport, for example. More innocently, someone may unintentionally bat out of turn in a neighborhood game of baseball. Given the frequency with which moral errors occur, another important social problem-solving skill is the ability to restore disrupted relationships.

Haan (Haan et al., 1985) again posits five levels of adequacy. Initially, the person, let us call her Gurra, does not consider the possibility that she may commit wrongs; rather, it is only others who wrong her. Unnecessary relationships quickly fracture at this level. At the second level, Gurra recognizes personal errors in the sense that she might try to take more than others will allow, in which case redress involves either giving back what she took or avoiding the relationship. At the third level, when wrongs are committed, Gurra believes a simple apology should suffice to restore relationship. At the fourth level, Gurra believes that apology by itself is insufficient and that people who do wrongs (whether self or others) must "pay" for them. Once a debt is paid, however, everything is thought to be restored to its former status. Finally, at the most adequate level, Gurra recognizes that irrespective of motives, wrongs are frequent in social life and they cannot be undone. Despite an inability to erase past actions and consequences, a variety of mechanisms can be employed, including forgiveness and redress, to restore relationships.

Personal Competencies—Summary

Although power hierarchies play an important role, personal competencies also contribute importantly to Process IV. The skills of self-regulation, summarized by the concept of autonomy, and social problem-solving are required for effective implementation of moral intentions. In the next section we examine ego-processing variables that relate to Process IV of our moral action model.

Ego-Processing Influences

In the actual production of moral behavior, a person's characteristic and situationally evoked ego processes are all relevant. Nonetheless, the attention-focusing category, comprising the single generic ego function of selective awareness, is particularly salient in Process IV. The coping alternative is referred to as *concentration* and is characterized by an ability to set aside disturbing or attractive feelings or thoughts to concentrate on the task at hand. A person who scores high in concentration is efficiently productive in difficult situations, whereas those who score low in concentration are easily distracted by the immediate requirements or attractions of the situation (Haan, 1977a). If a person fails to cope in attention-focusing efforts, the defending alternative is *denial*. Denial involves refusing to acknowledge present or past facts and feelings that are painful and focusing attention instead on the pleasant or benign. One of the interesting ways that selective awareness enters into moral action pertains to the tendency of some people to characteristically or situationally focus their attention inward to the relative neglect of awareness of others. Let's examine how self-concentration impacts moral action.

Self-Concentration

In our discussion of empathy in chapter 6 we noted the need to carefully distinguish it from personal distress, the self-focused negative emotion arising in situations where someone perceives another in need or distress. The person experiencing distress may act prosocially if that is the least costly way to relieve it, but she or he may also escape the situation if that is the most efficacious route to relief. One reason personal distress may inhibit prosocial responding is simply that attentional processes are focused on the self more than on the other. In an interpersonal context, self-concentration refers to the quantity and quality of self-focus rather than other-focus.

One interesting study that exemplifies the role of self-concentration in prosocial behavior was conducted by Karylowski (1979, cited in Reykowski, 1982). He had subjects engage in a task that produced profit for themselves and for a partner. He found that if subjects looked in a mirror during the task they decreased their effort to promote profits for their partners but not for themselves. However, this effect did not occur with people highly committed to a norm of helping.

The Polish psychologist Janusz Reykowski and his colleagues have systematically investigated self-concentration in relation to prosocial behavior. Reykowski (1982) suggests that self-concentration is related to issues of self-esteem. High self-concentration is likely to follow from either of two polar conditions: low self-regard or high self-regard. In contrast, self-concentration is relatively low in people with moderate self-esteem. This may account for the counterintuitive findings that self-esteem has a curvilinear relationship with prosocial behavior: Those with low and high self-esteem have been shown in some studies to exhibit less prosocial behavior than those with moderate self-esteem (Kowalczewska, 1972, cited in Reykowski, 1982; Reykowski & Jarymowicz, 1976, cited in Staub, 1979).

Reykowski (1982) cites evidence that high self-concentration has its detrimental impact on prosocial behavior through its effect on both perceptual and valuative processes. People who tend to focus their attention on the self may miss significant cues about others' interests, needs, and concerns (distorting Process I). Furthermore, as Flavell (1963) observed, one tends to overestimate the value and quantity of the objects in the center of one's attention. Thus, if one's attention is concentrated on the self, the self's interests are likely to take on greater value relative to the interests of others (distorting Processes II and III).

Reykowski (1982) also suggests that self-concentration does not always decrease prosocial behavior. Under some conditions or for some people it may actually buttress moral action. This may occur when the dimension of the self that becomes the focus of attention is the moral aspect. Based on the work of Damon and Blasi, we would hypothesize that those people who have come to define their core identity in largely moral terms will experience self-concentration as supporting moral action rather than inhibiting it. Reykowski has suggested that situational factors that amplify the focus on people's normative standards may also ameliorate the negative affects of self-concentration.

Self-Concentration and Sport

Learning and executing physical skills necessitates a significant level of self-concentration. In sport attention is often directed on the self. But sport helps us understand ways that the concept of self-concentration needs to be elaborated. The self-concentration characteristic of sport involvement does not mean that one is unaware of others—far from it. Self-concentration is characterized as much by its qualitative aspect as its quantitative division. When self-concentrated, one may be highly aware of others but interpret their interests and behaviors in light of their impact on the self. This is typically the situation in sport, where others' behaviors are assimilated into a strategically and behaviorally focused self-interest. Annitella, for example, may pay careful attention to the behavior of a teammate or opponent so she can quickly respond to her competitive advantage. This is entirely appropriate. But there are instances when self-concentration may promote a disregard for the normative structures of sport or the welfare of another. When victory is the only value associated with sport experience, self-concentration may result in a systematic screening of moral information. We suspect this is more characteristic of people with high ego and low task motivational orientations, though this has yet to be demonstrated empirically.

The Interaction of Processes

Before we conclude this chapter and part, it may be helpful to remind you that the four major moral action processes that we have been probing do not operate in isolation; they are quite interactive. Rest (1983, 1984) offers several illustrations of such interactions. Dienstbier, Hillman, Lehnhoff, Hillman, and Valkenaar (1975) marshal evidence to suggest that the moral ideals people hold (Process II) influence their interpretation of aroused affects (Process I). As another illustration, Darley and Batson (1973) manipulated the amount of time pressure that subjects experienced in completing a task (Process IV) and found that it related to their sensitivity to the needs of another (Process I). Cost calculations (Process III) have been shown to influence moral reasoning level (Process II) for both children (Eisenberg-Berg & Neal, 1981) and adults (Sobesky, 1983).

It is clear that future research on moral action might profitably investigate the relationship among processes and components. One particular set of interactions deserves special mention. It is a common observation that people who behave in a less-than-ideal manner often justify their behavior with moral rationalizations. Mischel and Mischel (1976) demonstrated empirically that when people deviate from what they believe to be right, they may adjust their moral thinking to rationalize their action (also Eisenberg-Berg & Neal, 1981; Sobesky, 1983). This is an example of Process III influencing Process II. Often when competing values supplant the moral value, people adjust their moral reasoning so as not to appear to themselves or others as morally inconsistent. This is evidence of the motivational significance of morality. Even when one acts contrary to moral precepts, it is important to maintain one's self-image as moral. Some have concluded from the existence of moral rationalization that moral reasoning is illusory and simply a cover for nonmoral motives, but moral rationalization does not mean that genuinely moral behavior does not exist. Although people may sometimes deceive themselves about their true motivations, other people (or the same people in other circumstances) may act with moral integrity, even at great personal sacrifice.

Summary and Conclusions

Let us conclude by noting a few implications and limitations of the model that we have sketched out over the past several chapters. First, our model emphasizes that moral behavior is the result neither of strictly internal structures and processes nor of contextual influences but of an interaction among them. This is a point of both common sense and sound theory. Unfortunately, in practice it is a point too often neglected. Researchers in the social learning tradition frequently employ research methodologies that neglect the active, constructive processes of the person. Similarly, structural developmentalists often neglect social influences in their effort to trace behavior to structures of personal meaning.

If research on moral action in sport is to progress, researchers need to systematically investigate how different processes and components of the model interact in the production of moral behavior. How do mood states influence an athlete's tendencies to empathize with her opponent? How does a person's ego processing affect the causal attributions he makes about other competitors' behaviors? Methodologies need to become more complex and sophisticated if we are to learn more about the mediators of moral action in sport.

The model also significantly expands the range of what might be considered moral research. The implications of sport involvement on participants' morality are not limited to possible influences on their moral reasoning maturity. Research on such diverse topics as achievement motivation and perspective-taking ability can help reveal how sport involvement influences moral functioning. We need to move beyond simplistic questions about whether sport has a positive or negative effect on participants' moral lives. Rather, we need to ask questions that help us identify the contributions, positive and negative, that different sport experiences make to the multiple aspects of moral functioning.

Finally, our moral action model helps underscore the fact that moral intervention programs need to be multidimensional in focus. Many moral problems in sport, for example, owe their source to structural characteristics of the competitive context rather than personal variables of the athletes themselves; to the extent that personal characteristics are implicated, the problems are probably due less to an inadequate ability to reason about abstract moral issues than to a complex set of affective, cognitive, and ego skills distributed throughout the four major processes. All of these need to be taken into account in designing intervention programs.

Three limitations of the model also need to be highlighted. First, the model itself is ahistorical and reflects only influences on the immediate production of moral action. The forces operative in the development of the various underlying competencies, traits, and skills are not reflected in the model. For this reason, the model is useful but incomplete as a guide for developing moral education or intervention programs.

The model also does not deal well with behaviors that are overlearned and habituated. It is based on the assumption that a given situation has enough novelty to arouse construction of meaning. Because much sport behavior is overlearned, this may seem to be a severe limitation. But even if an action is carried out habitually, unanticipated consequences can result. In such cases, habitual action may stimulate moral reflection that influences subsequent action. And habituated action itself has a learning history, and if the action has moral implications, then moral reflection was probably a part of that learning history.

Finally, despite our effort to expand it, the model remains excessively individualistic. The paradigm on which the model is built is an individual confronting a situation where a choice about how to act is required. This may fit many situations, but not all. Haan reminds us that many moral actions involve complex exchanges among people and that meaning and behavior are often subtly negotiated. Moral dialogue may influence how every process is experienced. How others perceive the relevant moral issues may influence how the self perceives them (Process I); moral meaning may be defined and refined through dialogue (Process II); what values are selected at one point may influence later negotiations (Process III); and moral behavior (Process IV) impacts the moral balance, which, in a cyclical, interactive fashion, impacts every other process once again, and so on.

Recognizing the imperfect nature of any model, we believe the present one is a useful heuristic for organizing theory and research on moral action in physical activity contexts.

Part III
Physical Activity and Character Development

To provide a context for this last part, we'd like to discuss *praxis*. Many dictionaries define the word by using its English cognate, *practice*, thus differentiating "practice" from "theory." But this distinction is not consistent with the original meaning of praxis, nor is it congruent with how the term is used in contemporary philosophy (Boff, 1987). As Robert McAfee Brown (1978) points out, praxis does incorporate practice, but it should not be used to fortify a dualism between theory and practice. Rather, the term *praxis* connotes an affinity between the two. They are not separable, and each continually influences and is influenced by the other. Praxis is theory-laden practice that cycles back into practice-rich theory.

The theme of praxis is woven throughout this part, the last in our volume. In chapter 10 we address the question, Does sport build character? We begin by reviewing the conceptual and empirical aspects of this topic; then, drawing from the 12-component model of moral action we presented in Part II, we offer a model of character based on the identification of four virtues.

The final chapter builds on the preceding ones, emphasizing moral praxis intended to enhance the character development of physical activity participants. We review pertinent literature and translate key concepts into practical advice for teachers, parents, coaches, and consultants who want to promote moral growth through physical education, informal games and sports, and organized youth sports.

Chapter 10
Does Sport Build Character?

In Part II we elaborated a model of moral action that can guide theory and research on moral behavior in sport. The present chapter draws from some of the material presented earlier, relating it directly to the question of sport and character. The notion that sport builds character is popular among many sport enthusiasts, and it is often pulled off the adage shelf when a sport program is in jeopardy. As Stevenson (1975) noted, "In the final analysis, it is the rationale of 'character-building,' of moral development, of citizenship development, of social development, that justifies the existence of physical education and athletics in educational institutions" (p. 287).

Although many claim that sport builds character, others disagree. In this chapter, we summarize both arguments, identify the historical roots of the idea, examine empirical research, discuss the relation between values fostered in sport and broader societal values, and offer a four-virtue characterization of "character" that can guide theory, research, and education.

Sport Builds Character: Arguments For and Against

The relation between sport and character has been discussed and debated in the public arena, among philosophers, and among researchers (Dowell, 1971). In this section, we introduce arguments for and against sport as a character builder. Later sections amplify what is said here, helping refine the discussion.

The Argument For

Those who maintain that sport builds character point to how sport participants must overcome difficult obstacles, persist in the face of opposition, develop self-control, cooperate with teammates, and learn to live with both victory and defeat. Sport is said to be a vehicle for learning such virtues as fairness, self-control, courage, persistence, loyalty, and teamwork.

In the banquet halls, talk shows, and sports pages, accolades to the character-building efficacy of sport usually come in the form of personal testimonies and anecdotal evidence. But some sport philosophers have extended and refined the public discussion of sport and character. Peter Arnold (1984a), for example, has offered a thoughtul essay; we summarize it here to illustrate the pro-sport approach. Arnold suggests that both the idea and practice of sport are concerned with fairness. Borrowing from Rawls's (1971) theory of justice, Arnold describes fairness as a confluence of freedom and equality. For Arnold, sport embodies these twin moral principles. Sport embodies freedom because individuals choose freely to participate. It embodies equality because, in choosing to participate, participants tacitly agree to abide by a shared set of rules impartially applied to all. Because players freely choose to participate knowing that sport is a rule-governed activity, they have a moral duty to abide by the rules, and furthermore to commit themselves to what the rules are designed to advance: fairness. When players deliberately cheat, the result is not bad sport, but no sport at all; sport ceases to exist because sport is premised on freedom and equality.

Because sport embodies moral principles, it can be a productive place for the practice of moral virtue. "Moral character is developed in sport, as in other spheres of life, in so far as much admired human qualities as loyalty, courage and resolution are cultivated and directed to the upholding of what is fair and just and in the interests of all" (Arnold, 1984a, p. 278). Sport is a particularly valuable locale for character formation because "there are not many situations in everyday life which provide either the kind of opportunities or the number of them evoking the qualities which are considered desirable" (Maraj, 1965, quoted in Arnold, p. 279).

Arnold concludes with a discussion of the Kantian notion of self-formation, which involves understanding the moral underpinnings of a practice and committing oneself as an autonomous being to the principles perceived. In sport, moral self-formation is possible as participants accept personal responsibility for how the practice of sport is conducted, rather than transferring responsibility to coaches or officials. To accept responsibility, participants need a developed sense of self-respect. In turn, self-respect is premised on valuing oneself and having confidence in one's ability to fulfill one's intentions. Again, sport is a potentially potent practice for developing these qualities.

Arnold's discussion is based on philosophical argument and, in principle, does not depend on empirical support. In fact, Arnold acknowledges that much of the activity that occurs under the sport umbrella is awash with miseducating influences and practices. Nonetheless, if sport can provide an optimal environment for building character, it would be reasonable to anticipate some positive socialization outcomes from participation. Later in the chapter we return to the empirical issue. Before we do, however, we'll summarize the counterargument.

The Argument Against

Many have countered the claim that sport builds character with bumper sticker arguments of their own. Leonard (1972) quips, "If competitive sports build character, it is character fit for a criminal" (p. 77). The oft-cited article by Ogilvie and Tutko (1971) is titled "Sport: If You Want to Build Character, Try Something Else."

Critiques of the character-forming potential of sport have generally taken one of three forms. Some argue that sport is neither a vehicle for moral education nor a facilitator of antisocial behavior, but rather morally neutral. Other people acknowledge that sport may encourage the development of desirable attributes, but they question whether these attributes transcend the sport context. Kari may learn to cooperate with her softball teammates, for example, but that does not mean she will be more cooperative with her professional colleagues.

Finally, some people criticize the character-building thesis because they believe sport does the opposite: that it builds characters, not character. It is easy to find stories of recruiting scandals, use of illegal performance-enhancing drugs, athletic aggression, playing-field cheating, and other exhibitions of antisocial behavior on and off the field. The prevalence of such occurrences, and the publicity given to them, provides fuel for this argument. Proponents may argue that competition itself promotes antisocial behavior (Kohn, 1986), that an overemphasis on competitive outcome generates moral problems (Orlick, 1978, 1990), that sport reflects negative values present in the broader culture (Sage, 1988), or that the special status or treatment given to athletes retards their development (e.g., Butt in Coakley, 1990).

Several of the critiques directed at modern sport are elaborated on later in this chapter. But first we will place the sports-builds-character motto in its historical context.

Sport and Character: Historical Introduction

The idea that sport participation is valuable to character formation is an ancient one, going back at least to Plato, who held that there is a close correspondence between physical and moral fitness. For our purposes, however, it is enough to begin the story in 19th-century Britain.

British Public Schools

In recent times the notion that sport is a medium for forming character is most prominently associated with 19th-century British "public" schools (which were really private boarding schools). It was there that team sports first were deliberately employed in educational settings to promote virtue (Mangan, 1981). The rationale of educational sport was expressed by the Royal Commission on Public Schools in 1864: "The cricket and football fields . . . are not merely places of exercise or amusement; they help to form some of the most valuable social qualities and manly virtues, and they hold, like the classroom and the boarding house, a distinct and important place in Public School education" (cited in McIntosh, 1957, p. 178). The "cult of athleticism" (Mangan) that developed was aimed at fostering the muscular Christian gentleman.

The particular virtues extolled in the British schools were those useful to an expanding and imperialistic Empire. The Christian gentleman was to be fortified with self-confidence, determination, physical and psychological strength, and bravery to empower him as a soldier, administrator, or missionary in the colonies.

In these 19th-century British schools a belief in the character-building efficacy of team sports was tied to an ideology of amateurism and self-governance. The ideology of amateurism paradoxically connected physical and moral strength but maintained a dualistic approach both to mind and body and to work and play. Professional sports were disdained because they united profit making with bodywork thereby, it was believed, undermining the potential of sport to cultivate the "higher" character of the participant. If material reward could be gained from sports, then spiritual and moral gains could not. It was a class-based ideology that effectively excluded the poor from participating in the lofty world of "moral" sport. Only those with means could afford to devote the time, energy, and attention to sport in the amateur model. Sport was believed to build character, but only so long as it was engaged in as a nonserious, leisure activity.

In the British boarding schools, sport was governed by the participants. The students organized, managed, and officiated their own sporting events. This was not an anomaly, because self-governance was widely practiced in areas outside of sport as well, but it was particularly important on the playing field. The importance of self-governance lay in the self-conscious way these schools trained the elite for leadership roles in business, industry, government, and the military.

It was thought that learning to lead and organize on the playing field would translate into skills useful in other leadership positions.

The British military was quick to pick up on the theme. A popular saying arose that "the Battle of Waterloo was won on the playing fields of Eton" (a private boarding school). Supposedly Arthur Wellington, a British general, gained his leadership capacities from his adolescent sporting experience at Eton. In truth, Wellington probably never participated in sports as an adolescent (Langford, 1969). Still, the idea of sport as a character builder was so entrenched that by World War I, sport was viewed as an essential preparation for soldiers. British military tacticians suggested that the way to defeat an adversary who possessed superior technology was to develop a superior soldier, and the way to do that was through team sports (Travers, 1979). Soldiers would develop manliness, discipline, courage, loyalty, and a capacity for self-sacrifice through their team sport preparation.

The Creed Moves to the United States

When the cult of athleticism was flourishing in Britain, educators in the United States were generally disinterested in sport. But cultural transformations occurring in the U.S. late in the 19th century and early in the 20th created a fertile environment for the introduction of the character-building philosophy (Sage, 1990). The most rapid growth of industry and capital in U.S. history occurred during this period, and a largely rural, agrarian society was rapidly transformed into an urban, industrial one. In addition, a large influx of immigrants arrived. As Sage points out, these transformations created numerous social problems. With one or both parents increasingly working outside the home, the need for an effective way to educate and socialize children was keen. And new immigrants needed to be integrated into the country's dominant values, customs, and language. To meet these demands, public education expanded rapidly.

Public educators initially resisted the tide of sports that were being organized by students in the latter part of the 19th and early 20th centuries, but eventually they came to embrace them as a vehicle for instilling culturally valued traits. Early physical educators were among the audiences receptive to the British idea that sport is a useful practice for the development of character.

American educators, however, were less concerned with training the cultural elite than with training new immigrants into the American way of life and educating all for jobs in the office and factory (O'Hanlon, 1980). The British emphasis on self-governance was discarded in favor of a hierarchy with school administrators in control. Sage (1990) notes that the resultant sport experience promulgated the dominant ideology, which served well the interests of the capitalist class by spreading a social consciousness willing to tolerate, and even embrace, structural social inequality.

As sport became accepted as a character-building social practice, it was increasingly shaped by both capitalist and patriarchal values (Coakley, 1990; Sage,

1988). The "character" sport was supposed to develop was a compliant yet "masculine" set of virtues well suited for the workplace. Because comparatively few girls and women participated, there was no perceived need to question these values.

By the mid-20th century the sport-builds-character creed was well established in America. To a limited extent, it became a topic of empirical investigation.

The Empirical Research

The theme of sport as a builder of character has never been a major topic of research (Stevenson, 1985). Fortunately, this may be changing; various contemporary textbooks now include chapters on sport and moral development or related themes, and research reports are becoming more common.

Let us state our conclusion first. The research does not support either position in the debate over sport building character. If any conclusion is justified, it is that the question as posed is too simplistic. The term *character* is vague, even if modified with the adjective *good*. More important, sport experience is far from uniform. There is certainly nothing intrinsically character-building about batting a ball, jumping over hurdles, or rolling heavy spheres toward pins. The component physical behaviors of sport are not in themselves moral or immoral. When we talk about building character through sport, we are referring to the potential influence of the social interactions that are fostered by the sport experience. The nature of those interactions varies from sport to sport, from team to team, from one geographical region to another, from one level of competition to another, and so on.

Several lines of research are relevant to the sport and character theme. In this review we summarize research relating sport participation to personality, behavioral propensities, value hierarchies, sportspersonship, and moral development.

Sport Participation and Personality

The word *character* is often used synonymously with *personality*. Not surprisingly, then, a number of early researchers were interested in whether sport influenced the personality characteristics of participants. Most studies conducted on this question have followed one or more of three strategies (Stevenson, 1975): a comparison of athletes with nonparticipants, a comparison of elite athletes with less-advanced sport participants or the general population, or a comparison of athletes participating in different sports. In all three cases, results are inconclusive.

Despite some evidence of personality differences that generally favor athletic participation, the conclusion that sport aids personality development is unwarranted. After carefully reviewing relevant studies, Stevenson (1975, 1985) concluded that there is little credible evidence of socialization effects through sport.

Similar conclusions were reached by other literature reviewers (Coakley, 1982; Eitzen & Sage, 1982; Loy, McPherson, & Kenyon, 1978; McPherson, 1978, 1981; Snyder & Spreitzer, 1983). Although some researchers have found differences on certain personality factors, in few instances have multiple investigators found support for any single personality factor. The lone exception may be that athletes tend to score higher on "dominance" than nonparticipants (Stevenson, 1975, 1985).

Most of the personality research has been methodologically flawed (Coakley, 1982; Fisher, 1976; Martens, 1975; McPherson, 1981; Morgan, 1980; Snyder & Spreitzer, 1983; Stevenson, 1975, 1985). The cross-sectional design employed in most studies allows for conclusions to be drawn only if the populations under study are similar in every meaningful respect except for their sport involvement, an assumption not typically warranted. Many studies did not try even minimally to match samples (Stevenson, 1975, 1985), though there have been notable exceptions (Geron, Furst, & Rotstein, 1986; R. Johnson & Morgan, 1981). Studies have used a wide range of psychological inventories, several of questionable validity, making comparisons among studies difficult. And the literature is replete with examples of unclear operationalization of variables, overgeneralized conclusions, and lack of adequate theoretical grounding.

Finally, it is important to note that the concept of "personality" has itself changed over the years (Martens, 1975; Vealey, 1989). Most early studies were conceived within a trait approach, such that an individual was characterized as possessing quantitative amounts of different specific traits that largely determined her or his behavior irrespective of situational factors (Martens, 1975). More recently, an interaction model of personality (Vealey), taking account of both person and situation, has gained prominence. There is still too little research reflecting this approach, however, to determine whether it will yield more satisfactory conclusions.

Sport Participation and Behavior

There may exist socialization-through-sport effects on personality. As yet, if such effects do occur, they are not well understood. Sport participation may also influence the behavioral tendencies of athletes. Although *character* is a term that refers to attributes rather than specific behaviors, most would acknowledge that character must bear some relation to behavior if it is to have useful meaning. In this section we examine literature related to prosocial behavior, delinquency, and aggression.

Prosocial Behavior

It is sometimes argued that sport participation encourages a range of prosocial behaviors, such as cooperation, altruism, and sharing. Cooper (1982) argues on philosophical grounds, for example, that team sports, through developing strong intrateam affiliations, mediate against egoism and provide the experiential base for altruistic behavior.

The claim that sport fosters prosocial behavioral tendencies is often echoed by parents. Skubic (1956), for example, obtained questionnaire responses from parents of male Little League baseball players. Ninety-five percent felt that the baseball experience helped their sons be more cooperative.

Seymour (1956) also examined the perceived influence of baseball experience on young players. He compared 10- to 12-year-old Little League players with nonplayers in terms of self, teacher, and peer ratings before and after the Little League season ($N = 228$). He found that teachers (but not others) rated participants higher in cooperation, social consciousness, and leadership both before and after the season; the differences were statistically significant only for leadership, however. Finally, Salz (1975) administered a personality test and found that boys who participated in competitive play, including the Little League World Series, were superior to their peers in cooperation and friendliness. It is not clear, however, that sport experience caused the observed differences, and the personality test approach to assessing behavior is notoriously fraught with validity problems.

Armstrong (1984) analyzed boarding schools in both England and the United States where sports play a prominent role. He concluded that sport encourages the acquisition of such lifelong values as teamwork, fair play, and being "a gentleman." Unfortunately, he presented no empirical data to support his analysis. It is possible that the observed values were learned through experiences in the school environment as a whole; whether a person participated in sport programs may have been irrelevant.

Not all behavioral studies support a correlation between prosocial behavior and sport. In fact, competition often has been associated with antisocial behavior. You will recall the famous "robbers cave" experiments (Sherif et al., 1961; Sherif, 1967) in which athletic competition appeared to incite a host of antisocial behaviors. Similarly, Raush (1965) observed hospitalized, but psychologically normal, 10- to 12-year-old boys and found that "friendly interactions" occurred 89% of the time when the boys were not competing in games, but when they were engaged in competitive games, 42% of their actions were "unfriendly."

A study by Kleiber and Roberts (1981) used an experimental design that, in principle, allows cause–effect relations to be established. In a field experiment with 54 fourth- and fifth-grade boys and girls, subjects were given the Social Behavior Scale (Knight & Kagen, 1977) before and after participating in a 2-week "Kick-Soccer World Series." The scale provides children 10 opportunities to obtain rewards for themselves and others. The pretest showed that those children with the most sport experience were significantly less altruistic. After controlling for the initial differences in scores, Kleiber and Roberts found that the kick-soccer experience had no reliable impact on the giving pattern of participants when all 10 test trials were considered. However, if only the last trial is examined (arguably the most significant), then the boys (but not the girls) displayed a significant decrease in generosity. For boys, at least, the study suggests a weak causal relationship between participation in the sport tournament and decreased altruism. Unfortunately, the short duration of the intervention, the reduction of "character" to an undifferentiated operationalization of altruism, and the questionable paralleling of the kick-soccer tournament with organized youth sport raise questions about the generalizability of the study's conclusions. The observed gender difference also points to the difficulty of assigning causality exclusively to the sport experience.

Burchard (1977, cited in 1979) examined the effects of sport competition on the attitudes and social behaviors of participants in a statewide youth hockey tournament for 11- and 12-year-old boys. Winning did not result in any hostility, nor did losing create hostility toward opponents. But losing did create hostility toward the self, teammates, and officials, especially if the team had not lost consistently. Burchard further investigated how the relationship between game outcome and hostility was mediated by individual motivational orientation. Each player was designated as either competition-motivated (by desire to win) or competence-motivated (by desire to play well) based on the amount of fun he reported when his team lost. Burchard found that when the competence-motivated players lost they did not express negative feelings toward anyone; when the competition-motivated players lost, however, they expressed negative feelings toward teammates, referees, and themselves.

Some effort also has been devoted to determining whether modified games that emphasize cooperation can promote prosocial behavior. Studies have provided support for this contention (Grineski, 1989a, 1989b; Mender, Keer, & Orlick, 1982; Orlick, 1981a, 1981b), but most have included only young children or populations with special needs.

Delinquency

One reason often cited by educators, sociologists, administrators, and parents for including sport programs in educational and community settings is their potential for diminishing delinquency (Donnelly, 1981). In his classic work on adolescents, for example, Coleman (1965) wrote that "if it were not for interscholastic athletics or something like it, the rebellion against school, the rate of drop, and the delinquency of boys might be far worse than they presently are" (pp. 44-45). Athletes themselves often reinforce this view through testimonial claims that were it not for sport, they would have drifted into drugs, vandalism, and crime (e.g., Connie Hawkins, cited in Wolf, 1972).

Indeed, there is considerable empirical evidence that sport participants are less likely than nonparticipants to engage in delinquent behavior (Donnelly, 1981; Hastad, Segrave, Pangrazi, & Peterson, 1984; Melnick, Vanfossen, & Sabo, 1988; Schafer, 1972; Segrave, 1983; Segrave & Chu, 1978; Segrave & Hastad, 1982, 1984). This is true for males (Segrave & Hastad, 1984) and females (Buhrman, 1977; Buhrman & Bratton, 1978; Melnick et al.; Segrave & Hastad, 1984) and for those in elementary school (Hastad et al.) and high school (Landers & Landers, 1977; Schafer, 1969; Segrave & Hastad, 1982, 1984). The negative relationship between sport participation and delinquency tends to be stronger among lower class youth (Buhrman; Buhrman & Bratton; Schafer, 1969; Segrave & Chu) and athletes in minor sports (Segrave & Hastad, 1982).

That a negative correlation exists between sport involvement and delinquency is well established. The reason for the correlation, however, is less clear. To comprehend better the sport–delinquency relationship requires understanding the etiology of delinquent behavior. Only then is it possible to develop a coherent theory about how sport may deter delinquent behavior.

Two theories about the causes of delinquency are particularly relevant to sport: differential association theory and control theory (Purdy & Richard, 1983). According to differential association theory (Sutherland & Cressy, 1966), deviant behavior is learned through contact with other deviants who communicate the techniques of deviancy, together with the ideological supports that legitimize the behavior in the eyes of perpetrators. Differential association theory focuses on such issues as the frequency, duration, and intensity of contact that an individual has with deviant associates and the age at which contact is made.

Sport may deter delinquency by encouraging less frequent, shorter, or less intense interaction with deviant others (Hastad et al., 1984; Segrave & Hastad, 1984). Also, the values emphasized in the sport context—such as teamwork, effort, and achievement—tend toward conventionality (Schafer, 1971) and correspondingly may discourage the legitimation of delinquent behavior. In this connection, we think it interesting that Snyder and Spreitzer (1979a) found that athletes were perceived by their classmates as more conventional than their nonathletic peers.

Control theory (Hirschi, 1969) emphasizes four sources of bonding between the individual and the broader society, any of which when violated creates the conditions for delinquent behavior. First, the "social bond" depends on feelings of respect and affection for a variety of individuals and institutions that represent the social order (e.g., parents and schools). Second, the social bond depends on a sense of commitment to obtaining the training necessary for entering adult roles in the social order. Third, it depends on a level of involvement in activities connected to the social order that leaves little unstructured time. Finally, the social bond is facilitated by a belief that one can obtain just and adequate rewards from the social system through personal effort.

It is easy to relate sport to the control theory of delinquency (Purdy & Richard, 1983). Sport participants, through contact with coaches and supportive others, are likely to develop a sense of attachment to significant others who represent the social order. Athletes have been shown to have somewhat higher educational aspirations (Braddock, 1980; Otto & Alwin, 1977; Picou & Curry, 1974; Snyder & Spreitzer, 1983; Spreitzer & Pugh, 1973), and there appears to be a slight positive correlation between sport participation and educational attainment (Braddock). The temporal demands of athletic involvement translate to less unstructured time, and sport certainly fosters a belief that hard work can lead to just reward.

In addition to the differential association and control theories, Purdy and Richard (1983) identify labeling theory and strain theory as potential contributors to a comprehensive approach to understanding the deterrent effect of athletic participation on delinquency. Labeling theory suggests that delinquency develops through a process by which one comes to be labeled, first by others and then by oneself, as delinquent. Once a person is labeled delinquent, a cyclical self-fulfilling prophecy is set in motion. Purdy and Richard (1983) note that athletes who engage in the same "delinquent" behavior as nonathletes may escape the negative label, may be treated less harshly, and may have sufficient alternative positive labels to escape self-labeling as delinquent, even if others so identify the athlete.

Strain theory suggests that delinquency results from a gulf between the standard of living that is prized in American society and avenues available to attain that standard of living, particularly among the poor, the racially and ethnically marginalized, and others who have suffered discrimination. Sport may provide an avenue to increase prestige, popularity, and status, thereby reducing the strain between ideal goals and beliefs about attainable goals.

Segrave and Hastad (1984) sought to determine the relative contributions of 12 theoretically derived sociopsychological factors involved in the etiology of delinquency in both athletes and nonathletes ($N = 1,693$). Though slight variations were present among athletes and nonathletes and males and females, the most powerful predictors of delinquent behavior among the entire sample were those drawn from differential association theory (namely, "delinquent associates") and control theory (namely, "attachment to school," "conventional value orientation," and "subcultural value orientations").

Despite reasonably uniform results in studies on sport and delinquency, it is still difficult to draw definitive conclusions (Segrave, 1983). Are individuals with tendencies toward delinquency less interested in sport and removed from sport teams when they do participate, or does sport itself have some inhibiting effect on delinquent behavior? Based on the empirical evidence, Segrave (1981) and others have argued that sport participation does in fact deter delinquency. However, this interpretation is challenged by Yiannakis (1980, 1981), who notes that the empirical evidence does not demonstrate a cause-and-effect link. Some have argued that the conventional value-set of traditional sports make them unattractive to delinquency-prone youth, who might benefit more from less traditional physical activity programs like Outward Bound (Donnelly, 1981; Sugden & Yiannakis, 1982).

One study that attempted to use sport as a treatment for delinquency provides some, but limited, insight into sport as a delinquency deterrent. Trulson (1986) matched 34 delinquent teenaged boys on age, socioeconomic background, and test scores on aggression and personality adjustment and then divided them into three groups. One group received traditional Tae Kwon Do training, which combined philosophical reflection, meditation, and physical practice of the martial art techniques. The second group received "modern" martial arts training, emphasizing only fighting and self-defense techniques. The third group ran and played basketball and football. For 6 months each group met three times a week for an hour.

After the 6 months posttests were given. Members of the Tae Kwon Do group were classified as normal rather than delinquent, scored below normal on aggression, and exhibited less anxiety, increased self-esteem, and improved social skills. The modern martial arts group scored higher on delinquency and aggression and were less well adjusted than when the experiment began. The traditional sports group showed little change on delinquency and personality measures, but their self-esteem and social skills improved. These findings underscore the point that whatever advantages or liabilities are associated with sport involvement, they do not come from sport per se but from the particular blend of social interactions and physical activities that comprise the totality of the sport experience. It is unfortunate that Trulson did not include a group receiving the philosophical training without the practice of Tae Kwon Do physical skills. Perhaps the integration of philosophical training with physical activity is so effective because the physical activity provides opportunities to "embody" the philosophy.

Aggression

Critics of the contemporary sport experience often raise the issue of athletic aggression. A quick perusal of sport news reveals plenty of anecdotes about athletes involved in aggressive behavior. On the other hand, some have argued that the relatively controlled level of aggression that occurs in sports provides a socially acceptable outlet for aggressive instincts, or a release for pent-up frustrations (e.g., Brill, 1963; P. Marsh, 1978, 1982).

It is important to distinguish aggression from assertion; the two terms are sometimes used interchangeably. *Aggression* can be defined as action initiated with the intent to cause pain or injury. Forceful, robust, energetic play that does not involve an intent to inflict pain or injury may be termed assertive, or competitive, play.

The literature on sport and aggression is vast, and we will not review it all here. It is replete with various theories, the most popular being the cathartic theory, the frustration-aggression hypothesis, and social learning theory. Space does not permit us to adequately describe and evaluate these different approaches, but three conclusions appear warranted.

First, there is little support for the cathartic theory, despite its intuitive appeal. Derived from Freud's psychodynamic approach, the cathartic theory holds that sport aggression provides a release for aggression instincts. In contrast to the predictions of cathartic theory, however, aggression that is exhibited increases rather than reduces the likelihood of future aggression (Bandura, 1973; Berkowitz, 1964).

Second, the frustration-aggression hypothesis, formulated by Dollard, Doob, Miller, Mowrer, and Sears (1939), also has received little support. According to the original formulation of this drive theory, aggression is always rooted in frustration and, conversely, frustration always leads to some form of aggression. Like the cathartic theory, the frustration-aggression hypothesis is not widely supported by social scientists. Michael Smith, one of the most influential researchers on sport violence, has labeled the idea that frustration needs to find an outlet in aggression "hockey's most durable folk theory" (1979, p. 76). The rejection of the frustration-aggression hypothesis does not mean that frustration plays no role in aggression. Berkowitz (1962, 1974) adapted parts of Dollard et al.'s model and proposed a new framework for understanding the antecedents of aggression. Frustration, according to Berkowitz, can arouse anger, creating a "readiness" for aggressive behavior. If aggression occurs, it is because previous learning and situational cues cause violent behavior to erupt (Berkowitz, 1969; Goldstein, 1983). Even then, other nonaggressive behavioral options may be selected.

Third, there is considerable support for the social learning theory that aggression is a learned response pattern under the influence of modeling and reinforcement (Bandura, 1973; Berkowitz, 1969). Most researchers in the field of sport aggression employ one or another of the variants of the social learning approach. Again, we simply summarize some of the main conclusions.

There is ample support for the idea that an in-sport socialization process occurs that tends to legitimize illegal or extralegal aggression, particularly in contact sports (Bredemeier, 1985; Silva, 1983; M.D. Smith, 1974, 1979, 1983; Vaz, 1982). However, the frequency and intensity of learned aggression vary considerably between sports and, within a given sport, from one region to another and from one level of competition to another (M.D. Smith, 1983).

In general, male athletes tend to be more aggressive than female athletes (Bredemeier, 1984; J.M. Brown & Davies, 1978; Silva, 1983; M.D. Smith, 1983); this difference parallels the nonsport literature. Though the differences are not great, males generally tend to express and accept more aggression than females (Hyde, 1986).

More violent societies also tend to experience higher levels of aggression in their sports. Coakley (1990) observes, "Instead of allowing people to release the pent-up energy that instinct theorists say is the foundation of all aggression, contact sports seem to be expressions of the same orientation that underlie warfare and high rates of murder, domestic violence, and assault" (p. 143). Homicide rates in the United States, for example, increase immediately after highly publicized and televised boxing matches (Phillips, 1983).

Structural developmental theory has been employed recently to shed light on athletic aggression (Bredemeier, 1983, 1985; Bredemeier & Shields, 1984b; Bredemeier, Weiss, Shields, & Cooper, 1986, 1987). In this approach, the sport participant's reflective moral evaluation is taken into account. It has been found, for example, that athletes with more mature moral reasoning are less approving of aggressive tactics than those with less mature moral reasoning (Bredemeier, 1985; Bredemeier & Shields). Furthermore, athletes with "principled" moral reasoning scores are rated as significantly less aggressive by their coaches (Bredemeier & Shields).

Does aggression in sport carry over into everyday life? This is one of the most critical questions for the person inquiring whether sport builds character. Are athletes who are aggressive on the playing field more aggressive than other people when they are not playing sports? The questions remain unanswered. Several scholars offer limited evidence of the opposite trend—that athletes tend to be less aggressive than most people in other areas of life (Nosanchuk, 1981; Thirer, 1978; Zillmann et al., 1974)—but their methodologies provide only indirect support for this conclusion. On the other hand, Bredemeier (1994) found that those children who tended to describe themselves as more aggressive in sport also tended to describe themselves as more aggressive in other areas of life. Once again, however, no cause-and-effect link can be established because of the correlational nature of the study.

Sport and Value Hierarchies

In addition to its affecting personality and behavior, some have suggested that sport influences the development of specific attitudes and values. These terms are often used in overlapping ways, as is evident in the "professionalization" literature that refers to changes in attitudes and/or values. We reviewed this literature in chapter 7 and will only briefly recap it here. In this line of research, investigators study the relative priority that people give to skill, fairness, winning, and (in some studies) fun in their view of sport. According to Webb (1969), children progress from an initial play orientation (fairness is of greatest concern, game outcome least) to a professional orientation (winning is most important, fairness least). The professional orientation is generally associated in the literature with males more than females, with elite athletes more than other athletes, and with those with a longer history of sport involvement.

One major methodological problem in the professionalization literature is the ambiguity of the meaning of "game" in the original Webb instrument. It appears that all people tend to use a more playful orientation when recreational games are specified and a more professional orientation when competitive sports are specified (Knoppers et al., 1986). Even if one accepts the general trends present in the literature, it is not clear that socialization through sport is occurring. Perhaps only those individuals who are already predisposed to a professionalized value hierarchy choose to participate in sport, stay in sport, or get selected for sport (Theberge et al., 1982). It may also be that it is not sport per se but the value orientation of coaches that is most influential (Albinson, 1973). Finally, the dichotomy between "play" and "professional" value orientations is itself problematic, as Knoppers (Knoppers et al.) has argued.

Dubois (1986) conducted one of the few longitudinal studies to examine changes of value preferences associated with sport participation. He studied participants in two youth sport leagues, one competitive ($n = 68$) and one instructional ($n = 42$), assessing them pre- and postseason, and, for the instructional league, pre- and postseason a second year. Participants were asked to rate the importance of 13 value items, such as winning, playing fair, sportsmanship, playing time, and having fun. Results suggested that involvement in the programs did in fact influence the participants' value preferences, with changes generally reflecting the different emphases of the two leagues. However, the lack of a control group and a second-year follow-up with the competitive league limits the study's generalizability.

Best (1985) investigated the comparative valuing of academic achievement, social skills, physical development, religion, self-control, honesty, and independence by interscholastic athletes and nonathletes ($N = 1,799$). The two groups differed significantly only with regard to physical development and religion. In both of these cases, athletes attached greater value to the item than nonathletes. Unfortunately, the sample was limited to boys and was correlational in design.

Lee (1977, 1986) has taken a somewhat different approach to the issue of value hierarchies in sport. Drawing from Rokeach's work (see chapter 1), Lee investigated the extent to which athletes embrace different classes of values. He reasons,

> If sport were effective in developing ''character'' we should expect to see athletes placing more emphasis on social and moral values than on competence and personal values. My research with college athletes in North America indicates that this does not happen and, insofar as there are differences in the values of athletes and nonathletes, it is only that athletes tend to place more value on being good at what they do. (Lee, 1986, pp. 250-251)

Unfortunately, Rokeach's method of separating moral from nonmoral values is problematic (see chapter 1). Also, Lee's research is cross-sectional, and therefore no cause-and-effect relations can be established. Finally, even if we accept the basic premises of the study, it does not follow that giving preference to competence values in an achievement setting like sport is contradictory to the sport-builds-character motif. Similar difficulties exist in a study by Davis and Baskett (1977), who used the Rokeach Value Survey and found that college athletes differed from nonathletes in their terminal but not instrumental values.

In short, we know little about the impact of sport on participants' values. It does appear from the professionalization literature that increased involvement in sport, or participation in higher levels of sport, is associated with less focus on fairness, particularly among males. But the existing literature does not let us conclude why this association exists, or even whether it is a desirable or undesirable trend. The issue, however, is closely tied to another, which is our next focus of analysis: sportspersonship.

Sportspersonship

Of all the virtues that sport supposedly fosters, sportspersonship is perhaps the most frequently cited. On a commonsense level, most people believe they know what sportspersonship is, but research continues to suffer from a lack of good instrumentation and a commonly accepted definition. The term's meaning has evolved over time (Abe, 1988; Chambers, 1984) and has generated an interesting philosophical debate (Arnold, 1984b; Feezell, 1986; Keating, 1964).

Feezell (1986), in an essay we found useful, connects the idea of sportspersonship with an Aristotelian balance between an "internal" perspective on sport that takes its goal and procedures quite seriously and an "external" perspective grounded in the recognition that sport is really quite inconsequential. Sport is at once, and in different ways, serious and nonserious; maintaining that binocular view enables the participant to be both devoted and playful. "Sportsmanship is a mean between excessive seriousness, which misunderstands the importance of the play-spirit, and an excessive sense of playfulness, which might be called frivolity and which misunderstands the importance of victory and achievement when play is competitive" (Feezell, p. 10).

The apparent decline in sportspersonship that many lament has usually been attributed to an overemphasis on winning. Kroll (1975) interestingly suggests that unless athletes place a high value on winning, sportspersonship has little meaning. For Kroll, the concept is relevant when success strategy and ethical strategy collide. Taking an ethical action that does not risk competitive success is right but not particularly noteworthy. The true test of sportspersonship comes when one foregoes a highly desired strategic gain for ethical reasons. Combining this perspective with Feezell's (1986), we suggest that *sportspersonship* involves an intense striving to win combined with a committment to the "play spirit" of sport, such that ethical standards will take precedence over strategic gain when the two conflict.

We noted that researchers have found that increased involvement in sport, or involvement in more elite levels of sport, is associated with a lower emphasis on fairness. This is congruent with most studies on sportspersonship. Despite the use of diverse instruments—from psychometers to content analysis of written stories, from a "study of values" test to a "critical incidents" inventory—a surprisingly uniform picture emerges. When compared to nonathletes, athletes tend to have less "sportsmanlike" attitudes or values, and more elite athletes have less "sportsmanlike" attitudes than other athletes (Allison, 1982; Bovyer, 1963; Kistler, 1957; Lakie, 1964; Richardson, 1962). One exception is reported by Dubois (1986), who found that good sportspersonship was among the top 5 of 13 value choices for participants in two youth sport programs and that sportspersonship gained in importance over the season. Unfortunately, Dubois did not employ a control group and left the meaning of "sportsmanship" unspecified; also, his results may be an artifact of a social desirability response set.

The work by Duda and Stephens (see chapter 8) may be helpful in clarifying underlying variables involved in the issue of sportspersonship. Duda (Duda et al., 1991) investigated the relationship between motivational orientation (task and ego) and sportspersonship attitudes. Results revealed a significant negative relationship between task orientation and cheating and a positive relationship between task orientation and fair play. Ego orientation, on the other hand, was positively related to self-reported cheating. Similar findings are reported by Stephens (1993) using different instrumentation.

Sport and Moral Development

A critical question pertinent to the issue of character building through sport is whether sport facilitates, impedes, or has little impact on moral reasoning development and how moral development, in turn, is related to the behavior of sport participants on and off the field. Having reviewed the relevant literature on moral reasoning and sport experience in chapter 7, we limit our comments here to a brief synopsis of main findings. But a preliminary comment is in order.

One major problem with most literature on "sport and character" is that it has typically followed what Kohlberg (1981) facetiously labeled a "bag of virtues" approach to defining character. In this approach, researchers arbitrarily select character or behavioral measures that reflect a preferred set of values and then equate their selection with character. For example, Blanchard (1946) selected an expressive set of traits in assessing the influence of a physical education program on students' character. Given Blanchard's particular bag of virtues, it is not surprising that she found girls' character benefited significantly more than boys'. Typically, however, the selection of character traits has subtly supported the "masculine" stereotype (Coakley, 1990; Sage, 1988). In either case, arbitrary selections of values pose as definitions for character.

Kohlberg argues that the way out of the relativist bag-of-virtues dilemma is to identify a universal competence underlying a wide range of moral behaviors. Because the moral quality of action is rooted, at least in part, in the moral meaning that it has for the actor, focusing on moral reasoning development is a particularly productive way to proceed. Although moral reasoning competence no more exhausts the meaning of "character" than "knowledge" does "wisdom," it certainly is an important component. With that comment in mind, what does the literature tell us?

Sport Participation and Moral Reasoning Maturity

No longitudinal studies have investigated moral reasoning development and sport, so the cause-and-effect relationship remains unexplored. The existing literature, however, suggests that involvement in collegiate basketball is associated with less mature moral reasoning than is characteristic of the general population (Bredemeier & Shields, 1984b, 1986c; Hall, 1981). The same, however, was not true of collegiate swimmers, whose moral reasoning scores were not significantly different from nonathletes (Bredemeier & Shields, 1986c). Among high school students, the difference between basketball players and nonathletes was not significant (Bredemeier & Shields, 1986c). At the collegiate and high school level, no moral reasoning studies have been published focusing on other sports. However, a study of middle elementary school children (Bredemeier, Weiss, Shields, & Cooper, 1986) found that the lengths of participation by boys in high-contact sports and girls in medium-contact sports were positively related to less mature moral reasoning, but participation in other sports was not. The similarity between the boys in high-contact and the girls in medium-contact sports may have resulted from the fact that no girls participated in high-contact sports, making medium-contact sports their equivalent to high-contact sports.

Moral reasoning is typically viewed as a structural competence that is relatively stable across diverse content areas. One of the interesting findings in the moral reasoning and sport literature (as we discussed in chapter 7) is that people tend to use different reasoning patterns when thinking about moral issues in sport than they do when thinking about moral issues in daily life contexts such as school or work. Analyzed from a structural perspective, "sport" reasoning tends to be scored lower than corresponding "life" reasoning (Bredemeier, in press; Bredemeier & Shields, 1984b; Bredemeier, Weiss, Shields, & Cooper, 1986). The implications for this divergence in reasoning patterns are not well understood, however. It may be that "sport" moral reasoning typically reflects a nonserious, playful regression congruent with the ludic character of sport. On the other hand, "game reasoning" may, at times, be a form of moral rationalization that seemingly legitimizes behavior that would ordinarily result in self-censure (Bredemeier & Shields, 1985, 1986a, 1986b; Shields & Bredemeier, 1984).

Moral Development and Moral Behavior in Sport

The studies just cited suggest that within some sports there is a relationship, generally negative, between participation and level or stage of moral reasoning development. If future research supports this association and, more importantly, demonstrates a cause-and-effect relationship, this would indeed be a serious problem. In the general psychology literature, there is ample evidence that less mature moral reasoning is associated with antisocial behaviors (Blasi, 1980; Smetana, 1990). As we noted in the section on aggression, it also has been found that levels of moral reasoning among athletes are a mediating factor in their aggressive behavior (Bredemeier, 1985, 1994; Bredemeier & Shields, 1984a, 1986a; Bredemeier, Weiss, Shields, & Cooper, 1986, 1987). Whether moral reasoning maturity among athletes is associated with other antisocial behaviors has not yet been studied.

Conclusion

Stevenson (1975, 1985) reviewed the literature addressing possible socialization effects through sport and concluded that little is known about the psychosocial effects of participation in sport. That remains true today. However, Stevenson concluded in 1985 that the whole area of research was essentially dead because interests had turned to other concerns. On that count, he was incorrect. Shortly after he pronounced the death, interest burgeoned. Though definitive conclusions are still few and far between, research methodologies have continued to improve. Indeed, though the area remains greatly understudied, the future looks promising.

Sport and Societal Values

Psychologists have had difficulty verifying specific relationships between sport involvement and various facets of psychosocial development. Still, few doubt that sport involvement has some impact. Sport is an intense experience to which many young people devote significant time and energy, and such a concentrated focus of social interaction is certain to have an effect on its participants.

Sociologists are quick to point out a correspondence between broader social values and those seemingly nourished in the world of sport. Rather than attempt to demonstrate that sport is a unique arena for developing specific traits or competencies, sociologists tend to emphasize how sport is integrated with other socializing institutions, passing on the norms and ethos of culture. Schafer (1971), for example, wrote that "interscholastic athletics serve first and foremost as a social device for steering young people—participants and observers alike—into the mainstream of American life through overt and covert teaching of attitudes, values, and behavior patterns" (p. 6). In his empirical report, Schafer found that coaches tended to be conventional in their behavior, and it is likely that they encourage or insist on similar behavior from their charges.

That a close connection exists between sport and the broader society is indisputable. In one carefully designed comparison of 10 peaceful societies and 10 societies with long traditions of fighting many wars, anthropologist Richard Sipes (1973, 1975, 1976) found that contact sports were popular in 90% of the warlike societies and in only 20% of the peaceful societies. Similarly, Keefer (Keefer, Goldstein, & Kasiarz, 1983) found that military activity is positively related to the popularity of contact sports.

George Sage (1988) has written incisively about "character building" from a sport and society perspective. As a critical theorist, he suggests that sport as a cultural practice promulgates an ideology that supports the position of the dominant powers in society:

Sport must be understood as a set of social practices and relations structured by the culture in which it exists. Treating sport as a social practice means situating it in the context of social power and culture. Mottoes and slogans, such as "sports builds character," must be seen in light of their ideological intent. . . . Ideology tends to be aligned with dominant and powerful interests in society, and its role is to institute *their* practices and vision of the world as universal. Ideology is a protective cocoon beneath which prevail structures and processes of domination and exploitation. . . . Modern sport forms are part of the terrain upon which the dominant ideology is constructed and sustained. (p. 634)

Sport functions as an instrument of ideological manipulation by helping to manufacture a social consensus about such values as hard work, corporate loyalty, and belief in hierarchical organization, specialization, meritocracy, and patriarchy.

These values and beliefs are necessary to maintain a compliant and productive work force in the modern capitalist state, a set of social arrangements that in turn tremendously benefit a few but disadvantage and disempower many.

A study by Berlage (1982a) bears out some of these reflections. Fathers of youth sport participants (soccer and ice hockey) were asked to identify three attributes that sports develop that they considered valuable. The values they selected were those most essential to a bureaucratic and corporate structure. Berlage (1982a, 1982b) places these findings in a broader discussion of how parents and coaches foster values like authoritarianism, team loyalty, and the performance principle that are conducive to assuming roles in corporate America.

Modern sport has been "commodified" and commercialized, testimony to the ubiquitous character of the capitalist impulse. Kleiber (1983) argues that this has undermined its special qualities of separateness and play. Even youth sports have increasingly become commodities: Young athletes are paraded as heroes, athletic teams have "bought into" uniforms and special equipment, and the whole organizational structure has become more bureaucratized, rationalized, and commercialized (Berlage, 1982b). Lombardo (1982) argues that the evident trend of youth sport coaches to model their training and goal orientation on professional sports does a profound disservice to the young, whose needs differ considerably from those of adult athletes.

The reflections of critical theorists like Sage point to the importance of clarity about what is meant by character. For research on "character building" through sport to advance, we need to clarify just what it is that we mean by character. What is needed is not simply a description of what passes as "character"—the term is used much too variably and imprecisely to garner any consensus about what it means—but a normative description that is critical, positive, and sufficiently focused to provide a direction for research. To that task we now turn.

What Is Character?

One of the most significant problems to plague the investigation of character building through sport is the extreme diversity of definitions attached to the word *character* (Hodge, 1988). Perhaps given its vague and multiple uses, it would be better to abandon it altogether. Still, we believe that the term communicates something vital about a person's being that is not well captured by other terms.

In the second part of this volume we elaborated a model of moral action that we believe can help give greater specificity to the concept of character. According to that model, moral action invariably involves four processes: interpreting a situation, constructing a situation-specific moral ideal, selecting the moral ideal over competing values, and fulfilling one's intention in action. Now we propose a concept of character that is rooted in this model of moral action. Essentially, we define character as the possession of those personal qualities or virtues that facilitate the consistent display of moral action. Accordingly, we describe character in terms of four virtues (one for each of the four processes of the moral action model): compassion, fairness, sportspersonship, and integrity.

We appeal to the concept of virtue in much the same way that Erikson (1964) did. Erikson distinguished virtues, or what he sometimes called "strengths," from ethical or moral ideas. According to Erikson, moral ideas, by themselves, are "non-vital" or "despirited." Moral ideas need the qualities of character that Erikson labeled virtues to animate them, give them spirit, root them deeply in personality. Ethical constructs or principles provide useful guides to action only as they are infused with the vitality of virtues arising from the core of one's being.

Let us summarize the meaning of the four virtues we have identified.

Compassion

Compassion is the character virtue that most closely corresponds to Process I of the moral action model: interpreting the situation. By compassion we do not mean a disposition to charity or sentimentality. Such tendencies reflect a self–other dichotomy and an element of paternalism. Compassion rather is a virtue akin to moral sensitivity, closely related to empathy and an ability to "feel with" others. Compassion opens us up, allowing us to indwell a moral situation; it engages both intellect and emotion. Compassion does not oppose reason, or even a limited sense of detachment. In fact, compassion demands the cooperation of intellect, because only when we use our reasoning capacities to their fullest can we be fully engaged with another. But if compassion does not oppose reason, it certainly opposes severing the bonds between intellect and the affective life.

Compassion is as relevant in sport as in other arenas of life. Though sport often discourages compassion, it is interesting to note that sport itself is often done *with passion*, that is, com-passionately. Compassion, however, does not connote simply intense feeling, but the activation of those feelings that emanate from and reinforce a sense of human solidarity. There is nothing intrinsic to competition ("to strive with") that mitigates against compassion, and players can be encouraged to see competitors as coparticipants, equally valuable, equally deserving of regard.

Fairness

Compassion engages one fully in a situation, but the virtue of fairness is needed to ensure that compassion is not overly influenced by our natural affinity with those who are similar to us, those whom we particularly like, or those simply closer to us. Fairness is the virtue most closely connected to the second process of the moral action model—constructing a moral ideal. Fairness involves even-handedness, equal consideration. It is not "blind justice" but suspended interest. One needs to be both engaged and disengaged to be fair.

Compassion and fairness typically join harmoniously and work in concert to bring about caring and just behavior, but there are times when they tend to split and counterbalance each other. In such instances, there is no necessary priority between them. It is essential to bring compassion and fairness into the greatest harmony possible. To completely sacrifice one for the other exhibits a lack of character.

Fairness is the primary virtue of sport. Sport is based on fairness and cannot exist apart from it. Imagine that someone were to say, "Let's create a new sport in which those with green eyes are advantaged." Who would play? Unless participants believe in the fairness of the contest, sport dissolves.

Sportspersonship

Some might think it odd that sportspersonship be identified as a central component of character. But it is a concept that transcends the world of sport. As Kroll (1975) observed, "the moral equivalents of sportsmanship are extrapolated beyond the boundaries of sport per se" (p. 1). Everyday conversations are punctuated with expressions that draw on sportspersonship themes: "hitting below the belt," "cheap shot," "out-of-bounds," and the like.

Sportspersonship is aligned with Process III of the moral action model—selecting the moral value from among competing values. As stated earlier, we believe sportspersonship involves an intense striving to succeed, tempered by commitment to a "play spirit," such that ethical standards will take precedence over strategic gain when the two conflict. Essentially, sportspersonship involves two complements: maintaining allegiance to one's moral vision in the face of attractive competing values and maintaining a fruitful tension between seriousness and nonseriousness, between work and play, between critique and affirmation. Both aspects are as essential in the nonsport world, especially in other competitive contexts, as they are in sport.

Integrity

Integrity is the character trait most closely associated with Process IV, the final one, of the moral action model—fulfilling our intentions in action. The virtue of integrity is the cornerstone of character, for it is the embodiment of our ideals. Without integrity, we fail to act on our moral values when obstacles interfere or when distractions surface. Integrity typically rests on two other qualities: a sense of *moral self-esteem* (a belief in one's moral worth and in one's ideal) and a sense of *moral self-efficacy* (a belief that one is capable of bringing to fulfillment one's moral intentions).

Integrity is a quality of character clearly relevant to the sport experience. Integrity enables one to act on one's convictions, even if such action is negatively received by a coach, teammates, or fans. Given the prevalence of rule breaking, drug use, and aggression in sport, there is ample opportunity and need for the display of integrity.

Summary

In this chapter we examined the research on sport and various character-related attributes and behaviors. In general, the literature supports a negative relation between sport participation and delinquency and a positive relation between sport participation and a lessening of restraints on aggression, at least aggression in sport. The impact of sport participation on personality and various prosocial behaviors is less clear. There is limited evidence that experience in some sports is correlated negatively with moral reasoning maturity, but this is not true for participants of all ages or in all sports. Clearly, sport does not automatically build either character or characters. The influence that sport has for its participants depends on a complex set of factors tied to the specific sport and the social interactions that are present.

We also proposed a definition of ''character'' in terms of four virtues: compassion, fairness, sportspersonship, and integrity. Each virtue is rooted in a specific set of psychological competencies and processes that relate to moral action. Many of these are amenable to educational intervention. In the final chapter, we use our description of character to discuss how physical activity experiences might be designed to encourage character formation.

Chapter 11
Promoting Moral Character Through Physical Education and Sport

According to Piagetian theory, physical activity is the taproot from which all psychological processes and structures grow. Morality, too, has its roots in the early physical activity of infants and toddlers. The extensive literature on such themes as attunement (e.g., Haft & Slade, 1989; Rayner, 1992; Szajnberg, Skrinjaric, & Moore, 1989), attachment (e.g., Hinde, 1991; Vaughn et al., 1992), and children's play (e.g., Booth, 1980, 1981; Bruner, Jolly, & Sylva, 1976; Mead, 1934; Peller, 1971; Piaget, 1932/1965, 1962; Sutton-Smith, 1971b) points to the importance of physical activities in the early underpinnings of moral development. Booth (1981), for example, notes that play enables learners to begin with action, rather than ideals, and that what is learned through action is readily cycled back into improved action. Perhaps it is for this reason that Karpova and Murzinova (1990) report that play with peers is more effective than regular school activities in fostering prosocial behavior in preschool children.

Although few scholars doubt the importance of play to early development, there is less consensus about the continuing role of physical activity in later childhood and adolescence. It is not so much that scholars challenge the significance of physical activity but that they simply neglect it. But what of physical activity? As children get older, much of their physical activity gets channeled into physical education classes and organized games and sports. What influences do these forms of physical activity have on moral formation? The previous chapter made it clear that sport does not necessarily promote character development. The same, no doubt, is true of physical education programs. On the other hand, both of these contexts can be, with deliberate effort, productive environments for development.

In this final chapter, we draw together insights from the previous chapters to make recommendations relevant to physical activity contexts, beginning with physical education programs. We then consider children's informal games and sports. We conclude with a discussion of adult-organized youth sport programs. But before addressing physical education, we'll recap a few themes from earlier chapters that help set the stage for the present discussion.

We have described moral character as comprising four virtues: compassion, fairness, sportspersonship, and integrity. For us, these four virtues define the primary content of moral education. The virtues correspond to the four processes that flow into moral action: interpretation, judgment, choice, and implementation. In turn, each process is undergirded by a set of psychological competencies, the most important of which include perspective taking and empathy (Process I), moral reasoning (Process II), the self-structure (Process III), and autonomy and social problem-solving skills (Process IV). Each virtue reflects the activation and utilization of its underlying competencies in the service of moral action. Moral action requires, in addition to these competencies, an ability to remain coping in one's ego processing and sufficient information to act critically and knowledgeably. Moral action is further facilitated, and virtues are sustained, in a supportive moral atmosphere where group norms are conducive to the display of virtuous behavior.

Development of virtues requires what Kant called *self-formation*, a process through which a person critically and self-consciously appropriates moral values and marshals the personal qualities and capacities needed to consistently display them (Arnold, 1984a). Psychological competencies, even moral reasoning capacity, are themselves morally neutral. It is the placing of one's competencies in the service of moral action guided by a coherent moral vision that infuses them with their moral significance. Only dedication to specific moral contents can provide the vision and concreteness necessary for self-formation. We offer the four virtues as one proposal (not the only possible one) for the defining content of moral education. Our model of moral education rests on five presuppositions:

1. Moral character can be summarized as a composite of four virtues: compassion, fairness, sportspersonship, and integrity.
2. Each virtue is premised on a set of psychological competencies, some of which develop through a regular, age-related sequence of stages or phases.

3. Each virute extends the underlying competencies by placing them in the service of moral action.

4. Moral action reflects the joint operation of the four virtues and is mediated by ego processes. From the standpoint of moral action, it is better to cope than to defend.

5. Moral education has five primary aims:

a. Development of a moral atmosphere conducive to the expression of virtuous behavior

b. Promotion of the full development of the underlying capacities of moral action

c. Development of ego flexibility and security, enabling one to maintain the most favorable balance possible of coping over defending

d. Development of a knowledge base that enables critical analysis of the moral circumstances in which one finds (or is likely to find) oneself

e. Promotion of a self-formative process through which one comes to deeply embrace the four character virtues

With that foundation laid, we'll turn to our first physical activity context—physical education.

Physical Education and Moral Character

Physical education is probably the most significant physical activity context for developing moral character. We say this for several reasons. First, physical education is less commercialized, bureaucratized, and formalized than organized sport. Physical education programs are traditionally structured with less emphasis on competition; certainly, there are fewer external social pressures to emphasize outcome. Situated in an educational setting, physical education benefits from the diverse range of values, goals, and objectives that permeate education more broadly. These combined factors allow physical educators flexibility in planning and implementation sometimes unavailable to leaders of more formal sport programs.

Physical education also provides a foundation on which other physical activities build. At least in theory, if not always in practice, the school gymnasium or playing field is where young people learn the techniques, skills, arts, and values of competitive sports and recreational physical activities. If modern competitive sport has become dominated by a win-at-all-costs ethos, part of the problem lies in the preparation provided by physical education classes.

Another reason for focusing on physical education as a context for moral development is its sheer number of participants. As Caine and Krebs (1986) remind us, "for every high school or college athlete there are another thousand or more participants involved in physical education" (p. 198). Organized youth sport programs certainly involve tremendous numbers, but physical education remains the largest organized setting for physical activity.

Of course, even more children and youths are involved in informal games and sports. But this brings up our final point: Physical education provides an optimal context for moral development because it is organized and structured by a trained educator. Again in theory at least, the physical educator can arrange an optimal environment for fostering growth in the various dimensions of moral character. Through both preservice and in-service training, the physical educator can learn the insights and skills needed to stimulate growth and development.

Before we discuss how physical education can foster moral character, we must mention one objection to our educational aims. Some might conclude incorrectly from what we have said so far that we embrace an instrumental approach to physical education. According to the instrumentalist view, education generally, and physical education in particular, are valued for their effectiveness in producing socially valued products (health, fitness, moral character, etc.). In contrast, others argue for an intrinsic approach to physical education that emphasizes play, dance, recreation, and sport as worthy simply for the fun, stimulation, and self-expression they embody (Bain, 1976; L.F. Locke, 1973; Siedentop, 1972). Our perspective is that the instrumental and intrinsic positions are not antithetical but rather complementary emphases. Physical education, we believe, should help people appreciate the intrinsic value and joy of physical expression and movement. A well-designed physical education program will simultaneously foster moral growth. We firmly believe that physical education has the potential to foster moral character without in the process abandoning an emphasis on physical activity as intrinsically valuable.

Moral Education Through Physical Education: Defining the Possibilities

A number of theorists and practitioners have argued persuasively that physical education can be a context and practice useful in the development of character (e.g., Arnold, 1986; Austin & Brown, 1978; Bain, 1975; Caine & Krebs, 1986; DeBusk & Hellison, 1989; Figley, 1982, 1984; Fraleigh, 1979; Giebink & McKenzie, 1985; Hellison, 1982, 1985, 1993; Meakin, 1981, 1982; Preston, 1979; Romance, 1988; Romance, Weiss, & Bockoven, 1986; Wandzilak, 1985; Wandzilak, Carroll, & Ansorge, 1988). In this section we analyze this possibility using our four-virtue depiction of character as a guide. Because we deal with sport separately, here we focus primarily on those contents of physical education, such as fitness training, educational gymnastics, and dance, that are not directly tied to competitive sport. Most of what we later say about sport, however, applies to the practice of sport in physical education as well.

What possibilities does physical education offer for fostering growth in moral character? First, a few general comments. Perhaps nowhere else in the curriculum is practical activity (activity directed toward practical outcomes) highlighted more than in physical education. This alone makes physical education particularly relevant to moral education because the arena of moral action is practical activity.

In physical education, ideas are "embodied." It also is clear that most students care deeply about their physical competence. In the early grades, this may be because children define themselves in largely physical terms (Damon, 1984). In older grades it may be because physical competence is a means for both self-expression and social acceptance. In either case, the degree of personal investment that students bring to physical education provides a rich environment for dealing with moral issues.

To review some of the possibilities for physical education's contributing to moral education, we first highlight how it can contribute to the growth of each of the four virtues. We then review some experimental physical education programs that have sought to promote moral growth. Finally, we conclude this section with specific recommendations for the physical educator.

Physical Education and Compassion

Moral sensitivity, the theme of Process I of moral action, is manifest in the virtue of compassion. The psychological competencies undergirding compassion include role taking, perspective taking, and empathy. Further, the goal structure of the situation is an important influence on how compassion will likely be displayed.

Can physical education contribute to compassion? We believe so. Role taking and perspective taking are competencies readily fostered in the physical education context, where teachers can give assignments that enable students to take differing roles and perspectives.

Meakin (1981, 1982) argues strongly for the physical educator's ability to foster empathy. He correctly points out that empathy builds on knowledge. The knowledge necessary for effective empathy pertains to things like what causes physical and psychological harm, what causes insecurity or fear, and so on. Relevant, too, is knowledge about the social-structural forces that impact people's lives, shaping their perspectives, opportunities, and circumstances. Thus, critical awareness of politics, economics, and other social dynamics is vital to a developed capacity for empathy.

Physical education can provide a setting for gaining the knowledge base on which empathy draws. For example, there is ample and obvious opportunity to learn about what causes physical harm. And physical education is a context of self-display in which participants' strengths and vulnerabilities are often evident. Embarrassment or elation may accompany failure or success at trying a new skill. In such an environment, it is relatively easy to learn about what causes fear, insecurity, psychological hurt, and so on.

The integration of children with physical disabilities into physical education classes may also provide a good environment to develop perspective taking and empathy. Sherrill (1985) presents evidence that the integration of "handicapped" students into mainstream physical education is helpful for both students with disabilities and those without.

Finally, the physical educator is free to develop and implement, perhaps in consultation with class members, a variety of goal structures. The class can experiment with various forms and combinations of cooperative and competitive games or exercises. In physical education students can gain critical insight into how they respond to environments with different goal structures. By becoming aware of the influence of goal structures on their behavior, students may learn to exercise more self-direction. Another goal should be helping students understand and appreciate the cooperative underpinnings of all forms of competition, thus breaking down the cooperative–competitive dualism.

Physical Education and Fairness

Moral decision making is the theme of Process II of moral action, manifest in the virtue of fairness. The psychological competencies undergirding fairness include moral reasoning ability and moral dialogue skills. The moral atmosphere is the contextual influence most likely to affect the display of fairness.

Physical education provides many opportunities for students to discuss hypothetical or real moral problems and develop moral reasoning and moral negotiation abilities. Who should decide, and why, about curriculum? Should risky physical skills be tried? Should grading be based on skill, effort, or performance—or should it be eliminated altogether? Should students who are not interested in learning a particular skill be compelled to do so? If so, why?

The physical education class, like any other, also can develop a sense of community with particular community norms. It is certainly possible to foster a constructive moral atmosphere supportive of efforts to be fair. Developing such an atmosphere will involve two component processes: encouraging an intrinsic valuing of the experience and community and promoting prosocial collective norms. Interdependent group work is essential to both processes.

Physical Education and Sportspersonship

Value choice is the theme of Process III, to which we tie the virtue of sportspersonship. The undergirding psychological competencies include motivational orientation and moral identity, two aspects of the self structure. A task orientation and a sense of identity closely aligned with the moral self help develop sportspersonship. The particular "domain cues" embedded in the context will influence what domains of social cognition are activated and, correspondingly, what motives need to be coordinated.

It is probably self-evident that sportspersonship has relevance to physical education. Unfortunately, there is little consensus on its meaning. Some people emphasize "conventional" behaviors corresponding to the rites, rituals, and customs of a particular sport. Others prefer to define sportspersonship in terms of "good manners": winning graciously, losing with dignity, being polite to opponents. Still others, ourselves included, accent the moral dimension.

One way to think of sportspersonship is in terms of "keeping perspective." Games are games; they are not of ultimate importance. Central to this ability to keep perspective is a "task orientation" to achievement contexts and a well-developed sense of "the moral self." Physical education can contribute to both areas. Teachers can encourage a strong task orientation, for example, by helping students define realistic and self-referenced goals. They can encourage the moral self simply by breaking down the walls of silence that often surround moral issues. Teachers can talk about morality and physical activity, letting students know that moral concerns are both relevant and important.

Sportspersonship requires that a person see the moral dimensions of contexts, even when other domains of social cognition might be applicable. Fairness in games and sports, for example, needs to be seen as a moral issue, not just a matter of the conventional structure. Certainly the physical educator can assist in this process.

Physical Education and Integrity

Implementing action is the theme of Process IV of the moral action model, featuring the virtue of integrity. Psychological autonomy and social problem-solving skills can facilitate integrity. The power dynamics of the context also play a critical role in the display of integrity.

In 1908, Royce (1978) argued that physical education can nurture "loyalty to loyalty," by which he meant something akin to integrity and justice. Physical education offers ample opportunities to promote integrity through buttressing autonomy and social problem-solving skills. Teachers can foster autonomy by encouraging self-selection of tasks, individualized goals, assumption of responsibility, and the like. Bain (1975, 1985) warns, however, that the "hidden curriculum" often operative in physical education may impede the development of autonomy; teachers need to be careful that concerns for control and order do not undermine espoused values. Finally, cooperative group work where students coordinate their activities can provide a valuable environment for fostering social problem-solving skills.

Physical activity contexts are rife with opportunities to help students understand and deal with issues of power. Power comes through many means, including institutional roles, physical prowess, leadership capabilities, and group cohesion. It is important to help students understand their own sources of power and respond with integrity when people with power encourage less-than-moral behavior.

Moral Education Through Physical Education: Research Interventions

Physical education, of course, does not automatically produce moral growth. It can be beneficial, neutral, or detrimental to character development, all hinging on the nature of the social interactions that actually take place in the physical education setting.

One problem in getting physical educators to implement effective moral education strategies may be inferred from a study by Henkel and Earls (1985), who found that physical educators were on average less developed in their moral reasoning capacities than most others of similar ages and educational backgrounds. It certainly would be beneficial if in the future physical educators received training in professional ethics to help stimulate their own moral reasoning. But there certainly are a great many dedicated and competent physical educators who could, especially with training, be quite effective moral educators. We now consider empirical studies that have investigated the potential of physical education to contribute to moral growth.

Social Learning Studies

Austin and Brown (1978) used social learning principles to fashion a physical education program designed to promote prosocial behavior. They developed a checklist of desirable behaviors (e.g., enthusiasm, effort, sharing responsibility, winning and losing graciously). Students then were given the responsibility to organize, play, and officiate floor hockey during physical education periods. The instructor kept tabs of negative and positive behavior and, at the conclusion of each class, reviewed game behaviors. Every month a trophy was presented to the team with the best "social" score. To encourage transfer of learning, student conduct was observed during recess. Any fighting or arguing caused a point deduction from the team to which the involved student belonged, and deductions were announced at the beginning of the next physical education period. Program evaluation was impressionistic, but both classroom teachers and the students themselves believed the program was effective in promoting prosocial behavior. An intervention based on similar principles was used by Giebink and McKenzie (1985), who also reported favorable results, but their small sample (four boys) makes it difficult to generalize.

Structural Developmental Studies

Improving behavior is certainly an important goal for moral educators, but it cannot be the only one. Figley (1984) articulates a point we have made repeatedly, and we hope you will not feel we belabor it by quoting the following passage:

> One could list numerous behaviors in physical education that could be classified as desirable moral behaviors. A child could share or trade a piece of equipment with another child who desired to play with that specific object. A child might be kind enough to ask a child who is usually rejected to be his or her partner. A child might admit to being tagged even though the tag was not obvious. These are but three of the many types of behaviors one would consider desirable, and certainly the qualities of sharing, kindness, and honesty, among others are valuable. These behaviors depict moral content. Moral content, however, is sometimes misleading. The first child could

have traded or shared the equipment because of wanting something the other child had. In the second incident a more skillful child might ask a less competent child to play because of the opportunity to dominate another and appear more competent by comparison. And the child who admitted being tagged may have merely wanted to sit out (be eliminated in an elimination type game) and have no conviction toward honesty. The rationale behind the choice of behavior (the process) determines the morality of behavior. (p. 94)

Corresponding to the insight that intent is central to the meaning of behavior, the four remaining empirical investigations all sought to impact moral reasoning as well as moral action.

Wandzilak, Carroll, and Ansorge (1988) designed a physical education program reflecting a model of values development proposed by Wandzilak (1985). The goal was to produce positive changes in moral reasoning, sportspersonship perceptions, and behaviors in junior high school boys. The intervention was carried out in the context of basketball practices. On the first day, to heighten awareness of sportspersonlike behavior, students were asked to define *sportsmanship* in writing. At the end of the practice, they were asked to offer examples of good and bad sportspersonship. The main intervention involved discussing moral issues and dilemmas relevant to basketball during a 15-minute period in each practice session. Results, however, were inconclusive. No significant differences between the intervention group and a control group were found, though insignificant changes in the predicted direction were observed.

A study by Bredemeier, Weiss, Shields, and Shewchuk (1986), conducted in a summer sports camp, was designed to compare the effectiveness of social learning and structural developmental prescriptions for moral pedagogy. Eighty-four children, aged 5 to 7, were matched on relevant variables and randomly assigned to one of three classes: social learning, structural developmental, or control. Each class was taught by two experienced physical educators who had been given special training on the instructional strategies of their assigned theoretical orientation. All classes shared similar curricula, and one moral theme was emphasized each week.

The social learning class was guided by an adult-centered modeling and reinforcement strategy. The structural developmental group used a peer-oriented intervention strategy based on the contention that dialogue aimed at resolving interpersonal conflicts is a potent means for promoting moral growth. The instructor watched for natural disruptions among the children and also created artificial conditions likely to result in conflicts of interest. The instructor then facilitated discussion and resolution.

Results indicated significant pre- to posttest gains on a Piagetian intentionality task and a measure of distributive justice in both experimental groups but not in the control group. However, the multivariate analysis demonstrating that the experimental groups were more effective than the control group only approached significance ($p < .07$). No clear differences between experimental groups were found on the moral measures.

In addition to the moral measures, coping and defending scores were obtained for the children both before and following the intervention (Shields & Bredemeier, 1989). Both coping and defending were significantly influenced by instructional strategies: The structural developmental group improved more in their coping skills than either of the other groups, which did not differ from each other. Defending scores in both experimental groups decreased (i.e., improved) significantly more than in the control group. The authors hypothesized that defensive processing declined in both experimental groups because both teaching strategies helped to create a low-stress, ego-affirming atmosphere that lessened the need to defend. However, the adult-dominated nature of the social learning pedagogy may have accounted for its failure to foster improvement in coping similar to the gains in the structural developmental group. Unfortunately, the ego-processing measure was an experimental, nonvalidated instrument, so results need to be viewed with caution.

A study by Romance, Weiss, and Bockoven (1986) is of considerable interest because of its creative structural-developmental teaching strategies. The study examined the effectiveness of a specially designed physical education program on the moral development of elementary school children. The program involved implementing five specific strategies:

1. Built-in dilemma/dialogue (BIDD)
2. Built-in dilemma/problem solve (BID-PS)
3. Create your own game (CYOG)
4. Two cultures
5. The listening bench

In the BIDD strategy, students participated in a game or a drill with a built-in moral dilemma. For example, they were asked to substitute themselves out of a game when they felt the need to do so. In the BID-PS strategy, the game or drill had a built-in dilemma, and the students were encouraged to change the game or drill as they wished. Students made up games in the CYOG strategy, adhering to guidelines of inclusion, fun, and opportunity. In the two-cultures strategy, a game or drill was presented in two different ways, one with a built-in dilemma and one without. Students played both ways and then discussed the difference. Finally, the listening-bench strategy dictated that when students were involved in a moral conflict they sit on the listening bench, turn on a tape recorder, and discuss their dilemma using posted guidelines.

The subjects were two fifth-grade PE classes ($N = 32$), one serving as the control group. Apart from implementing the specific strategies, the two groups used an identical physical activity curriculum during an 8-week program. Results were encouraging. The experimental group effectively promoted moral growth and did so significantly more than the control group.

Finally, Sharon Stoll and Jennifer Beller have designed a number of creative and noteworthy programs to promote moral development among intercollegiate athletes through workshops, courses, and seminars. One of their projects, which served as the basis for a study, was the implementation of a "Moral Reasoning in Sport" course (Beller & Stoll, 1992). The 37 student athletes enrolled in the course, together with 132 student athletes who served as controls, were pre-, post-, and post-posttested on the Hahm-Beller Values Choice Inventory in the Sport Milieu (an objectively scored instrument designed to assess the use of principled reasoning about sport dilemmas) and Rest's Defining Issues Test. The intervention consisted of a two-credit semester course emphasizing honesty, responsibility, justice, and beneficence taught using a modified Socratic method. Results were generally positive, with significant pre- to posttest gains on the Hahm-Beller, gains that were sustained at the time of the post-posttest. Oddly, the scores for the control student athletes actually declined significantly from pre- to posttest. In contrast, no significant changes on the Defining Issues Test scores were found. Unfortunately, validity and reliability data has not yet been published on the Hahm-Beller, and it appears to us to be vulnerable to a social desirability response set.

Before beginning our recommendations section, we need to mention one more model of physical education, though it does not neatly fit any theoretical category. Hellison's efforts to develop a model of physical education useful with "at-risk" youth is notable for its thoroughness and practicality.

Hellison's "Self-Responsibility" Model

Don Hellison (1978, 1983a, 1983b, 1985, 1986; Hellison & Templin, 1991) has described a model of physical education designed to promote participants' sense of responsibility. It has evolved over the years in the crucible of practical experience and is often referred to by curriculum experts as an exemplary approach to fostering social development through physical education (Bain, 1988; Jewett & Bain, 1985; Siedentop, Mand, & Taggart, 1986; Winnick, 1990). The model has received limited support from case study research (DeBusk & Hellison, 1989; Hellison, 1978).

In concept, the model is relatively simple and straightforward. It centers on the description of five heuristic levels, each level reflecting social goals toward which students can progressively work. The levels (summarized in Table 11.1) can be presented to students as a developmental progression or simply as an organized step-by-step process. Clearly, the levels are not intended as "stages" in the Piagetian sense but as useful devices for focusing attention and directing effort. In addition to outlining these levels, Hellison (1985) identifies sublevels and various teaching strategies (e.g., awareness, experience, choice, problem solving, self-reflection, and counseling time) that can be used across the levels.

We concur that Hellison has provided one of the best-articulated models for promoting social development through physical education. Nonetheless, we believe some problems are associated with it. Hellison (1985) clearly states that the levels at the center of the model are not developmental, but in practice they are often presented to students as reflecting a quasi-developmental progression.

Table 11.1   Hellison's Levels of Responsibility

Level 0—Irresponsibility. This level describes students who are unmotivated and whose behavior is disruptive. The goal of the physical educator is to help them get their behavior under control (thereby advancing them to Level 1) or to remove them from the setting so they do not interfere with others' rights.

Level 1—Self-control. Students at this level may not participate in the day's activities, but they control their behavior enough to not need to be removed from the setting. The goal of the physical educator is to help these students become involved in the activities (thereby advancing them to Level 2) or, minimally, to learn to respect the rights and feelings of others enough that their behavior and attitude do not interfere with teaching and learning.

Level 2—Involvement. Students at Level 2 participate in the physical education activities. Involvement may take many forms, from going through the motions to setting and pursuing objectives. The goal of the physical educator is to encourage students to take increasing responsibility for their own development and definitions of success. For example, students may come to define success as effort, improvement, goal setting, achievement of a norm or standard, or being socially responsible as a player or leader.

Level 3—Self-direction. This level describes students who can work effectively and independently on self-improvement in areas of personally identified need or aspiration. The goal of the physical educator is to enable them to acquire the skills needed to work independently and set realistic goals. A relevant knowledge base is also critical, and students need to be gradually confronted with broader philosophical issues that connect with their self-defined objectives: Who do I want to be? Why do I want to . . . ?''

Level 4—Caring. Up to this point, the only necessary regard for others is a respect for their fundamental rights. At Level 4, students move beyond the focus on self and are motivated by an other-regarding, prosocial orientation. The goal of the physical educator is to provide opportunities to cooperate, give support, show concern, help others, and the like.

Note. Summaries drawn from Hellison and Templin, 1991.

It is irrelevant, from one standpoint, whether the levels are intended in theory to be developmental. What is important is the communication that occurs. As we view the model, the organization of the levels communicates a view of the human person as more fundamentally egocentric than sociocentric, more prone to eruptions of uncontrolled destructive impulses than prone to shared experiences of cooperation, interdependency, and mutual regard. Perhaps these assumptions are useful in working with at-risk youths, but they may easily become self-fulfilling prophecies.

An alternate way to conceptualize the levels is as simultaneously operating components of responsible behavior. It may be that a person is caring (Level IV), self-directed (Level III), and involved (Level II), but she loses her temper

(Level I) on one day and fails in a different component on another day. Rather than asking, Where are you today in the sequence? better questions might be, Which component do you think might give you the most trouble today? and Where are you feeling strong? Unfortunately, this might undermine the motivation elicited by a progressive sequence of levels.

Another approach might be to retain the levels but to insert Level IV between the first and second levels. Perhaps a person may not feel ready for personal involvement but would like to assist others. Still another variation would be to redefine Level III from self-direction to group direction, with an emphasis on cooperatively designing goals for the entire class. Our point in offering these variations is to indicate that there are no *necessary* connections among the levels and to encourage educators to adapt them quite liberally to emphasize their own goals and values.

Finally, in our view, the goal of self-responsibility is too individual. Hellison (1985) acknowledges this limitation, and the inclusion of the fourth level is designed to partially overcome it. But the main thrust of the program remains *self*-responsibility. One way to overcome this limitation would be to add group goals, some of which relate to the development of a moral atmosphere that emphasizes community, corporate responsibility, cooperation, and mutual assistance. Combining Hellison's responsibility model with one that emphasizes the development of a sense of community and community norms might avoid the severance of the self and the social.

Promoting Moral Character Through Physical Education

In this section we summarize and extend the material we have presented, offering specific recommendations to physical educators. Rather than organize our recommendations according to the character virtues, we use the more instructionally useful categories of context, curriculum, and method. These three traditional teaching and learning categories loosely parallel the three dimensions of influence we identified as part of the moral action model: contextual, personal competence, and ego-processing influences.

Recommendations Pertaining to Context

The contextual variables that we identified as most central to moral action are the goal structure, the moral atmosphere, domain cues, and power relations. We offer recommendations related to each:

- The physical educator can create opportunities and cooperative activities in which participants need to coordinate perspectives and develop a sense of common purpose. These activities will encourage perspective taking, empathy, moral reasoning, and social problem-solving skills. Beedy (1988) suggests that cooperative activities are particularly important for children before they are introduced to competitive team sports.

- The moral atmosphere can be developed through group meetings in which children or youth are asked to reflect on what norms they want to guide the class. Frequent reflection on where they are relative to the norms may prove helpful. Activities that promote a sense of ''we-ness'' will help facilitate the sense of community necessary for a constructive moral atmosphere.
- Clearly differentiating moral from nonmoral issues will help students prioritize these appropriately. For example, Hellison (1985) requires students to recognize other students' moral rights without requiring, at the same time, that they obey the more conventional rules.
- Clearly, the physical educator is in a more powerful position than the students. Power can be employed as ''power over'' or ''power with.'' The physical educator should strive to exercise power in a way that enables students to claim their own power. This can be done by allowing students to assume as much responsibility as appropriate for their developmental level and individual needs. Also, the physical educator should seek to equalize power among students by working to reduce racism, sexism, classism, and other sources of group-based power differentials (see Shields, 1986).

Recommendations Relating to Curriculum

Compassion, fairness, sportspersonship, and integrity build on competencies in the areas of perspective taking, moral reasoning, the self-structure, and autonomy and social problem-solving skills. All these competencies can be promoted through physical education. Teachers need to be aware of the developmental characteristics of the age group with which they are working and tailor the general recommendations offered here to the appropriate level. Specifically, we recommend the following:

- Of first importance is simply incorporating moral themes into the curriculum. PE teachers need to engage students in dialogue about moral values involved in the activities of physical education. Moral issues arise not only in competitive sports but in every aspect of the curriculum. For example, it is worth discussing the moral issues raised by any physical activity that involves physical risk. Another issue is how to give everyone equal respect when people have different abilities. As Meakin (1982) notes, ''Just as worthy of discussion are the ethics of cooperation, the ideals of group loyalty, personal endeavor, and setting oneself challenges, all of which figure in PE activities'' (p. 80).
- Perspective-taking ability can be fostered by having students frequently rotate their activities so that each student is learning about a game or physical activity from multiple vantage points. Empathy and compassion can be fostered by helping students process the affective dimensions of these experiences. For example, say the teacher gives a lesson on gymnastics and students are divided into pairs. The teacher can help students be aware of and responsive to the partners' anxieties, fears, and frustrations as well as the pride,

joy, and exhilaration experienced when their partners face and eventually master challenging tasks.

- Perspective taking and empathy can also be fostered through cooperative games and reciprocal teaching (Horrocks, 1980). Orlick (1978) provides plenty of examples of cooperative games and a clear rationale for their use (see also Grineski, 1989a). Having older or more skilled students work with younger or less skilled students can also be beneficial for developing these psychological capacities.

- Development of moral reasoning ability can be easily incorporated into the curriculum. Figley (1984) suggests that hypothetical moral dilemmas about sport and physical activity issues might initially be used. Hypothetical dilemmas are useful in sensitizing students to moral issues, developing their dialogue skills, and sharpening their understanding of moral concepts (see Horrocks, 1980 for use of hypothetical "sport" dilemmas). Hypothetical dilemmas also enable the teacher to practice the art of facilitating moral discussion (see Reimer, Paolitto, & Hersh, 1983, for a good presentation of the topic). After an initial period of using hypothetical dilemmas, it is probably best to focus on real issues that arise in the gym or on the playground (Figley). Real issues are more engaging, challenging, and provocative. The various strategies devised by Romance (1984, 1988; Romance, Weiss, & Bockoven, 1986) are excellent means for creating real-life moral dilemmas in a physical activity setting.

- Teachers can facilitate moral reasoning development by including in their curricular planning opportunities for students to discuss games and sports as "moral" practices. Students can be encouraged to think about how game rules, for example, have been designed to give balanced opportunity to offense and defense, to protect the physical well-being of players, to ensure conditions of fairness—all of which are rooted in moral concepts. Also, students can be asked to design games that reflect moral principles.

- Moral identity and sportspersonship can be fostered through values clarification exercises that let students prioritize their values (Eskridge, 1977) and by giving them ample opportunities to act on their convictions. The process of clarifying values, acting, reflecting, and clarifying anew can be a regular part of the curriculum. The physical educator also needs to understand the distinction between moral values and conventional values and to communicate the priority of the moral over the conventional.

- Autonomy can be encouraged by including in the curriculum plenty of opportunity for selecting personal goals, taking responsibility, and acting independently. Galasso (1988), for example, argues that students should organize intramural programs, officiate their own games, and deal with discipline problems. Many of the recommendations built into Hellison's (1985) self-responsibility model are useful in promoting autonomy.

- Social problem-solving skills can be enhanced by including in the curriculum opportunities to negotiate perspectives. Again, many of the activities that

Romance recommends (in particular, create your own game and listening bench strategies) are useful in promoting social problem-solving skills.

Recommendations Regarding Process

How instructors teach is probably just as important as what they teach. It is crucial that the methods of teaching not contradict the content of what is taught. If, for example, the instructor verbally affirms the importance of autonomous moral action but uses autocratic methods, constructive moral education is unlikely.

The methods and processes of teaching impact the moral atmosphere, the communication of moral content, and the facilitation of ego processing. The first two of these are probably the most important to emphasize in educational planning because the development of coping processes is largely "self-actional" (Haan, 1977a). Individuals construct their preferred styles of coping through extended and intimate interaction with their most immediate social environment, typically the family. Furthermore, the simple notion of "like begets like" or "coping begets coping" does not hold. Highly defensive parents can have coping children, and parents who prefer one hierarchical organization of coping processes may have children who construct a different pattern of preference (Haan). The implication is that the physical educator should be more concerned with avoiding teaching methods and strategies that arouse considerable defense than in explicitly teaching to promote coping. However, the instructor should not entirely avoid arousing stress; moderate levels of stress tend to energize the coping processes and can provide a constructive environment for their practice and promotion. With these comments in mind, we offer four more recommendations to facilitate a positive moral atmosphere, promote moral content, and avoid the need to defend:

- PE teachers should model desired moral virtues. Whether modeling works through processes of imitation (as social learning theorists believe) or by providing context-sensitive information cues (as structural developmentalists believe) is not of great practical significance. In either case, the instructor needs to model those virtues that the students are being encouraged to adopt. Similarly, every available means should be used to provide role models from the world of sport and physical activity who embrace the virtues. Real stories of real athletes who sacrificed a chance at victory to aid an opponent, for example, will help clarify and make realistic the virtue of sportspersonship.
- Physical educators should use organized small group activity extensively. Small groups tend to keep everyone engaged, provide a setting in which interpersonal issues are likely to arise and be dealt with, and encourage the growth of a supportive social environment. Figley (1984) suggests that a group of five or six is small enough to allow involvement yet large enough to provide a number of viewpoints. Small groups can be used to teach and practice physical skills, discuss value issues, play games, construct games, and any number of other activities.

- To help students reason about rules and requirements, rather than just obey dictates, teachers should seek to move as much as possible from the declarative to the interrogative in their communications (Figley, 1984). For example, imagine that Marisol is the batter in a softball game. She hits the ball and throws the bat wildly on her way to first base. Rather than telling Marisol, "Don't throw the bat," it would be more educationally sound to ask, "What might happen if you continue to throw the bat like that?" Teachers should get in the habit of posing questions: "How would it feel if . . . ?" "Who has an idea of how we can . . . ?" "If everyone did . . . what would happen?"
- Perhaps most importantly, we recommend that physical educators incorporate as much democracy into their classes as feasible given the developmental level with which they are working (Figley, 1984). Even elementary school children are quite able to democratically decide on some of the goals and contents of their education, though this clearly cannot be left entirely in their hands.

Informal Games and Moral Character

Before we address organized sports, a few comments are in order about the role of informal games and child-organized sports. These often occupy something of a middle ground between play and organized sport. Although they display more organization and structure than children's play, informal games remain continuous with the play impulse.

Devereux (1976) has written provocatively about the importance of informal games to children's social and moral development. He cites disturbing evidence that organized youth sport programs have eroded the once rich culture of children's games, drawing his argument from cross-cultural and historical analyses, combined with no small amount of nostalgic reflection on his own childhood. His observations in Japan and Israel led him to conclude that children in those societies have a rich repertoire of games that they play with little or no adult supervision. His somewhat informal observations are buttressed by more rigorous studies, such as those done by Eifermann (1971) in Israel documenting the existence of more than 2,000 children's games and by Opie and Opie (1969) documenting more than 2,500 different games spontaneously played by English children. In contrast to these game-rich children's cultures, Devereux observed, American children suffer from game poverty. Rather than spend their time playing informal games, American children watch television! Furthermore, Devereux (1976) has suggested,

the availability of a mass television audience has had a lot to do with the extraordinary ascendancy of Big Leaguism in America, and, perhaps indirectly, of Little Leaguism as well. By focusing the attention of millions of viewers on a handful of major sports, and on the heroic teams and individual stars within them, we have converted ourselves to a nation of spectators. (p. 40)

The problem, as Devereux (1976) has defined it, is not so much that children are attracted to the model of professional sports (though some are) but that they have become aware of the cultural importance of selected elite sports, and particularly how seriously parents and other close adults take them. Even for children with no special sport talent or interest, the model of the "major" sports is present and salient. As Devereux noted, "Against the heroic, if perhaps somewhat myopic, standards of Big League or Little League sports, who would dare propose a simple game of puss in the corner, capture the flag, or red rover?" (p. 41).

The decline of an informal games culture is significant in part because of the unique psychosocial benefits that informal games provide. Coakley (1983) has posited that when children play informal games, they are interested primarily in four things: action, involvement, maintaining a close score, and opportunities to reaffirm friendships. Except for maintaining a close score, these closely parallel Devereux's (1976) observations. The psychosocial benefits of informal games are derived from the fact that children can experiment endlessly with game variations and relational interactions in their pursuit of such goals. This gives them the opportunity to gain experience in a variety of cognitive and emotional processes that parallel in a scaled-down form those needed for mature participation in the broader culture. The availability of a rich repertoire of games of varying complexity and peculiar mixes of skill, strategy, and chance enables children to become increasingly adept at modifying their cognitive and emotional approaches to differing contextual demands and configurations. Throughout the process of development, games provide a "buffered learning environment" because, as Lewin (1944) noted, they function on a "plane of unreality" wherein failures are not serious, dangers are not overwhelming, and risks lack finality.

To make concrete and tangible the beneficial context that informal games provide for development, Devereux recalls a game he used to play in his own childhood called "one-o-cat," a variation on baseball. After describing the game, Devereux (1976) observes that

> precisely because there was no official rule book and no adult or even other child designated as rule enforcer, we somehow had to improvise the whole thing; this entailed endless hassles about whether a ball was fair or foul, whether a runner was safe or out, or more generally, simply about what was fair. We gradually learned to understand the invisible boundary conditions of our relationships to each other. Don't be a poor sport or the other kids won't want you to play with them. Don't push your point so hard that the kid with the only catcher's mitt will quit the game. Pitch a bit more gently to the littler kids so they can have some fun, too.
>   . . . The game was so structured that it required us to use our utmost ingenuity to discover and understand the hidden rules behind the rules—the

general principles which make games fair, fun, and interesting, and which had to govern our complex relationships with each other; the recognition of the subtle differences in skills, including social skills, which gave added respect and informal authority to some; the ability to handle poor sports, incompetents, cry-babies, little kids, and girls, when the easy out of excluding them from the game entirely was somehow impractical.*

Many of the practices that Devereux (1976) found so helpful about informal games are connected with what Haan (1978, 1991; Haan et al., 1985) calls moral dialogue. Indeed, informal games provide optimal conditions for promoting moral growth, according to Haan's perspective. There are many opportunities for dialogue and negotiation, disruptions and restorations in a context where participants are interdependent and mutual interests need to be coordinated. Crossley (1988) similarly suggests that informal games provide an ideal context for learning moral values because they allow for the creation of rights and correlated obligations through the formation of agreements.

Unfortunately, many of the benefits that children's informal games provide are threatened by adult-organized youth sports, where rules are set, not negotiated. The plethora of informal games is replaced by a relatively few standardized sports. Self-regulation is turned over to coaches and umpires. The buffered environment is replaced by a pressure cooker as sports become observed and evaluated by anxious parents and coaches. Fun is sapped by the need to perform and win. Internal motivation gives way to external.

Organized sport programs may have several deficits for those who participate, but, worse still, many children have had the informal game culture removed without even being able to participate in the world of organized youth sports. Devereux (1976) referred to the high school setting to make this point:

In a high school of 2,000 students, only a relative handful get to participate even on the squads of any of the major teams. All the rest are consigned to the role of frenzied spectators at interscholastic meets, or, still worse, in many sport-minded communities, to being nonparticipant nonspectators, perceived by adults and peers alike as odd-balls or pariahs. (p. 53)

Perhaps Devereux has exaggerated the situation. Research by Kleiber and Roberts (1983), for example, suggests that the existence of organized youth sport programs is not always associated with low rates of participation in informal games, as Devereux seems to suggest. In fact, some researchers suggest that participation in organized sport programs can provide stimulation and prototypes for involvement in informal games (Lever, 1976, 1978; Wohl, 1970, 1979).

---

*Note. From "Backyard versus Little League Baseball: The Impoverishment of Children's Games" by E.C. Devereux. In *Social Problems in Athletics* (pp. 48-49) by D. Landers (Ed.), 1976, Urbana: University of Illinois Press, 1976. Reprinted by permission.

Informal games are also not necessarily the moral paradise that Devereux implies. As Coakley (1990) points out, bigger and stronger children may exploit smaller and weaker ones, methods of team selection can leave less skilled children feeling embarrassed or rejected, and cruel comments may be directed toward the unskilled or those who simply differ from local peer group norms. Informal games and organized sports alike often mirror the prejudices and distortions of the broader culture. As Devereux perhaps unintentionally communicated in one of the earlier quotes, informal games reflect the sexist patterns of the culture, with girls sometimes being excluded, given lesser attention, or ridiculed (Lever, 1976, 1978). Coakley and Westkott (1984) argue that organized programs provide a better opportunity for equalizing sport involvement and are especially important for girls because they provide a working knowledge of game models that can be carried over into informal games.

Despite these major qualifications, the main lines of Devereux's (1976) argument are valid. Informal games provide an extremely rich environment for moral development, and it does seem that children in contemporary America have an impoverished repertoire. If this is so, what can be done? Unfortunately, as Devereux himself notes, not very much. Very broad cultural forces have congealed to promote the competitive, institutionalized, and commodified model of youth sports. It would be idealistic in the extreme to suggest that a handful of individuals could reverse this trend. Furthermore, "in the long run, nothing extinguishes self-organized play more effectively than does action to promote it" (Opie & Opie, 1969, p. 16). Still, a few recommendations seem in order:

- Physical educators and adults involved in youth recreation and youth sport programs can provide opportunities for children to organize and play their own games as well as those the adults promote.
- Physical educators and adults involved in youth recreation and sport can reaffirm the value of informal games and spontaneous play in their contacts with parents, school administrators, and community organizations.
- Adults who work with children can introduce them to games that are in danger of being lost. Many marvelous games that have existed for generations, passed on through oral tradition in youth culture, are now endangered species. These can be taught, but the best role for the adult after introducing them is simply to get out of the way (Devereux, 1976).
- Finally, adults who work with children can modify sport contexts to incorporate some of the advantages of informal games. Because this recommendation is mirrored in other parts of this chapter, we won't elaborate here.

Youth Sport and Moral Character

Sport has been the main physical activity considered throughout our book, so some of what we say here has been developed more completely in other places.

Nonetheless, it may help you to have key points rehearsed. Because organized and interscholastic youth sports encompass the age range during which developmental change is most concentrated, we focus our comments and recommendations there. Other levels of sport also are important, but they are probably less amenable to changes in their goals and practices. In a different discussion we will address more specifically collegiate sport, professional sport, and adult recreational sport. Still, many of our points here would apply equally to older sport participants as well.

Before we discuss the potential of youth sport to contribute to character formation, however, we will respond to two challenges to the notion that sport can be useful for moral education. Some suggest that sport provides a context for the "display" of character but not for its formation. Others suggest that combining character-building goals with competition is no less than contradictory. Both arguments need to be addressed.

Sport as Context for the Display of Character

Kniker (1974) gives sportscaster Heywood Hale Broun credit for first quipping "Sports do not build character but reveal it." The argument is that sport action reveals the athlete's character but does not itself contribute to the athlete's character (Edwards, 1973; Ogilvie & Tutko, 1971; Sheehan & Alsop, 1972). Such a claim calls into question the usefulness of sport to moral education. But the claim is deficient because it fails to recognize that every display of character contributes to character. When action is taken, the consequences of that action provide feedback to the actor and other observers of the act. The feedback then informs future action.

The display argument also can be premised on the assumption that sport is so removed from daily life that action occurring in sport will have no relevance to everyday action (e.g., Reddiford, 1981). In contrast, we assume that sport is not so severed from the everyday world that transfer of learning is improbable. Because sport is a cultural practice in which people often invest considerable emotional and temporal resources, and because these resources are quite "real," our assumption seems plausible. As Arnold (1984a) points out, sport, just like numerous other practices, is a vehicle for self-expression and self-fulfillment. It is therefore to be taken seriously from a moral viewpoint.

The realness of sport does not mean, however, that participants don't experience an element of "unreality" or "separateness." Much like the "world within a world" of play (Huizinga, 1955), sport exists in a bracketed spatial-temporal reality (Weiss, 1969). Coutts (1968) has suggested that one motive for sport participation is precisely its separateness and the attendant freedom it entails.

To clarify the meaning of the separateness of sport it is essential to understand the frame of reference or mode of discourse being used. From the phenomenological perspective—the perspective of the experiencing subject—sport clearly is separated from everyday life. However, from a sociological perspective, sport processes closely resemble those in other arenas of life. Both of these frames of reference are necessary when considering the educative potential of sport.

Sport certainly embodies cultural values (both positive and negative), and sport provides opportunities for moral reflection and action. It also is possible, however, for the participant to psychologically isolate the sport experience so that the moral norms of everyday life are not experienced as binding. This can be done in a coping or defending way. To the extent that the usual moral demand of equalization is set aside in a playful and nonserious way, a form of "game reasoning" can be engaged in that is simply an enjoyable deviation and a limited release from standard moral obligation. In such a circumstance, the underlying necessity to maintain fairness and avoid harm is observed. However, sport can also be used as a defensive rationalization for immoral action. The defensive mode of game reasoning is revealed when the moral underpinnings of sport are themselves set aside. This is most likely to occur when extrinsic motivations become salient, so that game outcome becomes more important than game process.

Competition and Moral Education

Another argument against sport as a viable context for moral education comes from those who maintain that all competition is diametrically opposed to the goals of the moral educator. Fielding (1976), for example, asks whether approval of competition in schools, competitive sports included, could render legitimate "behavior within whose boundaries there thrived a form of compulsive narcissism whose staple diet consisted largely in the humiliation of fellow pupils" (pp. 126-127). Similarly, Kohn (1986) states that "competition entails a kind of perverse interdependence: our fates are linked in that I cannot succeed unless you fail. Thus I regard you merely as someone over whom to triumph. . . . This dynamic is found in virtually all exploitative relationships" (p. 138).

We do not accept the view that competition is inherently evil. When the internal aim of competition—winning—is not the exclusive aim of the participant, competition can be a mutually enjoyable and satisfying means of improving abilities, challenging boundaries, and expressing one's affective need for exhilaration, joy, and community. In other words, sport participants need to strive to win (otherwise the competition would collapse), but fulfilling that internal demand of competition does not need to be the only (or even primary) goal. In chapter 10 we spoke of sportspersonship as the virtue that straddles play and work, nonseriousness and seriousness, process and product orientations—the art of keeping perspective.

Though we do not accept the extreme view of competition, we do believe that there are many pitfalls associated with competition, particularly in a culture like the North American one that puts such a premium on competitive outcome. This can be seen, for example, in the way some sports in their elite or professional form have acquired an ethos that clearly violates moral norms. The violence associated with sports like professional ice hockey is one example; the drug use in sports like bodybuilding is another. However, the fact that some sports are associated with unscrupulous behavior does not mean that youth should be shielded from these sports or that participation in them is necessarily miseducative. No doubt the young ice hockey competitor is well aware of the sport's ethos but, as Meakin (1982) suggests, that awareness can provide an educational opportunity. Young people can learn to distinguish between *is* and *ought* and—more important, because most already make that distinction in theory—can learn to take personal responsibility for moving an immoral *is* toward the *ought*. Some sports may exhibit high levels of immoral action, but they need not, and participants can learn to take responsibility for the norms that guide their own sport involvement.

Moral Education Through Youth Sport: Defining the Possibilities

Youth sport provides a fertile environment for the development of character. Time with a team is frequently an intense emotional experience, rich in social interaction, abundant in moral challenges, replete with opportunity for the exercise of moral virtue. To amplify on the character-building potential of sport, we return to our four-virtue model of moral character.

Youth Sport and Compassion

Compassion, as the term implies, involves a "feeling with" others. It is rooted in moral capacities that enable us to perceive and interpret moral situations with sensitivity and responsiveness. Compassion builds on such structural competencies as role taking and perspective taking; it reflects the extensive use of empathy.

As we noted in chapter 6, sport likely contributes to role-taking and perspective-taking competence. Game strategy invariably requires the exercise of these skills. On the other hand, competition may inhibit the use of empathy because experiencing the emotions of one's competitors may be interpreted as distracting. But if competition tends to inhibit empathy, the skillful coach can put that fact to the player's advantage. One of the problems with empathy is that it tends to be selective. We are naturally more empathic toward those we know, those similar to us, or those close at hand. Hoffman (1987), in fact, encourages a moral education program where children learn to overcome the natural selectiveness of empathy. Since opponents are among those to whom empathy is not readily extended, sport may provide an excellent context for practicing the extension of empathy beyond usual bounds. A coach can encourage empathy for an opponent who has been injured or who has suffered a disappointing loss. Similarly, in our highly competitive society, people need to cultivate the capacity for compassion in contexts where the goal structure pushes in the opposite direction. If sport can be a learning ground for handling competition constructively, it can enhance development of the virtue of compassion in its participants.

Youth Sport and Fairness

Sport philosophers often have argued that fairness is essential to sport and game experience (e.g., Fraleigh, 1984; McIntosh, 1979; Meakin, 1981, 1982; Simon, 1991; Zeigler, 1984). In connection with the idea that fairness undergirds sports, Meakin (1981) writes,

> Take, for instance, the "ibw" law in cricket: while this is functional in that it helps to define what counts as "being out," it is of a moral character in that its purpose is to secure a fair balance in the contest between bowler and batsman. . . . Again, the rule proscribing scything tackles in soccer is moral in being designed not only to prevent injury but also to allow fair scope to the talents of the [player] with the ball. (p. 245)

Though fairness might be implicit in sport experiences, many participants may not consciously reflect on this dimension. A major aim of all those involved in sport should be to encourage such reflection and to encourage action congruent with a mature appreciation of the centrality of fairness. This is not an optional educational task tacked on to the already heavy responsibilities of the coach or physical educator. To paraphrase philosopher John Rawls (1971), fairness is the first virtue of sport, as truth is of systems of thought. If this is true, those responsible for teaching sport skills are necessarily involved in teaching fairness, for the exercise of those skills is tethered to a social practice that is grounded in fairness. To teach sport without concomitantly helping participants appreciate fairness is equivalent to teaching mathematics without concern for truth or counseling techniques without regard for mental health.

Fairness is nurtured best in the context of a supportive community. And sport is a setting where it is possible, in theory, for participants to experience moral community. In fact, Park (1980) draws from the anthropological and philosophical literature to support the claim that sport is a primary institution in contemporary society for the experience of "communitas" (i.e., an experience of creativity, freedom, and human solidarity) and that communitas is essential for promoting moral growth. Berlage (1982b) makes a related point, that the family's involvement in children's sport may provide a sense of community that is largely absent in the broader culture. Just what type of community surrounds particular sport experiences is not determined by sport per se, but it can be formed and shaped by the participants. The possibility exists that a community can be developed in keeping with high moral standards.

Youth Sport and Sportspersonship

In the sport context, sportspersonship is the virtue of coordinating the play impulse with the competitive one in light of moral goals. The underlying competencies most directly relevant to this virtue are a task motivational orientation and a moral-centered self-structure. Sport is clearly an arena where these orientations can be fostered and where sportspersonship can be exercised. The coach, for example, can help her players overcome dualisms of product and process, victory and defeat, ends and means, all of which interfere with the coordination of play and seriousness.

Youth Sport and Integrity

Integrity is rooted in the ability to unify one's complex and sometimes contradictory psychological dynamics—desires, impulses, cognitions, affects—so that one can act in a self-consciously coherent and deliberate way. Integrity also demands that one have the interpersonal skills to negotiate in good faith with others who may take a different position on critical issues.

The concentration needed for successful sport action may provide a good model for psychological integration through focused action. Remembering that sport is an action arena made possible by a mutual commitment to fairness on the part of participants, sport leaders can integrate moral concerns right along with strategic ones when teaching sport skills.

A great deal of sport action is habitual, and sport behavior comprises largely overlearned skills. This fact, sometimes advanced as a reason that sport action is amoral, provides a window of opportunity for exercising integrity. At all stages of the learning of sport skills, a moral commitment both to fairness and to the avoidance of harm can be integrated with a focus on strategic, competitive action so that habitual sport behavior will reflect the full unification of the participant's goals.

Youth sport also provides ample opportunity for the development of social problem-solving skills. For example, deviations from the ideal sport contest are frequent, whether intentional or otherwise, and sometimes result in disruptions of relationships. If Risto hurts Kwon while they are wrestling and Kwon is upset, the two may need to negotiate both their relationship and the appropriate wrestling tactics.

Promoting Moral Character Through Youth Sport

The concern for promoting moral character through sport, as we saw in the last chapter, is an ancient one. With the increasing popularity of youth sports over past decades, however, practitioners and researchers are giving renewed emphasis to their potential role in psychosocial development. Of course, as we have stated repeatedly, the quality of the sport experience is what matters. This quality in turn derives from the quality of the leadership, the structural qualities of the sport itself, the social milieu in which it occurs, and the characteristics of the participants, to name only the most salient factors. Keeping our moral education objectives in mind, we offer recommendations relevant to coaches, athletes, sports administrators, and parents.

Recommendations for Coaches

1. We recommend that coaches carefully reflect on their own coaching philosophies and objectives. Martens (1988) recommends a simple philosophy grounded in the slogan "Athletes first, winning second" (p. 299). Devereux (1976) suggests that coaches keep their eye on the child, not on the ball. Stoll (1993) has written a helpful book that can assist coaches in identifying their moral presuppositions. After coaches clarify philosophy and objectives, they must reflect on their actions to see if there is congruence with their stated aims.

2. Stated very generally, we recommend that coaches treat each child in a manner that encourages full and integrated development as a human being. As Galasso (1988) put it, "The coach must be mindful that the rights of children must be respected and that they must not be sacrificed at the altar of gold" (p. 336).

3. Coaches should encourage sport participants to reflect on the moral underpinnings of sport. Ideally, this reflection should have begun in physical education classes, but it may well not have. And if it has, continued reflection is important as the sport participant matures and gains experience in the world of sport.

4. Coaches should expect players to treat opponents with respect, helping them understand that playing well does not require dehumanizing opponents, even in high-contact sports. They should also help players understand that the exhilaration that often accompanies victory need not result in a lack of empathy for opponents, nor does the disappointment of defeat necessarily make it impossible to share in the victor's sense of accomplishment.

5. Coaches should tailor their styles and emphases to the appropriate age level. Lombardo (1982) accurately notes that most youth sport coaches model their coaching style and objectives after coaches of professional athletes. The needs of children and professional athletes, however, are quite distinct. And the needs of all ages of children are likewise not the same. We will take a moment to elaborate on this crucial point.

Beedy (1988) divides youth sport programs into four age levels (8-10, 11-12, 13-15, 16-18) and makes recommendations relevant to each. At the youngest level, ages 8 to 10, cooperation takes precedence over competition, particularly within the team. This means that children should not compete to obtain positions or playing time. Equal participation, cooperation, and skill development should be the major goals. Beedy (1988) further suggests that sport rules be modified to emphasize perspective taking and empathy. For example, in soccer the rules can be modified so that all players have to touch the ball before a shot can be made or no player can make two successive shots. Coaches can also have players rotate positions frequently to experience the game from different perspectives.

When children are 11 and 12 years old, they can be given various opportunities for exercising leadership, such as coaching younger players. Players might also learn to officiate their own games and organize practices. By the time the players reach the next age bracket, 13 to 15, they are ready for a strong emphasis on the team as a moral community. Beedy (1988) notes that young adolescents feel that "closeness" is one of the most important aspects of a good team. This opens the way for a deeper appreciation for the moral underpinnings of sport and team relationships.

At the most mature level of youth sport participation, which Beedy identifies as ages 16 to 18, young athletes want to be physically challenged. They also need considerable emotional support and an opportunity to converse about their budding ideas and often tumultuous feelings. Most adolescents have a strong interest in issues of fairness, and it is an excellent time to assist them in developing a mature understanding of the moral norms undergirding sport. The theme of sportspersonship, which often poses a choice between acting on a success strategy or an ethical strategy, is one that adolescents need to confront, both intellectually and in the heat of competition. Helping athletes develop their own moral code for sport participation is an appropriate goal for this age group.

6. Coaches are in a superb position to promote self-esteem. Excellent training programs are available to teach coaches how to promote self-esteem in their charges (e.g., Smith, Smoll, & Curtis, 1979), but the fundamental idea is to provide a positive experience wherein children are challenged but able to succeed and develop their skills.

7. Coaches should minimize external motivations for sport participation. We concur with Hill and Kochendorfer (1969), who recommend no trophies, medals, or awards contingent on sport victories. Such awards only reinforce the already strong tendency to overemphasize game outcome rather than game process.

8. To help promote their decision-making skills and autonomy, coaches should give youths as much responsibility as possible (Martens, 1988). Even at the youngest ages, Beedy (1988) recommends, "every team member should be given a purpose (i.e., organize equipment, video tape, keep score, etc.) to promote a sense of belonging, responsibility, and accountability" (p. 136). Older children can share responsibility for organizing games and practices. In particular, children and youth should be involved in (minimally) or given total responsibility for (maximally) developing their own strategies for games. Placing strategy decisions in the hands of the participants themselves may have the added benefit of helping the coach focus attention on the players, not the game outcome. Again, however, as Beedy reminds us, responsibility without accountability is not particularly useful. Coaches need to give plenty of affirmation and encouragement, but they need also to help players reflect on their decisions—both strategic and moral—in light of their outcomes and accepted norms.

9. Coaches should set up at least one meeting for parents to discuss the moral dimensions of their coaching philosophy. Parents should be given an opportunity to contribute to the goals of the sport program, and coaches should make clear the dangers of an excessive emphasis on winning.

10. Finally, coaches need to provide information to athletes about their rights. Athletes' rights are discussed in the next section.

Recommendations for Athletes

1. Athletes should be aware of their rights and take responsibility to see that they are observed. A number of resources are available for reflecting on one's rights as an athlete, such as the "Bill of Rights for Young Athletes" developed by the American Alliance of Health, Physical Education, Recreation and Dance (Martens & Seefeldt, 1976). Galasso (1988) has done a fine job in summarizing this topic from the perspective of Canadian youth sports.

2. Athletes should reflect on their own philosophy of "fair play." Again, excellent resources are available, such as Warren Fraleigh's (1984) book *Right Actions in Sport*. The budding international fair play movement also can provide guidance. Fair play codes devised by others may be useful as a point of departure, but ultimately athletes need to embrace moral perspectives that they claim as their own.

3. Athletes need to take ultimate responsibility for their own behavior. When issues of fairness or potential harm are involved, the decision about how to act rests with the athlete, not the coach or game official. Athletes need to see themselves as both responsible and accountable for their own actions.

Recommendations for Sport Administrators

1. Sport administrators should ensure that moral education goals are not neglected in sport programs. Chissom (1978) justifiably worries that the existing knowledge about how to promote moral growth will never be effectively implemented because it is difficult to pinpoint who is responsible to make the necessary changes. Clearly, sport administrators, whether professional or volunteer, have important responsibilities in this area.

2. Sport administrators should insure that comprehensive training programs are provided for all those who work directly with athletes regularly and intensely. Training programs should include units on athletes' rights, strategies for promoting moral character, and professional ethics.

3. Sport administrators should provide opportunities for members of different teams to work cooperatively toward achieving shared goals. For example, having work parties groom a common playing field could serve as a superordinate goal and emphasize the cooperative underpinning of the competitive process.

4. Those in a position to do so should encourage children to become involved in lifelong sport activities (such as swimming, golf, tennis, and racquetball) as well as the popular team sports.

Recommendations for Parents

1. Parents have a responsibility to investigate the sponsoring organization before enrolling a child in a youth sport program. Parents should investigate the

organization's philosophy, statement of athletes' rights, mode of operation, and control structure.

2. Parents should discuss the coach's philosophy of coaching with the coach, particularly as that philosophy relates to the range of responsibilities that children are allowed to assume and the relative emphasis given to process and outcome. Parents should observe coaches in action to see if their behavior matches their philosophy. Finally, parents should provide the coach with honest feedback when the coach's behavior deviates from what the parent considers positive leadership.

Summary

In this book we tried to make the case that moral psychology is relevant to physical activity contexts. Our main focus has been on sport, and we have suggested that sport is a rich arena of moral action. We have summarized major theoretical approaches to moral development and proposed a model for conceptualizing and investigating moral action in sport. We have sought as well to review the major empirical work that has been done in this field of interest and have offered suggestions for how physical education and youth sport programs can become more efficacious in promoting moral growth. Much work has yet to be done theoretically, empirically, and educationally on this vital topic. We invite you to join us in that rewarding task so that physical activity participants can embody their fullest capacity for compassion, fairness, sportspersonship, and integrity.

Bibliography

(Note: An asterisk indicates a source with a specific focus on sport and morality.)

Abe, I. (1988). A study of the chronology of the modern usage of "sportsmanship" in English, American and Japanese dictionaries. *International Journal of the History of Sport, 5*, 3-28.

Acosta, R.V., & Carpenter, L.J. (1992). As the years go by—Coaching opportunities in the 1990s. *Journal of Physical Education, Recreation and Dance, 63*, 36-41.

*Adams, D.L. (1982). *The development of a prosocial behavior inventory related to participation in high school physical education classes.* Unpublished master's thesis, California State University, Long Beach.

Ainsworth, M.D.S., Blehar, M., Waters, E., & Wall, S. (1978). *Patterns of attachment.* Hillsdale, NJ: Erlbaum.

*Albinson, J. (1973). Professionalized atitudes of volunteer coaches. *International Review of Sport Sociology, 8*, 77-88.

Allison, M.T. (1979). On the ethnicity of ethnic minorities in sport. *Quest, 31*, 50-56.

*Allison, M.T. (1982). Sportsmanship: Variations based on sex and degree of competitive experience. In A.O. Dunleavy, A.W. Miracle, & C.R. Rees (Eds.), *Studies in the sociology of sport* (pp. 153-165). Ft. Worth: Texas Christian University Press.

Allison, M., & Luschen, G. (1979). A comparative analysis of Navajo Indian and Anglo basketball sport systems. *International Review of Sport Sociology, 3-4*, 75-85.

Alterman, A., Druley, K., Connolly, R., & Bush, D. (1978). A comparison of moral reasoning in drug addicts and nonaddicts. *Journal of Clinical Psychology, 34*, 790-794.

Anderson, D.F., & Gill, K.S. (1983). Occupational socialization patterns of men's and women's interscholastic basketball coaches. *Journal of Sport Behavior, 6*, 105-116.

Armstrong, C.F. (1984). The lessons of sports: Class socialization in British and American boarding schools. *Sociology of Sport Journal, 1*, 314-331.

*Arnold, P.J. (1982). Competitive games and education. *Physical Education Review, 5*, 126-130.

*Arnold, P.J. (1984a). Sport, moral education and the development of character. *Journal of Philosophy of Education, 18*, 275-281.

*Arnold, P.J. (1984b). Three approaches towards an understanding of sportsmanship. *Journal of the Philosophy of Sport, 10*, 61-70.

*Arnold, P.J. (1986). Moral aspects of an education in movement. In G. Stull & H. Eckert (Eds.), *Effects of physical activity on children* (pp. 14-21). Champaign, IL: Human Kinetics.

Aronfreed, J. (1968). *Conduct and conscience: The socialization of internalized control over behavior.* New York: Academic Press.

Aronfreed, J., & Paskal, V. (1965). *Altruism, empathy, and the conditioning of positive affect.* Unpublished manuscript, University of Pennsylvania, Philadelphia.

Aronson, E., Bridgman, D.L., & Geffner, R. (1978). The effects of a cooperative classroom structure on student behavior and attitudes. In D. Bar-Tal, & L. Saxe (Eds.), *Social psychology of education: Theory and research* (pp. 257-272). Washington, DC: Hemisphere.

*Austin, D.A., & Brown, M. (1978). Social development in physical education: A practical application. *Journal of Physical Education and Recreation, 49*, 81-83.

Ausubel, D.P. (1952). *Ego development and the personality disorders.* New York: Grune & Stratton.

*Bain, L.L. (1975). The hidden curriculum in physical education. *Quest, 24*, 92-101.

Bain, L.L. (1976). Play and intrinsic values in education. *Quest, 26*, 75-80.

*Bain, L.L. (1985). The hidden curriculum re-examined. *Quest, 37*, 145-153.

Bain, L.L.. (1988). Curriculum for critical reflection in physical education. In R.S. Brandt (Ed.), *Context of the curriculum: 1988 ASCD yearbook* (pp. 133-147). Washington, DC: Association for Supervision and Curriculum Development.

Bandura, A. (1969). *The principles of behavior modification.* New York: Holt, Rinehart and Winston.

Bandura, A. (1973). *Aggression: A social learning analysis.* Englewood Cliffs, NJ: Prentice-Hall.

Bandura, A. (1977). *Social learning theory.* Englewood Cliffs, NJ: Prentice-Hall.

Bandura, A. (1986). *Social foundations of thought and action: A social cognitive theory.* Englewood Cliffs, NJ: Prentice-Hall.

Bandura, A. (1991). Social cognitive theory of moral thought and action. In W.M. Kurtines & J.L. Gewirtz (Eds.), *Handbook of moral behavior and development: Vol. 1. Theory* (pp. 45-103). Hillsdale, NJ: Erlbaum.

Barden, R.C., Garber, J., Leiman, B., Ford, M.E., & Masters, J.C. (1985). Factors governing the effective remediation of negative affect and its cognitive and behavioral consequences. *Journal of Personality and Social Psychology, 49*, 1040-1053.

Barker, R. (1968). *Ecological psychology: Concepts and methods for studying the environment of human behavior.* Stanford, CA: Stanford University Press.

Barnett, M.A., & Bryan, J.H. (1974). Effects of competition with outcome feedback on children's helping behavior. *Development Psychology, 10*, 838-842.

Barnett, M.A., Howard, J.A., Melton, E.M., & Dino, G.A. (1982). Effect of inducing sadness about self or other on helping behavior in high and low empathic children. *Child Development, 53*, 920-923.

Barnett, M.A., Matthews, K.A., & Howard, J.A. (1979). Relationship between competitiveness and empathy in 6- and 7-year-olds. *Developmental Psychology, 15*, 221-222.

Bartek, S., Krebs, D., & Taylor, M. (1993). Coping, defending, and the relations between moral judgment and moral behavior in prostitutes and other female juvenile delinquents. *Journal of Abnormal Psychology, 102*, 66-73.

Bateson, G. (1955). A theory of play and fantasy. *Psychiatric Research Reports, 2*, 39-51.

Batson, C.D., & Coke, J.S. (1981). Empathy: A source of altruistic motivation for helping. In J.P. Rushton & R.M. Sorrentino (Eds.), *Altruism and helping behavior: Social personality and developmental perspectives* (pp. 167-211). Hillsdale, NJ: Erlbaum.

Batson, C.D., Fultz, J., & Schoenrade, P.A. (1987). Adults' emotional reactions to the distress of others. In N. Eisenberg & J. Strayer (Eds.), *Empathy and its development* (pp. 163-184). New York: Cambridge University Press.

Batson, C.D., O'Quin, K., Fultz, J., Vanderplus, M., & Isen, A.M. (1983). Influence of self-reported distress and empathy on egoistic versus altruistic motivation to help. *Journal of Personality and Social Psychology, 45*, 706-718.

*Bauslaugh, G. (1986). Ethics in professional sports. *Humanist, 46*(6), 30-31.

Bear, G. (1989). Social cognitive influences on early adolescents' decision to copy software in hypothetical situations. *Journal of Early Adolescence, 9*, 499-515.

*Beedy, J.P. (1988). *Understanding the interpersonal world of youth sports.* Unpublished doctoral dissertation, Harvard University, Cambridge, MA.

*Beller, J.M. (1990). *A moral reasoning intervention program for Division I athletes. Can athletes learn not to cheat?* Unpublished doctoral dissertation, University of Idaho, Moscow.

*Beller, J.M., & Stoll, S.K. (1992, Spring). A moral reasoning intervention program for student-athletes. *Academic Athletic Journal*, pp. 43-57.

Benedict, R. (1961). *Patterns of culture.* Boston: Houghton Mifflin.

Berkowitz, L. (1962). *Aggression: A social psychological analysis.* New York: McGraw-Hill.

Berkowitz, L. (1964). *Development of motives and values in a child.* New York: Basic Books.

Berkowitz, L. (1969). *Roots of aggression: A reexamination of the frustration-aggression hypothesis.* New York: Atherton Press.

Berkowitz, L. (1973). Sports, competition, and aggression. In I. Williams & L. Wankel (Eds.), *Fourth Canadian symposium on psychology of motor learning and sport* (pp. 59-61). Ottawa, ON: University of Ottawa Press.

Berkowitz, L. (1974). Some determinants of impulsive aggression: The role of mediated associations with reinforcement for aggression. *Psychological Review, 81*, 165-176.

*Berlage, G.I. (1982a). Are children's competitive team sports teaching corporate values? *Arena Review, 6*, 15-21.

Berlage, G.I. (1982b). Children's sports and the family. *Arena Review, 6*, 15-21.

Berndt, T.J. (1981). The effects of friendship on prosocial intentions and behavior. *Child Development, 52*, 636-643.

Berndt, T.J. (1982). The features and effects of friendship in early adolescence. *Child Development, 53*, 1447-1460.

*Best, C. (1985). Differences in social values between athletes and nonathletes. *Research Quarterly for Exercise and Sport, 34*, 282-287.

Bettelheim, B. (1977). *The uses of enchantment.* New York: Vintage Books.

Betts, E. (1983). Keepers of the crown jewels. *Quest, 35*, 75-81.

*Bibliography of sports and value-oriented concerns. (1979). In E.W. Gerber & W.J. Morgan (Eds.), *Sport and the body: A philosophical symposium* (2nd ed.). Philadelphia: Lea & Febiger.

*Blair, S. (1985). Professionalization of attitude toward play in children and adults. *Research Quarterly in Exercise and Sport, 56*, 82-83.

*Blanchard, B. (1946). A comparative analysis of secondary-school boys' and girls' character and personality traits in physical education classes. *Research Quarterly, 17*, 33-39.

Blasi, A. (1980). Bridging moral cognition and moral action: A critical review of the literature. *Psychological Bulletin, 88*, 1-45.

Blasi, A. (1983a). Moral cognition and moral action: A theoretical perspective. *Developmental Review, 3*, 178-210.

Blasi, A. (1983b). The self and cognition: The roles of the self in the acquisition of knowledge, and the role of cognition in the development of the self. In B. Lee and G. Noam (Eds.), *Development approaches to the self* (pp. 189-213). New York: Plenum.

Blasi, A. (1984). Moral identity: Its role in moral functioning. In W. Kurtines & J. Gerwitz (Eds.), *Morality, moral behavior, and moral development* (pp. 128-139). New York: Wiley.

Blasi, A. (1985). The moral personality: Reflections for social science and education. In M. Berkowitz & F. Oser (Eds.), *Moral education: Theory and application* (pp. 433-444). Hillsdale, NJ: Erlbaum.

Blasi, A. (1987). Comment: The psychological definitions of morality. In J. Kegan and S. Lamb (Eds.), *The emergence of morality in young children* (pp. 83-90). Chicago: University of Chicago Press.

Blasi, A. (1988). Identity and the development of the self. In D.K. Lapsley and F.C. Power (Eds.), *Self, ego, and identity: Integrative approaches* (pp. 226-242). New York: Springer-Verlag.

Blasi, A. (1989). The integration of morality in personality. In I.E. Bilbao (Ed.), *Perspectivas acerca de cambio moral: Posibles intervenciones educativas* [Perspectives on moral change: Possible educational interventions]. San Sebastian, Spain: Servico Editorial Universidad del Pais Vasco.

Blasi, A. (1990a). How should psychologists define morality? or, The negative side effects of philosophy's influence on psychology. In T.E. Wren (Ed.), *The moral domain: Essays in the ongoing discussion between philosophy and the social sciences*. Cambridge, MA: MIT Press.

Blasi, A. (1990b). Kohlberg's theory and moral motivation. In D. Schrader (Ed.), *New directions in child development: Vol. 47. The legacy of Lawrence Kohlberg* (pp. 51-57). San Francisco: Jossey-Bass.

Blasi, A., & Oresick, R. (1986). Emotions and cognitions in self-inconsistency. In D.J. Bearison & H. Zimiles (Eds.), *Thought and emotion: Developmental perspectives* (pp. 147-165). Hillsdale, NJ: Erlbaum.

Blasi, A., & Oresick, R. (1987). Self-inconsistency and the development of self. In P. Young-Nisdendrafth & J. Hall (Eds.), *The book of the self: Person, pretext, and process* (pp. 69-87). New York: University Press.

Block, J., & Block, J.H. (1973, January). *Ego development and the provenance of thought: A longitudinal study of ego and cognitive development in young children*. Progress report for the National Institute of Mental Health (Grant No. MH16080).

Blum, L.A. (1980). *Friendship, altruism and morality*. Boston: Routledge & Kegan Paul.

Boff, C. (1987). *Theology and praxis*. Maryknoll, NY: Orbis Books.

*Booth, B.F. (1980). Play and the socio-cultural process in moral education. *Recreation Research Review, 8*, 37-42.

*Booth, B.F. (1981). Socio-cultural aspect of play and moral development. *Physical Education Review, 4*, 115-120.

*Bovyer, G. (1963). Children's concepts of sportsmanship in the 4th, 5th, and 6th grade. *Research Quarterly, 34*, 282-287.

Bowlby, J. (1958). The nature of the child's tie to his mother. *International Journal of Psychoanalysis, 39*, 350-373.

Bowlby, J. (1969). *Atachment and loss*. New York: Basic Books.

Braddock, J.H. (1980). Race, sport, and social mobility. *Sociological Symposium, 30*, 18-38.

*Brandi, J.F. (1989). *A theory of moral development and competitive school sports*. Unpublished doctoral dissertation, Loyola University of Chicago, IL.

Bredemeier, B.J. (1980). *The assessment of expressive and instrumental power value orientations in sport and in everyday life*. Unpublished doctoral dissertation, Temple University, Philadelphia.

*Bredemeier, B.J. (1982). Gender, justice and non-violence in sport. *Perspectives, 4*, 106-114.

*Bredemeier, B.J. (1983). Athletic aggression: A moral concern. In J. Goldstein (Ed.), *Sports violence* (pp. 42-81). New York: Springer-Verlag.

*Bredemeier, B.J. (1984). Sport, gender, and moral growth. In J.M. Silva & R.S. Weinberg (Eds.), *Psychological foundations of sport* (pp. 400-413). Champaign, IL: Human Kinetics.

*Bredemeier, B.J. (1985). Moral reasoning and the perceived legitimacy of intentionally injurious sport acts. *Journal of Sport Psychology, 7*, 110-124.

*Bredemeier, B.J. (1986). Character and competition. In *Idrettog Oppvekstvilkar [Proceedings from the Annual Conference of the Norwegian Research Council of Science and Humanities]* (pp. 21-35). Oslo: Lie & Co.s Boytrykkeri A.S.

*Bredemeier, B.J. (1987). The moral of the youth sport story. In E. Brown & C. Branta (Eds.), *Competitive sports for children and youth* (pp. 285-296). Champaign, IL: Human Kinetics.

*Bredemeier, B.J. (1994). Children's moral reasoning and their assertive, aggressive, and submissive tendencies in sport and daily life. *Journal of Sport and Exercise Psychology, 16*, 1-14.

*Bredemeier, B.J. (in press). Divergence in children's moral reasoning about issues in daily life and sport specific contexts. *International Journal of Sport Psychology.*

Bredemeier, B.J.L., Desertrain, G., Fisher, Getty, D., Slocum, N., Stephens, D., & Warren, J. (1991). Epistemological perspectives among women who participate in physical activity. Journal of Applied Sport Psychology, 3, 87-107.

*Bredemeier, B.J., & Shields, D.L. (1983). *Body and balance: Developing moral structures through physical education.* Eugene: Microform Publications, University of Oregon.

*Bredemeier, B.J., & Shields, D.L. (1984a). Divergence in moral reasoning about sport and life. *Sociology of Sport Journal, 1*, 348-357.

*Bredemeier, B.J., & Shields, D.L. (1984b). The utility of moral stage analysis in the investigation of athletic aggression. *Sociology of Sport Journal, 1*, 138-149.

*Bredemeier, B.J., & Shields, D.L. (1985). Values and violence in sport. *Psychology Today, 10*, 22-32.

*Bredemeier, B.J., & Shields, D.L. (1986a). Athletic aggression: An issue of contextual morality. *Sociology of Sport Journal, 3*, 15-28.

*Bredemeier, B.J., & Shields, D.L. (1986b). Game reasoning and interactional morality. *Journal of Genetic Psychology, 147*, 257-275.

*Bredemeier, B.J., & Shields, D.L. (1986c). Moral growth among athletes and nonathletes: A comparative analysis. *Journal of Genetic Psychology, 147*, 7-18.

*Bredemeier, B.J., & Shields, D.L. (1987). Moral development through physical activity: An interactional approach. In D. Gould & M. Weiss (Eds.), *Advances in pediatric sport sciences* (pp. 145-165). Champaign, IL: Human Kinetics.

*Bredemeier, B.J.L., & Shields, D.L.L. (1992). Moral psychology in the context of sport. In R. Singer, M. Murphey, & L.K. Tennant (Eds.), *Handbook of research in sport psychology* (pp. 587-599). New York: Macmillan.

*Bredemeier, B.J., Weiss, M.R., Shields, D.L., & Cooper, B. (1986). The relationship of sport involvement with children's moral reasoning and aggression tendencies. *Journal of Sport Psychology, 8*, 304-318.

*Bredemeier, B.J., Weiss, M.R., Shields, D.L., & Cooper, B. (1987). The relationship between children's legitimacy judgments and their moral reasoning, aggression tendencies and sport involvement. *Sociology of Sport Journal, 4*, 48-60.

*Bredemeier, B.J., Weiss, M.R., Shields, D.L., & Shewchuk, R.M. (1986). Promoting moral growth in a summer sport camp: The implementation of theoretically grounded instructional strategies. *Journal of Moral Education, 15*, 212-220.

Brickman, P. (1977). Crime and punishment in sports and society. *Journal of Social Issues, 33*, 140-164.

Brill, A.A. (1963). Why man seeks sport. *North American Review, 248*, 85-99.

Brown, J.M., & Davies, N. (1978). Attitude toward violence among college athletes. *Journal of Sport Behavior, 1*, 61-70.

Brown, L.M., Debold, E., Tappan, M., & Gilligan, C. (1991). Reading narratives of conflict and choice for self and moral voices: A relational method. In W. Kurtines & J. Gewirtz (Eds.), *Handbook of moral behavior and development: Vol. 2. Research* (pp. 25-61). Hillsdale, NJ: Erlbaum.

Brown, L.M., & Gilligan, C. (1990, August). Listening for self and the relational voice: A responsive/resisting reader's guide. In M. Franklin (Chair), *Literary theory as a guide to psychological analysis.* Symposium conducted at the annual meeting of the American Psychological Association, Boston.

Brown, R.M. (1978). *Theology in a new key: Responding to liberation themes.* Philadelphia: Westminster Press.

Bruner, J., Jolly, A., & Sylva, K. (Eds.) (1976). *Play: Its role in evolution and development.* New York: Penguin.

Bryan, J.H. (1977). Prosocial behavior. In H.L. Horn & P.A. Robinson (Eds.), *Psychological processes in early education* (pp. 233-259). New York: Academic Press.

Bryant, B.K. (1983). Context of success, affective arousal, and generosity: The neglected role of negative affect in success experience. *American Educational Research Journal, 20*, 553-562.

Buhrman, H.G. (1977). Athletics and deviance: An examination of the relationship between athletic participation and deviant behavior of high school girls. *Review of Sport and Leisure, 2*, 17-35.

Buhrman, H.G., & Bratton, R. (1978). Athletic participation and status of Alberta high school girls. *International Review of Sport Psychology, 12*, 57-67.

*Burchard, J.D. (1979). Competitive youth sports and social competence. In M. Kent (Ed.), *Social competence in children* (pp. 171-196). Hanover, NH: University Press of New England.

Burton, R., Allinsmith, W., & Maccoby, E. (1966). Resistance to temptation in relation to sex of child, sex of experimenter and withdrawal of attention. *Journal of Personality and Social Psychology, 3*, 253-258.

Burton, R., Maccoby, E., & Allinsmith, W. (1961). Antecedents of resistance to temptation in four-year-old children. *Child Development, 32*, 689-710.

Butler, L., & Meichenbaum, D. (1981). The assessment of interpersonal problem-solving skills. In P. Kendall & S. Hollon (Eds.), *Assessment strategies for cognitive-behavioral assessment* (pp. 197-225). New York: Academic Press.

*Caine, D.J., & Krebs, E. (1986). The moral development objective in physical education: A renewed quest. *Contemporary Education, 57*, 197-201.

Candee, D. (1976). Structure and choice in moral reasoning. *Journal of Personality and Social Psychology, 34*, 1293-1301.

*Card, A. (1981, April). *Orientation toward winning as a function of athletic participation, grade level, and gender.* Paper presented at the annual meeting of the American Alliance for Health, Physical Education, Recreation and Dance, Detroit.

Carlson, M., & Miller, N. (1987). Explanation of the relation between negative mood and helping. *Psychological Bulletin, 102*, 91-108.

Carter, R.E. (1980). What is Lawrence Kohlberg doing? *Journal of Moral Education, 9*, 2.

*Case, B.W., Greer, H.S., & Lacourse, M.G. (1987). Moral judgment development and perceived legitimacy of spectator behavior in sport. *Journal of Sport Behavior, 10*, 147-156.

Chambers, R. (1984). *Sportsmanship in a sporting America: Traditions, ideal, reality.* Unpublished doctoral dissertation, Temple University, Philadelphia.

*Chandler, T. (1988a). Building and displaying character through sport, and striving to win in sport: Values at odds or in concert? In S. Ross and L. Charette (Eds.), *Persons, minds and bodies* (pp. 161-169). North York, ON: University Press of Canada.

*Chandler, T. (1988b). Sports, winning and character building: What can we learn from Goffman's notion of self-formulation? *Physical Education Review, 11*, 3-10.

*Chissom, B. (1978). Moral behavior of children participating in competitive sport. In R. Magill, M. Ash, & F. Smoll (Eds.), *Children in sport: A contemporary anthology* (pp. 193-199). Champaign, IL: Human Kinetics.

Chodorow, N. (1978). *The reproduction of mothering: Psychoanalysis and the sociology of gender.* Berkeley: University of California Press.

Cialdini, R.B., Baumann, D.J., & Kenrick, D.T. (1981). Insights from sadness: A three-step model of the development of altruism as hedonism. *Developmental Review, 1*, 207-223.

Cialdini, R.B., Darby, B.L., & Vincent, J.E. (1973). Transgression and altruism: A case for hedonism. *Journal of Experimental Social Psychology, 9*, 502-516.

Cialdini, R.B., Kenrick, D.T., & Baumann, D.J. (1982). Effects of mood on prosocial behavior in children and adults. In N. Eisenberg (Ed.), *The development of prosocial behavior* (pp. 339-359). New York: Academic Press.

*Coakley, J.J. (1981, May). The professionalization of attitude scale: What does it measure? *Sport Sociology Academy Newsletter*, pp. 7-11.

Coakley, J.J. (1982). *Sport in society: Issues and controversies* (2nd ed.). St. Louis: Times Mirror/Mosby.

*Coakley, J.J. (1983). Play, games, and sport: Development implications for young people. In J.C. Harris and R.J. Park (Eds.), *Play, games and sports in cultural contexts* (pp. 431-450). Champaign, IL: Human Kinetics.

Coakley, J.J. (1984). *Mead's theory on the development of the self: Implications for organized youth sport programs.* Paper presented at the Olympic Scientific Congress, Eugene, OR.

Coakley, J.J. (1990). *Sport in society: Issues and controversies* (4th ed.). St. Louis: Times Mirror/Mosby.

*Coakley, J., & Bredemeier, B.J. (1988). *Youth sports: Development of ethical practices.* Unpublished manuscript.

Coakley, J., & Westkott, M. (1984). Opening doors for women in sport: An alternative to old strategies. In D.S. Eitzen (Ed.), *Sport in contemporary society.* New York: St. Martin's Press.

Colby, A., Kohlberg, L., Speicher, B., Hewer, A., Candee, D., Gibbs, J., & Power, C. (1987). *The measurement of moral judgment* (two volumes). New York: Cambridge University Press.

Coleman, J.S. (1965). *Adolescents and the schools.* New York: Basic Books.

Cooper, W.E. (1982). Association: An answer to Egoism. *Journal of the Philosophy of Sport, 9*, 66-68.

Corsaro, W.A. (1981). Friendship in the nursery school: Social organization in a peer environment. In S.R. Asher & J.M. Gottman (Eds.), *The development of children's friendships.* Cambridge, England: Cambridge University Press.

*Cote, B. (1981). *Moral development in intramurals.* Unpublished manuscript, York University, Toronto.

Coutts, C.A. (1968). Freedom in sport. [Monograph] *Quest, 10*, 68-71.

Cowan, P.A. (1982). The relationship between emotional and cognitive development. *New Directions for Child Development, 16*, 49-81.

Crossley, D. (1988). Unorganized sport as a model of political values. In S. Ross & L. Charette (Eds.), *Persons, minds, and bodies* (pp. 183-190). North York, ON: University Press of Canada.

*Crown, J., & Heatherington, L. (1989). The costs of winning? The role of gender in moral reasoning and judgments about competitive athletic encounters. *Journal of Sport and Exercise Psychology, 11*, 281-289.

Cunningham, M.R., Steinberg, J., & Grev, R. (1980). Wanting to and having to help: Separate motivations for positive mood and guilt-induced helping. *Journal of Personality and Social Psychology, 38*, 181-192.

*Dahl, P.J. (1992). *The relationship of coaching goal orientations to sportsmanship attitudes and the perceived legitimacy of potentially injurious sports acts.* Unpublished master's thesis, San Diego State University, San Diego.

Damon, W. (1975). Early conceptions of positive justice as related to the development of logical operations. *Child Development, 46*, 301-312.

Damon, W. (1977). *The social world of the child.* San Francisco: Jossey-Bass.

Damon, W. (1980). Patterns of change in children's social reasoning: A two-year longitudinal study. *Child Development, 51*, 1010-1017.

Damon, W. (1984). Self-understanding and moral development from childhood to adolescence. In W.M. Kurtines & J.L. Gewirtz (Eds.), *Morality, moral behavior, and moral development* (pp. 109-127). New York: Wiley.

Darley, J., & Batson, C.D. (1973). From Jerusalem to Jericho: A study of situational and dispositional variables in helping behavior. *Journal of Personality and Social Psychology, 27*, 100-108.

Davidson, P., Turiel, E., & Black, A. (1983). The effect of stimulus familiarity on the use of criteria and justifications in children's social reasoning. *British Journal of Developmental Psychology, 1*, 49-65.

*Davis, H., & Baskett, G. (1979). Do athletes and non-athletes have different values? *Athletic Administration, 13*, 17-19.

Debellefeuille, B. (1990). *The influence of cooperative learning activities on the perspective-taking ability and prosocial behavior of kindergarten students.* Unpublished doctoral dissertation, McGill University, Montreal.

*DeBusk, M., & Hellison, D. (1989). Implementing a physical education self-responsibility model for delinquency-prone youth. *Journal of Teaching Physical Education, 8*, 104-112.

Declaration on fair play. (n.d.) International Council of Sport and Physical Education. Paris, France.

Deutsch, M. (1985). *Distributive justice: A social-psychological perspective.* New Haven, CT: Yale University Press.

Devereux, E. (1976). Backyard vs. Little League baseball: The impoverishment of children's games. In D. Landers (Ed.), *Social problems in athletics* (pp. 37-56). Champaign, IL: University of Illinois Press.

Dewey, J. (1929). *Experience and nature* (2nd ed.). New York: Norton.

Dewey, J. (1959). *Moral principles in education.* New York: Philosophical Library.

Diab, L.N. (1970). A study of intragroup and intergroup relations among experimentally produced small groups. *Genetic Psychology Monographs, 82*, 49-82.

Dienstbier, R.A., Hillman, D., Lehnhoff, J., Hillman, J., & Valkenaar, M.C. (1975). An emotion-attribution approach to moral behavior: Interfacing cognitive and avoidance theories of moral development. *Psychological Review, 82*, 299-315.

Dollard, J., Doob, L.W., Miller, N.E., Mowrer, O.H., & Sears, R.R. (1939). *Frustration and aggression.* New Haven, CT: Yale University Press.

Donnelly, P. (1981). Athletes and juvenile delinquents: A comparative analysis based on a review of the literature. *Adolescence, 16*, 415-431.

Dowell, L.J. (1971). Environmental factors of childhood competitive athletics. *Physical Educator, 28*, 17-21.

*Dubois, P.E. (1986). The effect of participation in sport on the value orientations of young athletes. *Sociology of Sport Journal, 3*, 29-42.

*Dubois, P.E. (1990). Gender differences in value orientation toward sports: A longitudinal analysis. *Journal of Sport Behavior, 13*, 3-14.

Duda, J.L. (1981). Achievement motivation in sport: Minority considerations for the coach. *Journal of Sport Behavior, 4*, 24-31.

Duda, J.L. (1989a). Goal perspectives and behavior in sport and exercise settings. In C. Ames & M. Maehr (Eds.), *Advances in motivation and achievement, 6*, 81-115.

Duda, J.L. (1989b). The relationship between task and ego orientation and the perceived purpose of sport among male and female high school athletes. *Journal of Sport and Exercise Psychology, 11*, 318-335.

Duda, J.L. (1992). Motivation in sport settings: A goal perspective approach. In G. Roberts (Ed.), *Motivation in sport and exercise* (pp. 57-92). Champaign, IL: Human Kinetics.

Duda, J.L., & Nicholls, J.G. (1992). Dimensions of achievement motivation in schoolwork and sport. *Journal of Educational Psychology, 84*, 1-10.

*Duda, J.L., Olson, L.K., & Templin, T.J. (1991). The relationship of task and ego orientation to sportsmanship attitudes and the perceived legitimacy of injurious acts. *Research Quarterly for Exercise and Sport, 62*, 79-87.

*Duquin, M.E. (1984). Power and authority: Moral consensus and conformity in sport. *International Review for Sociology of Sport, 19*, 295-303.

*Duquin, M.E., Bredemeier, B.J., Oglesby, C., & Greendorfer, S.L. (1984). Teacher values: Political and social justice orientations of physical educators. *Journal of Teaching Physical Education, 3*, 9-19.

Durkheim, E. (1961). *Moral education.* New York: Free Press. (Original work published 1925)

Eagley, A.H., & Himmelfarb, S. (1978). Attitudes and opinions. *Annual Review of Psychology, 29*, 517-554.

Edwards, H. (1973). *Sociology of sport.* Homewood, IL: Dorsey.

Eifermann, R. (1971). Social play in childhood. In R. Herron & B. Sutton-Smith (Eds.), *Child's play* (pp. 270-297). New York: Wiley.

Eisenberg, N. (1976). *The development of prosocial moral judgment and its correlates.* Unpublished doctoral dissertation, University of California at Berkeley.

Eisenberg, N. (1982). The development of reasoning regarding prosocial behavior. In N. Eisenberg (Ed.), *The development of prosocial behavior* (pp. 219-249). New York: Academic Press.

Eisenberg, N. (1986). *Altruistic emotion, cognition, and behavior.* Hillsdale, NJ: Erlbaum.

Eisenberg, N., Cialdini, R.B., McCreath, H., & Shell, R. (1987). Consistency-based compliance: When and why do children become vulnerable? *Journal of Personality and Social Psychology, 52*, 1174-1181.

Eisenberg, N., Fabes, R.A., Miller, P.A., & Fultz, J. (1989). Relation of sympathy and personal distress to prosocial behavior: A multimethod study. *Journal of Personality and Social Psychology, 57*, 55-66.

Eisenberg, N., Fabes, R.A., Miller, P.A., & Shell, R. (1990). Preschoolers' vicarious emotional responding and their situational and dispositional prosocial behavior. *Merrill-Palmer Quarterly, 36*, 507-529.

Eisenberg, N., & Lennon, R. (1983). Sex differences in empathy and related capacities. *Psychological Bulletin, 94*, 100-131.

Eisenberg, N., & Miller, P. (1987). The relation of empathy to prosocial and related behaviors. *Psychological Bulletin, 101*, 91-119.

Eisenberg, N., & Mussen, P. (1989). *The roots of prosocial behavior in children.* Cambridge, England: Cambridge University Press.

Eisenberg, N., & Shell, R. (1985, April). *The relation of prosocial moral judgment and behavior in children.* Paper presented at the biennial meeting of the Society for Research in Child Development, Toronto.

Eisenberg, N., & Shell, R. (1986). Prosocial moral judgment and behavior in children: The mediating role of cost. *Personality and Social Psychology Bulletin, 12*, 426-433.

Eisenberg, N., & Strayer, J. (1987). Critical issues in the study of empathy. In N. Eisenberg & J. Strayer (Eds.), *Empathy and its development* (pp. 3-13). Cambridge, England: Cambridge University Press.

Eisenberg-Berg, N. (1979). Development of children's prosocial moral judgment. *Developmental Psychology, 15*, 128-137.

Eisenberg-Berg, N., & Hand, M. (1979). The relationship of preschoolers' reasoning about prosocial moral conflicts to prosocial behavior. *Child Development, 50*, 356-363.

Eisenberg-Berg, N., & Neal, C. (1981). Effects of identity of the story character and costs of helping on children's moral judgment. *Personality and Social Psychology Bulletin, 7*, 17-23.

Eitzen, D.S., & Sage, G.H. (1982). *Sociology of American sports* (2nd ed.). Dubuque, IA: Brown.

Ekstein, R. (1978). Psychoanalysis, sympathy, and altruism. In L.G. Wispe (Ed.), *Altruism, sympathy, and helping: Psychological and sociological principles* (pp. 165-175). New York: Academic Press.

Elder, J.L.D. (1983, April). *Role-raking and prosocial behavior revisited: The effects of aggregation.* Paper presented at the biennial meeting of the Society for Research in Child Development, Detroit.

Emde, R., Johnson, W., & Easterbrooks, M. (1987). The do's and don'ts of early moral development: Psychoanalytic tradition and current research. In J. Kagan & S. Lamb

(Eds.), *The emergence of morality in young children* (pp. 245-276). Chicago: University of Chicago Press.

Ennis, P.H. (1976, April). *Expressive symbol systems and the institutions of release.* Paper presented at the Third Annual Conference on Theory and the Arts, State University of New York, Albany.

Enright, R., Lapsley, D., & Olson, L. (1986). Moral judgment and the social cognitive development research programme. In S. Modgil & C. Modgil (Eds.), *Lawrence Kohlberg: Consensus and controversy* (pp. 313-324). Philadelphia: Falmer.

Epstein, R. (1965). *The development of children's conceptions of rules in the years four to eight.* Unpublished manuscript, University of Chicago.

Erikson, E.H. (1958). *Young man Luther.* New York: Norton.

Erikson, E.H. (1962). *Childhood and society.* New York: Norton.

Erikson, E.H. (1964). *Insight and responsibility.* New York: Norton.

Erikson, E.H. (1968). *Identity: Youth and crisis.* New York: Norton.

Erikson, E.H. (1969). *Gandhi's truth.* New York: Norton.

*Eskridge, V.L. (1977). Clarifying values. *Journal of Physical Education and Recreation, 48,* 17.

Eysenck, H.J. (1976). The biology of morality. In T. Lickona (Ed.), *Moral development and behavior: Theory, research, and social issues* (pp. 108-123). New York: Holt, Rinehart and Winston.

**Fair play codes for children in sport.* (1979). National Task Force on Children's Play, 1974-1977. Canadian Council on Children and Youth.

*Feezell, R.M. (1986). Sportsmanship. *Philosophy of Sport, 8,* 1-13.

Feffer, M.H., & Gourevitch, V. (1960). Cognitive aspects of role-taking in children. *Journal of Personality, 28,* 383-396.

Fielding, M. (1976). Against competition. *Proceedings of the Philosophy of Education Society of Great Britain, 10,* 124-145.

*Figley, G.E. (1982). *Characteristics of an upper elementary school physical education curriculum based on Kohlberg's cognitive-developmental approach to moral development.* Unpublished doctoral dissertation, University of Arkansas, Fayetteville.

*Figley, G.E. (1984). Moral education througyh physical education. *Quest, 36,* 89-101.

*Fine, G.A. (1979). Preadolescent socialization through organized athletics: The construction of moral meanings in Little League baseball. In M.L. Krotee (Ed.), *The dimensions of sport sociology* (pp. 79-105). Champaign, IL: Leisure Press.

*Fine, G.A. (1987). *With the boys: Little League baseball and preadolescent culture.* Chicago: University of Chicago Press.

Firth, R. (1973). *Symbols public and private.* New York: Cornell University Press.

Fisher, A.C. (1976). *Psychology of sport: Issues and insights.* Palo Alto, CA: Mayfield.

*Fisher, L. (1993). *Moral orientations and gender conceptions in female professional bodybuilders.* Unpublished doctoral dissertation, University of California at Berkeley.

Fiske, D.W., & Shweder, R.A. (1986). *Metatheory in social science.* Chicago: University of Chicago Press.

Flavell, J.H. (1963). *The developmental psychology of Jean Piaget.* Princeton, NJ: Van Nostrand.

Flavell, J.H., Fry, C., Wright, J., & Jarvis, P. (1968). *The development of role-taking and communication skills in children.* New York: Wiley.

*Fraleigh, W.P. (1979). A philosophic basis for curriculum content in physical education for the 1980s. *Academy Papers, 13,* 20-25.

*Fraleigh, W.P. (1984). *Right actions in sport: Ethics for contestants.* Champaign, IL: Human Kinetics.

Frankena, W. (1973). *Ethics* (2nd ed.). Englewood Cliffs, NJ: Prentice-Hall.

*Frankl, D. (1989). *Sport participation and moral reasoning: Relationships among aspects of hostility, altruism, and sport involvement.* Unpublished doctoral dissertation, Southern Illinois University at Carbondale.

Freud, S. (1959). The dissolution of the Oedipus-complex. In *The standard edition of the complete works of Sigmund Freud: Vol. XIX* (pp. 173-182). London: Hogarth Press. (Original work published 1924)

Freud, S. (1961). Some psychical consequences of the anatomical distinction between the sexes. In *The standard edition of the complete works of Sigmund Freud: Vol. XIX* (pp. 243-260). London: Hogarth Press. (Original work published 1925)

Freud, S. (1962). *Three essays on the theory of sexuality.* New York: Avon. (Original work published 1905)

Freud, S. (1965). *New introductory lectures in psychoanalysis.* New York: Norton. (Original work published 1933)

Friedman, M. (1985). Abraham, Socrates, and Heinz: Where are the women? In C.G. Harding (Ed.), *Moral dilemmas: Philosophical and psychological issues in the development of moral reasoning* (pp. 25-41). Chicago: Precedent Publishing.

*Frost, R.B., & Sims, E.J. (1974). *Development of human values through sport.* Washington, DC: American Alliance for Health, Physical Education and Recreation.

*Galasso, P. (Ed.) (1988). *Philosophy of sport and physical activity: Issues and concepts.* Toronto: Canadian Scholars' Press.

*Gelfand, D.M., & Hartmann, D.P. (1978). Some detrimental effects of competitive sports on children's behavior. In R.A. Magill, M.J. Ash, & F.L. Smoll (Eds.), *Children in sport: A contemporary anthology* (pp. 165-174). Chicago, IL: Human Kinetics.

Gelfand, D.M., & Hartmann, D.P. (1982). Response consequences and attributions: Two contributors to prosocial behavior. In N. Eisenberg (Ed.), *The development of prosocial behavior* (pp. 167-196). New York: Academic Press.

Geron, E., Furst, D., & Rotstein, P. (1986). Personality of athletes participating in various sports. *International Journal of Sport Psychology, 17,* 120-135.

Gerson, R., & Damon, W. (1978). Moral understanding and children's conduct. In W. Damon (Ed.), *New directions for child development: Vol. 1. Moral Development* (pp. 41-59). San Francisco: Jossey-Bass.

Gibbs, J.C. (1977). Kohlberg's stages of moral judgment: A constructive critique. *Harvard Educational Review, 47,* 43-61.

Gibbs, J.C. (1979). Kohlberg's moral stage theory: A Piagetian revision. *Human Development, 22,* 89-112.

Gibbs, J.C. (1991). Toward an integration of Kohlberg's and Hoffman's theories. In W. Kurtines & J. Gewirtz (Eds.), *Handbook of moral behavior and development: Vol. 1. Theory* (pp. 183-222). Hillsdale, NJ: Erlbaum.

*Giebink, M.P., & McKenzie, T.L. (1985). Teaching sportsmanship in physical education and recreation: An analysis of interventions and generalization effects. *Journal of Teaching in Physical Education, 4,* 167-177.

Giffin, H.L.N. (1982). *The metacommunicative process in a collective make-believe play.* Unpublished doctoral dissertation, University of Colorado, Boulder.

Gill, D.L. (1986). Competitiveness among females and males in physical activity classes. *Journal of Sex Roles, 15,* 233-247.

Gill, M., & Holtzman, P. (Eds.) (1976). Psychology versus metapsychology: Psychoanalytic essays in memory of George S. Klein. *Psychological Issues* (Monograph 36). New York: International Universities.

Gilligan, C. (1982). *In a different voice: Psychological theory and women's development.* Cambridge, MA: Harvard University Press.

Gilligan, C. (1986). Remapping the moral domain: New images of self in relationship. In T.C. Heller, M. Sosna, & D.E. Wellbery (Eds.), *Reconstructing individualism: Autonomy, individuality, and the self in Western thought* (pp. 237-252). Stanford, CA: Stanford University Press.

Gilligan, C., & Attanucci, J. (1988). Two moral orientations: Gender differences and similarities. *Merrill-Palmer Quarterly, 34,* 223-237.

Gilligan, C., Brown, L.M., & Rogers, A.G. (1990). Psyche embedded: A place for body, relationships, and culture in personality theory. In A.I. Rabin, R.A. Zucker, R.A. Emmons, & S. Frank (Eds.), *Studying persons and lives* (pp. 86-124). New York: Springer.

Gilligan, C., Lyons, N., & Hanmer, T. (Eds.) (1990). *Making connections: The relational worlds of adolescent girls at Emma Willard School.* Cambridge, MA: Harvard University Press.

Gilligan, C., Ward, J., & Taylor, J. (Eds.) (1988). *Mapping the moral domain.* Cambridge, MA: Harvard University Press.

Gilligan, C., & Wiggins, G. (1987). The origins of morality in early childhood relationships. In J. Kegan & S. Lamb (Eds.), *The emergence of morality in young children* (pp. 277-305). Chicago: University of Chicago Press.

Goldstein, J. (Ed.) (1983). *Sports violence.* New York: Springer-Verlag.

*Goodger, M., & Jackson, J. (1985). Fair play: Coaches' attitudes towards the laws of soccer. *Journal of Sport Behavior, 8,* 34-41.

*Gould, D. (1981). Sportsmanship: Building character or characters? In V. Seefeldt, F.L. Smoll, R.E. Smith, & D. Gould (Eds.), *A winning philosophy for youth sports programs* (pp. 25-37). East Lansing, MI: Youth Sports Institute.

*Gould, D. (1984). Psychosocial development and children's sport. In J. Thomas (Ed.), *Motor development during childhood and adolescence* (pp. 212-234). Minneapolis: Burgess.

Green, T. (1971). *The activities of teaching.* New York: McGraw-Hill.

*Greendorfer, S.L. (1987). Psycho-social correlates of organized physical activity. *Journal of Physical Education, Recreation and Dance, 58,* 59-64.

Grim, P., Kohlberg, L., & White, S. (1968). Some relationships between conscience and attentional processes. *Journal of Personality and Social Psychology, 8,* 239-253.

Grinder, R. (1961). New techniques for research in children's temptation behavior. *Child Development, 32,* 679-688.

Grinder, R. (1962). Parental child-rearing practices, conscience, and resistance to temptation of sixth-grade children. *Child Development, 33,* 803-820.

*Grineski, S.C. (1989a). Children, games, and prosocial behavior: Insight and connections. *Journal of Physical Education, Recreation and Dance, 60,* 20-25.

*Grineski, S.C.(1989b). *Effects of cooperative games on the prosocial behavior interactions of young children with and without impairments.* Unpublished doctoral dissertation, University of North Dakota, Grand Forks.

Haan, N. (1971). Moral redefinition in the family as the critical aspect of the generation gap. *Youth and Society, 2,* 259-283.

Haan, N. (1975). Moral reasoning in hypothetical and an actual situation of civil disobedience. *Journal of Personality and Social Psychology, 32,* 255-270.

Haan, N. (1977a). *A manual for interactional morality.* Unpublished manuscript, Institute of Human Development, University of California at Berkeley.

Haan, N. (1977b). *Coping and defending: Processes of self-environment organization.* New York: Academic Press.

Haan, N. (1978). Two moralities in action contexts: Relationship to thought, ego regulation, and development. *Journal of Personality and Social Psychology, 36,* 286-305.

Haan, N. (1982). Can research on morality be "scientific"? *American Psychologist, 37,* 1096-1104.

Haan, N. (1983). An interactional morality of everyday life. In N. Haan, R. Bellah, P. Rabinow, & W. Sullivan (Eds.), *Social science as moral inquiry* (pp. 218-250). New York: Columbia University Press.

Haan, N. (1985). Processes of moral development: Cognitive or social disequilibrium? *Developmental Psychology, 21,* 996-1006.

Haan, N. (1986). Systematic variability in the quality of moral action as defined by two formulations. *Journal of Personality and Social Psychology, 50,* 1271-1284.

Haan, N. (1991). Moral development and action from a social constructivist perspective. In W.M. Kurtines & J.L. Gewirtz (Eds.), *Handbook of moral behavior and development: Vol. 1. Theory* (pp. 251-273). Hillsdale, NJ: Erlbaum.

Haan, N., Aerts, E., & Cooper, B.B. (1985). *On moral grounds: The search for a practical morality*. New York: New York University Press.

Haan, N., Langer, J., & Kohlberg, L. (1976). Family moral patterns. *Child Development, 47*, 1204-1206.

Haan, N., Smith, M., & Block, J. (1968). Moral reasoning of young adults: Political-social behavior, family background, & personality correlates. *Journal of Personality and Social Psychology, 10*, 183-201.

Habermas, J. (1971). *Knowledge and human interests*. Boston: Beacon.

Habermas, J. (1973). *Theory and practice*. Boston: Beacon.

Habermas, J. (1979). *Communication and the evolution of society*. Boston: Beacon.

Habermas, J. (1983). *The theory of communicative action* (2 vols.). Boston: Beacon.

Habermas, J. (1988). *On the logic of the social sciences*. Cambridge, MA: Massachusetts Instutite of Technology.

Habermas, J. (1990). *Moral consciousness and communicative action*. Cambridge, MA: Massachusetts Institute of Technology.

Haft, W.L., & Slade, A. (1989). Affect attunement and maternal attachment: A pilot study. *Infant Mental Health Journal, 10*, 157-172.

*Hahm, C.H. (1989). *Moral reasoning and development among general students, physical education majors, and student athletes (Korea, United States)*. Unpublished doctoral dissertation, University of Idaho, Moscow.

*Hahm, C.H., Beller, J.M., & Stoll, S.K. (1989a). *The Hahm-Beller value choice inventory in the sport mileau*. Moscow: University of Idaho, Institute for Ethics.

*Hahm, C.H., Beller, J.M., & Stoll, S.K. (1989b). *A new moral values inventory*. Paper presented at the annual convention of the Northwest District of the American Alliance for Health, Physical Education, Recreation and Dance, Boise, ID.

*Hall, E.R. (1981). *Moral development levels of athletes in sport-specific and general social situations*. Unpublished doctoral dissertation, Texas Woman's University, Denton.

*Hall, E.R. (1986). Moral development levels of athletes in sport-specific and general social situations. In L. Vander Velden & J.H. Humphrey (Eds.), *Psychology and sociology of sport: Current selected research* (pp. 191-204). New York: AMS Press.

Hampshire, S. (1983). *Morality and conflict*. Cambridge, MA: Harvard University Press.

Handelman, D. (1977). Play and ritual: Complementary frames of metacommunication. In A.J. Chapman & H.C. Foot (Eds.), *It's a funny thing, humour* (pp. 185-192). Oxford: Pergamon Press.

Hanson, N.R. (1958). *Patterns of discovery*. Cambridge, England: Cambridge University Press.

Hartmann, H. (1960). *Psychoanalysis and moral values*. New York: International University Press.

Hartshorne, H., & May, M.A. (1928). *Studies in the nature of character: Vol. 1. Studies in deceit*. New York: Macmillan.

Hartshorne, H., May, M.A., & Maller, J.B. (1929). *Studies in the nature of character: Vol. 2. Studies in service and self-control*. New York: Macmillan.

Hartshorne, H., May, M.A., & Schuttleworth, F.K. (1929). *Studies in the nature of character: Vol. 3. Studies in the organization of character*. New York: Macmillan.

Hastad, D.N., Segrave, J.O., Pangrazi, R., & Petersen, G. (1984). Youth sport participation and deviant behavior. *Sociology of Sport Journal, 1*, 366-373.

Hefferline, R.F., Bruno, L.J.J., & Davidowitz, J.E. (1970). Feedback control of covert behavior. In K. Connolly (Ed.), *Mechanisms of motor skill development* (pp. 245-278). New York: Academic Press.

Hellison, D. (1978). *Beyond balls and bats: Alienated (and other) youth in the gym*. Washington, DC: American Alliance for Health, Physical Education, Recreation and Dance.

*Hellison, D. (1982). Attitude and behavior change in the gym: The Oregon story. *Physical Educator, 39,* 67-70.

Hellison, D. (1983a). It only takes one case to prove a possibility . . . and beyond. In T.J. Templin & J.K. Olson (Eds.), *Teaching in physical education* (pp. 102-106). Champaign, IL: Human Kinetics.

*Hellison, D. (1983b). Teaching self-responsibility (and more). *Journal of Physical Education, Recreation and Dance, 54,* 23, 28.

*Hellison, D. (1985). *Goals and strategies for teaching physical education.* Champaign, IL: Human Kinetics.

Hellison, D. (1986). Cause of death: Physical education. *Journal of Physical Education, Recreation and Dance, 57,* 27-28.

*Hellison, D. (1993). The coaching club: Teaching responsibility to inner-city students. *Journal of Physical Education, Recreation and Dance, 64,* 66-71.

Hellison, D., & Templin, T. (1991). *A reflective approach to teaching physical education.* Champaign, IL: Human Kinetics.

*Hendry, L. (1982). The hidden curriculum in physical education and sports. In J. Partington, T. Orlick, & J. Samela (Eds.), *Sport in perspective* (pp. 32-47). Ottawa, ON: Coaching Association of Canada.

*Henkel, S., & Earls, N. (1985). The moral judgment of physical education teachers. *Journal of Teaching in Physical Education, 4,* 178-189.

*Hetherington, C. (1932). Character and moral training through physical education. In J. Nash (Ed.), *Interpretations of physical education: Vol. 3. Character education through physical education* (pp. 101-107). New York: A.S. Barnes.

Higgins, A. (1991). The just community approach to moral education: Evolution of the idea and recent findings. In W. Kurtines & J. Gewirtz (Eds.), *Handbook of moral behavior and development: Vol. 3. Application* (pp. 111-141). Hillsdale, NJ: Erlbaum.

Higgins, A., Power, C., & Kohlberg, L. (1984). The relationship of moral judgment to judgments of responsibility. In W. Kurtines & J. Gewirtz (Eds.), *Morality, moral behavior, and moral development* (pp. 74-106). New York: Wiley.

Hill, J.P., & Kochendorfer, R.A. (1969). Knowledge of peer success and risk of detection as determinants of cheating. *Developmental Psychology, 1,* 231-238.

Hinde, R.A. (1991). Relationships, attachment, and culture: A tribute to John Bowlby. *Infant Mental Health Journal, 12,* 154-163.

Hirschi, T. (1969). *Causes of delinquency.* Berkeley: University of California Press.

*Hodge, K.P. (1988). *A conceptual analysis of character development in sport.* Unpublished doctoral dissertation, University of Illinois at Urbana-Champaign.

*Hodge, K.P. (1989). Character-building in sport: Fact or fiction. *New Zealand Journal of Sports Medicine, 17,* 23-25.

*Hodge, K., & Jackson, S. (1986, October). *Moral reasoning in sports: The issue of athletic aggression.* Paper presented at the First Annual Meeting of the Association for the Advancement of Applied Sport Psychology, Jekyll Island, GA.

Hoffman, M.L. (1970). Conscience, personality, and socialization techniques. *Human Development, 13,* 90-126.

Hoffman, M.L. (1975a). Developmental synthesis of affect and cognition and its implications for altruistic motivation. *Developmental Psychology, 11,* 607-622.

Hoffman, M.L. (1975b). Sex differences in moral internalization and values. *Journal of Personality and Social Psychology, 32,* 720-729.

Hoffman, M.L. (1976). Empathy, role-taking, guilt, and development of altruistic motives. In T. Lickona (Ed.), *Moral development and behavior: Theory, research and social issues* (pp. 124-143). New York: Holt, Rinehart and Winston.

Hoffman, M.L. (1978). Empathy, its development and prosocial implications. In C.B. Keasey (Ed.), *Nebraska Symposium on Motivation, Vol. 25* (pp. 169-218). Lincoln: University of Nebraska Press.

Hoffman, M.L. (1981). Is altruism part of human nature? *Journal of Personality and Social Psychology, 40*, 121-137.

Hoffman, M.L. (1982). The measurement of empathy. In C.E. Izard (Ed.), *Measuring emotions in infants and children* (pp. 279-296). Cambridge, England: Cambridge University Press.

Hoffman, M.L. (1984). Empathy, its limitations, and its role in a comprehensive moral theory. In W.M. Kurtines & J.L. Gewirtz (Eds.), *Morality, moral behavior, and moral development* (pp. 283-302). New York: Wiley.

Hoffman, M.L. (1986). Affect, cognition, and motivation. In R.M. Sorrentino & E.T. Higgins (Eds.), *Handbook of motivation and cognition: Foundations of social behavior* (pp. 244-280). New York: Guilford Press.

Hoffman, M.L. (1987). The contribution of empathy to justice and moral judgment. In N. Eisenberg & J. Strayer (Eds.), *Empathy and its development* (pp. 47-80). Cambridge, England: Cambridge University Press.

Hoffman, M.L. (1989). Empathy and prosocial activism. In N. Eisenberg, J. Reykowski, & E. Staub (Eds.), *Social and moral values: Individual and societal perspectives* (pp. 65-85). Hillsdale, NJ: Erlbaum.

Hoffman, M.L. (1990). Empathy and justice motivation. *Motivation and Emotion, 14*, 151-171.

Hoffman, M.L. (1991). Empathy, social cognition, and moral action. In W. Kurtines & J. Gewirtz (Eds.), *Handbook of moral behavior and development: Vol. 1. Theory* (pp. 275-301). Hillsdale, NJ: Erlbaum.

Hoffman, M.L., & Saltzstein, H.D. (1967). Parent discipline and the child's moral development. *Journal of Personality and Social Psychology, 5*, 45-57.

Hogan, R. (1970). A dimension of moral judgment. *Journal of Counseling and Clinical Psychology, 35*, 205-212.

Hogan, R. (1973). Moral conduct and moral character: A psychological perspective. *Psychological Bulletin, 79*, 217-232.

Holder, A. (1982). Preoedipal contributions to the formation of the superego. *Psychiatric Study of the Child, 37*, 245-272.

*Horrocks, R.N. (1977). Sportmanship. *Journal of Physical Education and Recreation, 48*, 20-21.

*Horrocks, R.N. (1979). *The relationship of selected prosocial play behaviors in children to moral reasoning, youth sports, participation, and perception of sportsmanship.* Unpublished doctoral dissertation, University of North Carolina, Greensboro.

*Horrocks, R.N. (1980). Sportsmanship: Moral reasoning. *Physical Educator, 37*, 208-212.

Howard, G.S. (1985). The role of values in the science of psychology. *American Psychologist, 40*, 255-265.

Huizinga, J. (1955). *Homo ludens: A study of the play element in culture.* Boston: Beacon.

Huston, L., & Duda, J. (1992). *The relationship of goal orientation and competitive level to the endorsement of aggressive acts in football.* Unpublished manuscript.

Hutslar, J. (1982). Second national forum on youth sports: Conference summary with commentary. *Arena Review, 6*, 3-14.

Hyde, J.S. (1986). Gender differences in aggression. In J.S. Hyde & M.C. Linn (Eds.), *The psychology of gender: Advances through meta-analysis* (pp. 51-66). Baltimore, MD: Johns Hopkins University Press.

Isen, A.M. (1970). Success, failure, attention and reaction to others: The warm glow of success. *Journal of Personality and Social Psychology, 15*, 294-301.

Jackson, P.W. (1968). *Life in the classroom.* New York: Holt, Rinehart and Winston.

*Jantz, R.K. (1975). Moral thinking in male elementary pupils as reflected by perception of basketball rules. *Research Quarterly, 46*, 414-421.

Jarymowicz, M. (1977). Modification of self-worth and increment of prosocial sensitivity. *Polish Psychological Bulletin, 8*, 45-53.

Jewett, A.E., & Bain, L.L. (1985). *The curriculum process in physical education*. Dubuque, IA: Brown.

Johnson, D., & Johnson, R. (1989). *Cooperation and competition: Theory and research*. Edina, MN: Interaction Books.

Johnson, D.W. (1975). Cooperativeness and social perspective-taking. *Journal of Personality and Social Psychology, 31*, 241-244.

Johnson, D.W., Johnson, R.T., & Maruyama, G. (1983). Interdependence and interpersonal attraction among heterogeneous and homogeneous individuals: A theoretical formulation and a meta-analysis of the research. *Review of Educational Research, 53*, 5-54.

Johnson, D.W., Maruyama, G., Johnson, R.T., Nelson, D., & Skon, L. (1981). Effects of cooperative, competitive, and individualistic goal structures on achievement: A meta-analysis. *Psychological Bulletin, 89*, 47-62.

Johnson, R., & Johnson, D. (1983). Effects of cooperative, competitive, and individualistic learning experiences on social development. *Exceptional Children, 49*, 323-329.

Johnson, R., & Morgan, W. (1981). Personality characteristics of college athletes in different sports. *Scandinavian Journal of Sport Science, 3*, 41-49.

*Kalliopuska, M. (1987). Relation of empathy and self-esteem to active participation in Finnish baseball. *Perceptual and Motor Skill, 65*, 107-113.

Kalliopuska, M. (1989). Empathy, self-esteem and creativity among junior ballet dancers. *Perceptual and Motor Skills, 69*, 1227-1234.

*Kane, M.J. (1982). Influence of level of sport participation and sex-role orientation on female professionalization of attitudes toward play. *Journal of Sport Psychology, 4*, 290-294.

Karpova, S., & Murzinova, N. (1990). The importance of play and schoolwork in the assimilation of moral norms by 6-7 year-olds. *Soviet Psychology, 28*, 56-65.

*Keating, J.W. (1964). Sportsmanship as a moral category. *Ethics, 75*, 25-35.

*Keating, J.W. (1988). Sportsmanship as a moral category. In W.J. Morgan & K.V. Meier (Eds.), *Philosophic inquiry in sport* (pp. 241-250). Champaign, IL: Human Kinetics.

Keefer, R., Goldstein, J.H., & Kasiarz, D. (1983). Olympic games participation and warfare. In J.H. Goldstein (Ed.), *Sports violence* (pp. 183-193). New York: Springer-Verlag.

Keller, M., Eckensberger, L.H., & Von Rosen, K. (1989). A critical note on the conception of preconventional morality: The case of stage 2 in Kohlberg's theory. *International Journal of Behavioral Development, 12*, 57-69.

Keller, M., & Edelstein, W. (1991). The development of socio-moral meaning making: Domains, categories, and perspective-taking. In W.M. Kurtines & J.L. Gewirtz (Eds.), *Handbook of moral behavior and development: Vol. 2. Research* (pp. 89-114). Hillsdale, NJ: Erlbaum.

Kelley, H.H., & Stahleski, A.J. (1970). Social interaction basis of cooperators' and competitors' beliefs about others. *Journal of Personality and Social Psychology, 16*, 66-91.

Kelley, H.H., & Thibant, J.W. (1978). *Interpersonal relations: A theory of interdependence*. New York: Wiley-Interscience.

Kennedy, H., & Yorke, C. (1982). Steps from outer to inner conflict viewed as superego precursors. *Psychiatric Study of the Child, 37*, 221-228.

*Kew, F.C. (1978). Values in competitive games. *Quest, 29*, 103-111.

Kidd, R.F., & Berkowitz, L. (1976). Dissonance, self-concept, and helpfulness. *Journal of Personality and Social Psychology, 33*, 613-622.

*Kidd, T., & Woodman, W. (1975). Sex and orientation toward winning in sport. *Research Quarterly, 46*, 476-483.

Kirschenbaum, H. (1977). *Advanced value clarification*. La Jolla, CA: University Associates.

*Kistler, J.W. (1957). Attitudes expressed about behavior demonstrated in specific situations occurring in sports. *Proceedings of the National College Physical Education Association for Men, 60*, 55-58.

Kleiber, D.A. (1983). Sport and human development: A dialectical interpretation. *Journal of Humanistic Psychology, 23*, 76-95.

Kleiber, D.A., & Roberts, G.C. (1983). The relationship between game and sport involvement in later childhood: A preliminary investigation. *Research Quarterly for Exercise and Sport, 54*, 200-203.

*Kleiber, D.A., & Roberts, G.C. (1981). The effects of sport experience in the development of social character: An exploratory investigation. *Journal of Sport Psychology, 3*, 114-122.

Knight, G.P., & Kagen, S. (1977). Development of prosocial and competitive behaviors in Anglo-American and Mexican-American children. *Child Development, 48*, 1385-1394.

*Kniker, C.R. (1974). The values of athletics in schools: A continuing debate. *Phi Delta Kappan, 56*, 116-120.

Knoppers, A. (1988). Equity for excellence in physical education. *Journal of Physical Education, Recreation and Dance, 59*, 54-58.

*Knoppers, A. (1985). Professionalization of attitudes: A review and critique. *Quest, 37*, 92-102.

*Knoppers, A., Schuiteman, J., & Love, B. (1986). Winning is not the only thing. *Sociology of Sport Journal, 3*, 43-56.

*Knoppers, A., Schuiteman, J., & Love, B. (1988). Professional orientation of junior tennis players. *International Review for the Sociology of Sport, 23*, 243-254.

*Knoppers, A., Zuidema, M., & Meyer, B. (1989). Playing to win or playing to play? *Sociology of Sport Journal, 6*, 70-76.

Kohlberg, L. (1969). Stage and sequence: The cognitive-developmental approach to socialization. In D.A. Goslin (Ed.), *Handbook of socialization theory and research* (pp. 347-480). Chicago: Rand McNally.

Kohlberg, L. (1971). Stages of moral development as a basis for moral education. In C.M. Beck, B.S. Crittenden, & E.V. Sullivan (Eds.), *Moral education: Interdisciplinary approaches* (pp. 23-92). Toronto: University of Toronto Press.

Kohlberg, L. (1976). Moral stages and moralization: The cognitive-developmental approach. In T. Lickona (Ed.), *Moral development and behavior: Theory, research and social issues* (pp. 31-53). New York: Holt, Rinehart and Winston.

Kohlberg, L. (1978). Forward. In P. Scharf (Ed.), *Readings in moral education* (pp. 2-16). Minneapolis: Winston Press.

Kohlberg, L. (1981). *Essays on moral development: Vol. 1. The philosophy of moral development.* San Francisco: Harper & Row.

Kohlberg, L. (1984). *Essays on moral development: Vol. 2. The psychology of moral development.* San Francisco: Harper & Row.

Kohlberg, L., & Candee, D. (1984). The relationship of moral judgment to moral action. In W. Kurtines & J. Gewirtz (Eds.), *Morality, moral behavior, and moral development* (pp. 52-73). New York: Wiley.

Kohlberg, L., Hickey, J., & Scharf, P. (1972). The justice structure of the prison: A theory and intervention. *Prison Journal, 51*, 3-14.

Kohlberg, L., & Higgins, A. (1987). School democracy and social interaction. In W. Kurtines & J.L. Gewirtz (Eds.), *Moral development through social interaction* (pp. 102-128). New York: Wiley.

*Kohn, A. (1986). *No contest: The case against competition.* Boston: Houghton Mifflin.

Krebs, R. (1967). *Some relationships between moral judgment, attention and resistance to temptation.* Unpublished doctoral dissertation, University of Chicago.

*Kroll, W. (1975, March). *Psychology of sportsmanship.* Paper presented at the Sports Psychology meeting, National Association for Sport and Physical Education, Atlantic City, NJ.

*Kroll, W., & Petersen, K.H. (1965). Study of values test and collegiate football teams. *Research Quarterly, 36*, 441-447.

Kuhn, T. (1970). *The structure of scientific revolutions* (2nd ed.). Chicago: University of Chicago Press.

Kupfersmid, J.H., & Wonderly, D.M. (1982). Disequilibrium as a hypothetical construct in Kohlbergian moral development. *Child Study Journal, 12*, 171-185.

Kurdek, L.A. (1977). Structural components and intellectual correlates of cognitive perspective taking in first- through fourth-grade children. *Child Development, 48*, 1503-1511.

Kurdek, L.A. (1978). Perspective taking as the cognitive basis of children's moral development: A review of the literature. *Merrill-Palmer Quarterly, 24*, 3-28.

Kurtines, W. (1974). Autonomy: A concept reconsidered. *Journal of Personality Assessment, 38*, 243-246.

Kurtines, W. (1978). A measure of autonomy. *Journal of Personality Assessment, 42*, 253-257.

Kurtines, W.M., Alvarez, M., & Azmitia, M. (1990). Science and mortality: The role of values in science and the scientific study of moral phenomena. *Psychological Bulletin, 107*, 283-295.

Kurtines, W.M., & Gewirtz, J.L. (1984). Certainty and morality: Objectivistic versus relativistic approaches. In W.M. Kurtines & J.L. Gewirtz (Eds.), *Morality, moral behavior, and moral development* (pp. 3-23). New York: Wiley.

Kurtines, W.M., & Gewirtz, J.L. (Eds.) (1987). *Moral development through social interaction.* New York: Wiley.

Kurtines, W., & Gewirtz, J.L. (Eds.) (1991a). *Handbook of moral behavior and development: Vol. 1. Theory.* Hillsdale, NJ: Erlbaum.

Kurtines, W., & Gewirtz, J.L. (Eds.) (1991b). *Handbook of moral behavior and development: Vol. 2. Research.* Hillsdale, NJ: Erlbaum.

Kurtines, W., & Gewirtz, J.L. (Eds.) (1991c). *Handbook of moral behavior and development: Vol. 3. Application.* Hillsdale, NJ: Erlbaum.

*Lakie, W.L. (1964). Expressed attitudes of various groups of athletes toward athletic competition. *Research Quarterly, 35*, 497-503.

Landers, D.M., & Landers, D.M. (1977). Socialization via interscholastic athletics: Its effect on delinquency. *Sociology of Education, 51*, 299-303.

Langer, E.J., Blank, A., & Chanowitz, B. (1978). The mindlessness of ostensibly thoughtful action. *Journal of Personality and Social Psychology, 36*, 635-642.

Langford, E. (1969). *Wellington: The years of the sword.* New York: Harper & Row.

*Lee, M. (1977). *Expressed values of varsity football players, intramural football players, and non-football players.* Eugene, OR: Microform Publications.

*Lee, M. (1986). Moral and social growth through sport: The coach's role. In G. Gleeson (Ed.), *The growing child in competitive sport* (pp. 248-255). London: Hodder and Stoughton.

*Lee, M. (1988). Values and responsibilities in children's sports. *Physical Education Review, 11*, 19-27.

Leonard, G.B. (1972). *The transformation: A guide to the inevitable changes in humankind.* New York: Delacorte Press.

Lever, J. (1976). Sex differences in the games children play. *Social Problems, 23*, 4.

Lever, J. (1978). Sex differences in the complexity of children's play and games. *American Sociological Review, 43*, 471-483.

Levi-Strauss, C. (1969). *Elementary structure of kinship.* Boston: Beacon.

Levine, L.E., & Hoffman, M.L. (1975). Empathy and cooperation in 4-year-olds. *Developmental Psychology, 11*, 533-534.

Lewin, K. (1944). Level of aspiration. In J.M. Hunt (Ed.), *Personality and behavior disorders* (Vol. 1, pp. 333-378). New York: Ronald Press.

Lickona, T. (1976a). Critical issues in the study of moral development and behavior. In T. Lickona (Ed.), *Moral development and behavior: Theory, research, and social issues* (pp. 3-27). New York: Holt, Rinehart and Winston.

Lickona, T. (1976b). Research on Piaget's theory of moral development. In T. Lickona (Ed.), *Moral development and behavior: Theory, research, and social issues* (pp. 219-240). New York: Holt, Rinehart and Winston.

Lind, G., Hartmann, H., & Wakenhut, R. (1985). *Moral development and the social environment*. Chicago: Precedent Publishing.

Lind, G., Sandberger, J., & Bargel, T. (1981). Moral judgment, ego strength, and democratic orientations: Some theoretical contiguities and empirical findings. *Political Psychology, 3*, 70-110.

Lindley, R. (1986). *Autonomy*. London: Macmillan.

Locke, D. (1979). Cognitive stages or developmental phases? A critique of Kohlberg's stage-structural theory of moral reasoning. *Journal of Moral Education, 8*, 168-181.

Locke, D. (1980). The illusion of stage six. *Journal of Moral Education, 9*, 103-109.

Locke, L.F. (1973). Are sports education? *Quest, 19*, 87-90.

*Lombardo, B. (1982). The behavior of youth sport coaches: Crisis on the bench. *Arena Review, 6*, 48-55.

Long, G.T., & Lerner, M.J. (1974). Deserving the "personal contract" and altruistic behavior by children. *Journal of Personality and Social Psychology, 29*, 551-556.

*Loy, J., Birrell, S., & Rose, D. (1976). Attitudes held toward agonetic activities as a function of selected social identities. *Quest, 26*, 81-93.

Loy, J., McPherson, B.D., & Kenyon, G. (1978). *Sport and social systems*. Reading, MA: Addison-Wesley.

*Lueschen, G. (1976). Cheating in sport. In D.M. Landers (Ed.), *Social problems in athletics: Essays on the sociology of sport* (pp. 67-77). Champaign: University of Illinois Press.

Madsen, M.C. (1967). Cooperative and competitive motivation of children in three Mexican sub-cultures. *Psychological Reports, 20*, 1307-1320.

Madsen, M.C. (1971). Developmental and cross-cultural differences in the cooperative and competitive behavior of young children. *Journal of Cross-Cultural Psychology, 2*, 365-371.

Madsen, M.C., & Shapiro, A. (1970). Cooperative and competitive behavior of urban Afro-American, Anglo-American, Mexican-American, and Mexican village children. *Developmental Psychology, 3*, 16-20.

Madsen, M.C., & Yi, S. (1975). Cooperation and competition of urban and rural children in the Republic of Korea. *International Journal of Psychology, 10*, 269-274.

*Maloney, T.L., & Petrie, B. (1972). Professionalization of attitude toward play among Canadian school pupils as a function of sex, grade, and athletic participation. *Journal of Leisure Research, 4*, 184-195.

Mangan, J.A. (1981). *Athleticism in the Victorian and Edwardian public school*. London: Cambridge University Press.

Manicas, P.T., & Secord, P.F. (1983). Implications for psychology of the new philosophy of science. *American Psychologist, 38*, 399-413.

*Mantel, R.C., & Vander Velden, L. (1974). The relationship between the professionalization of attitude toward play of preadolescent boys and participation in organized sport. In G. Sage (Ed.), *Sport and American society* (2nd ed.) (pp. 172-178). Reading, MA: Addison-Wesley.

*Marczynski, G.J. (1989). *The effect of a moral dilemma discussion group on the social behavior of male college athletes*. Unpublished doctoral dissertation, University of South Dakota, Vermillion.

*Mark, M., Bryant, F., & Lehman, D. (1983). Perceived injustice and sports violence. In J.H. Goldstein (Ed.), *Sports violence* (pp. 83-109). New York: Springer-Verlag.

Marsh, D.T., Serafica, F.C., & Barenboim, C. (1981). Interrelationships among perspective taking, interpersonal problem solving, and interpersonal functioning. *Journal of Genetic Psychology, 138*, 37-48.

Marsh, P. (1978). *Aggro: The illusion of violence*. London: Dent.

Marsh, P. (1982). Social order on the British soccer terraces. *International Social Science Journal, 34*, 247-256.

Martens, R. (1975). The paradigmatic crisis in American sport psychology. *Sportwissenschaft, 1*, 9-24.

*Martens, R. (1976). Kid sports: A den of iniquity or land of promise. In R. Magill, M. Ash, & F. Smoll (Eds.), *Children in sport: A contemporary anthology* (pp. 201-216). Champaign, IL: Human Kinetics.

*Martens, R. (1978). *Joy and sadness in children's sports.* Champaign, IL: Human Kinetics.

*Martens, R. (1988). Helping children become independent, responsible adults through sports. In E.W. Brown & C.F. Branta (Eds.), *Competitive sports for children and youth: An overview of research and issues* (pp. 297-307). Champaign, IL: Human Kinetics.

*Martens, R., & Seefeldt, V. (1976). *Bill of rights for young athletes.* Washington, DC: American Alliance for Health, Physical Education, Recreation and Dance.

Matsumoto, D., Haan, N., Yabrove, G., Theodorou, P., & Carney, C. (1986). Preschoolers' moral actions and emotions in Prisoner's Dilemma. *Developmental Psychology, 22*, 663-670.

*Maxwell, T. (1985). Kidsport: How to finally achieve what we say are the benefits of the program. *CAHPER/ACSEPL Journal, 51*, 4-8.

May, L. (1985). The moral adequacy of Kohlberg's moral development theory. In C.G. Harding (Ed.), *Moral dilemmas: Philosophical and psychological issues in the development of moral reasoning* (pp. 115-136). Chicago: Precedent Publishing.

*McElroy, M., & Kirkendall, D.R. (1980). Significant others and professionalized sport attitudes. *Research Quarterly for Exercise and Sport, 51*, 645-667.

McGuire, J.M., & Thomas, M.H. (1975). Effects of sex, competence, and competition on sharing behavior in children. *Journal of Personality and Social Psychology, 32*, 490-494.

McGuire, W.J. (1985). Attitudes and attitude change. In G. Lindzey & E. Aronson (Eds.), *Handbook of social psychology* (3rd ed.): *Vol. 2. Special fields and applications* (pp. 233-346). New York: Random House.

McIntosh, P.C. (1957). Games and gymnastics for two nations in one. In J.G. Dixon, P.C. McIntosh, A.D. Munrow, & R.F. Willetts (Eds.), *Landmarks in the history of physical education* (pp. 177-208). London: Routledge & Kegan Paul.

*McIntosh, P.C. (1979). *Fair play: Ethics in sport and education.* London: Heinemann.

McPherson, B.D. (1978). Socialization and sport involvement. In G.H. Sage & G.R.F. Luschen (Eds.), *Encyclopedia of physical education* (Vol. 2). Reading, MA: Addison-Wesley.

McPherson, B.D. (1981). Socialization into and through sport. In G.R.F. Luschen & G.H. Sage (Eds.), *Handbook of social science of sport* (pp. 246-273). Champaign, IL: Stipes.

Mead, G.H. (1934). *Mind, self, and society.* Chicago: University of Chicago Press.

*Meakin, D.C. (1981). Physical education: An agency of moral education? *Journal of Philosophy of Education, 15*, 241-253.

*Meakin, D.C. (1982). Moral values and physical education. *Physical Education Review, 5*, 62-82.

Melnick, M.J., Vanfossen, B.E., & Sabo, D.F. (1988). Developmental effects of athletic participation among high school girls. *Sociology of Sport Journal, 5*, 22-36.

*Mender, J., Keer, R., & Orlick, T. (1982). Cooperative games program for learning disabled children. *International Journal of Sport Psychology, 13*, 222-233.

Messner, M.A., & Sabo, D.F. (Eds.) (1990). Introduction: Toward a critical feminist reappraisal of sport, men, and the gender order. *Sport, men, and the gender order: Critical feminist perspectives* (pp. 1-15). Champaign, IL: Human Kinetics.

Midlarsky, E., & Midlarsky, M. (1973). Some determinants of aiding under experimentally induced stress. *Journal of Personality, 41*, 305-327.

Milgrim, S. (1963). Behavioral study of obedience. *Journal of Abnormal and Social Psychology, 67*, 371-378.

Milgrim, S. (1974). *Obedience to authority: An experimental view.* New York: Harper & Row.

*Miller, D.M. (1980). Ethics in sport: Paradoxes, perplexities and a proposal. *Quest, 32*, 3-7.

*Miller, R.F., & Jarman, B.O. (1988). Moral and ethical character development: Views from past leaders. *Journal of Physical Education, Recreation and Dance, 59*, 72-78.

Mischel, W., & Mischel, H. (1976). A cognitive social learning approach to morality and self-regulation. In T. Lickona (Ed.), *Moral development and behavior: Theory, research, and social issues* (pp. 84-107). New York: Holt, Rinehart and Winston.

Modgil, S., & Modgil, C. (Eds.) (1985). *Lawrence Kohlberg: Consensus and controversy.* Philadelphia: Falmer.

Morgan, W. (1980). The trait psychology controversy. *Research Quarterly for Exercise and Sport, 51*, 50-76.

*Moriarty, D., & McCabe, A.E. (1977). Studies of television and youth sport. In *Ontario: Royal commission on violence in the communications industry. Report: Vol. 5— Learning from the media.* [Research reports]. Toronto: Queen's Printer for Ontario.

*Musgrave, P.W. (1978). *The moral curriculum: A sociological analysis.* London: Methuen.

Mussen, P., Rutherford, E., Harris, S., & Keasey, C. (1970). Honesty and altruism among preadolescents. *Developmental Psychology, 3*, 169-194.

Mwamwenda, T.S. (1992). Moral development and behavior. *Psychological Reports, 71*, 499-502.

*Naples, R.J. (1987). *The discussion of sport-specific dilemmas to enhance the moral development of club sport participation.* Unpublished doctoral dissertation, Temple University, Philadelphia.

Naraváez, D. (1993). *Moral perception.* Unpublished manuscript, University of Minnesota, Minneapolis.

*Nash, J. (Ed.) (1932). *Character education through physical education.* New York: A.S. Barnes.

*Nelson, K., & Cody, C. (1979). Competition, cooperation, and fair play. *International Review of Sport Sociology, 1*, 97-104.

Nelson, L.L., & Kagan, S. (1972). Competition: The star-spangled scramble. *Psychology Today, 5*, 53-56, 90-91.

Nicholls, J.G. (1983). Conceptions of ability and achievement motivation: A theory and its implications for education. In S.G. Paris, G.M. Olson, & H.W. Stevenson (Eds.), *Learning and motivation in the classroom* (pp. 211-237). Hillsdale, NJ: Erlbaum.

Nicholls, J.G. (1989). *The competitive ethos and democratic education.* Cambridge, MA: Harvard University Press.

Nicholls, J.G. (1992). The general and the specific in the development and expression of achievement motivation. In G.C. Roberts (Ed.), *Motivation in sport and exercise* (pp. 31-56). Champaign, IL: Human Kinetics.

*Nicholson, C. (1979). Some attitudes associated with sports participation among junior high school females. *Research Quarterly, 50*, 661-667.

*Nideffer, R.M. (1981). *The ethics and practice of applied sport psychology.* Ithaca, NY: Mouvement.

*Nixon, H. (1980). Orientation toward sports participation among college students. *Journal of Sport Behavior, 3*, 29-45.

Noam, G.G., & Wolf, M. (1991). Lawrence Kohlberg 1927-1987. In W. Kurtines & J. Gewirtz (Eds.), *Handbook of moral behavior and development: Vol. 1. Theory* (pp. 21-24). Hillsdale, NJ: Erlbaum.

Noddings, N. (1984). *Caring: A feminine approach to ethics and moral education.* Berkeley: University of California Press.

Nosanchuk, T.A. (1981). The way of the warrior: The effects of traditional martial arts training on aggressiveness. *Human Relations, 34*, 435-444.

Nucci, L. (1981). The development of personal concepts: A domain distinct from moral or societal concepts. *Child Development, 52*, 114-121.

Nunner-Winkler, G. (1984). Two moralities? A critical discussion of an ethic of care and responsibility versus an ethic of rights and justice. In W. Kurtines & J. Gewirtz (Eds.), *Morality, moral behavior, and moral development* (pp. 348-361). New York: Wiley.

*Nyquist, E.B. (1985). The immorality of big-power intercollegiate athletics. In D. Chu, J.O. Segrave, & B.J. Becker (Eds.), *Sport and higher education* (pp. 101-114). Champaign, IL: Human Kinetics.

*Oberteuffer, D. (1963). On learning values through sport. *Quest, 1*, 23-29.

*Oberteuffer, D. (1977). *Concepts and convictions.* Washington, DC: American Alliance for Health, Physical Education, Recreation and Dance.

*Ogilvie, B., & Tutko, T. (1971). Sport: If you want to build character, try something else. *Psychology Today, 5*, 60-63.

O'Hanlon, T. (1980). Interscholastic athletics, 1900-1940: Shaping citizens for unequal roles in the modern industrial state. *Educational Theory, 30*, 89-103.

Olson, S.L., Johnson, J., Parks, K., Barrett, E., & Belleau, K. (1983a, April). *Behavior problems of preschool children: Dimsnions and social and cognitive correlates.* Paper presented at the biennial meeting of the Society for Research in Child Development, Detroit.

Olson, S.L., Johnson, J., Parks, K., Barrett, E., & Belleau, K. (1983b, April). *Social competence in preschool children: Interrelations with sociometric status, social problem-solving, and impulsivity.* Paper presented at the biennial meeting of the Society for Research in Child Development, Detroit.

Opie, I., & Opie, P. (1969). *Children's games in street and playground.* Oxford: Clarendon Press.

*Orlick, T. (1978). *Winning through cooperation: Competitive insanity, cooperative alternatives.* Washington, DC: Acropolis Press.

*Orlick, T. (1979). Children's games: Following the path that has heart. *Elementary School Guidance and Counseling, 14*, 156-161.

*Orlick, T. (1981a). Cooperative play socialization among preschool children. *Journal of Individual Psychology, 37*, 54-63.

*Orlick, T. (1981b). Positive socialization via cooperative games. *Developmental Psychology, 17*, 126-129.

Orlick, T. (1990). *In puirsuit of excellence.* Champaign, IL: Human Kinetics.

Otto, L.B., & Alwin, D.F. (1977). Athletics, aspirations, and attainments. *Sociology of Education, 42*, 102-113.

*Park, R.J. (1980). Play and sport as moral education: The problem of is and ought. *Academy Papers, 14*, 34-42.

*Park, R.J. (1983). Three major issues: The Academy takes a stand. *Journal of Physical Education, Recreation and Dance, 54*, 52-53.

*Parsons, T.W. (1984). Gamesmanship and sport ethics. *Coaching Review, 71*, 28-30.

*Partington, J. (1982). Sport values: The "Jekyll and Hyde" syndrome. In L. Wankel & R. Wilberg (Eds.), *Psychology of sport and motor behavior: Research and practice* (pp. 129-134). XIV Annual Conference Proceedings CSMLSP, Edmonton, Alberta.

Pearl, R. (1985). Children's understanding of others' need for help: Effects of problem explicitness and type. *Child Development, 56*, 735-745.

Peller, L.E. (1971). Models of children's play. In R.E. Herron & B. Sutton-Smith (Eds.), *Child's play* (pp. 110-125). New York: Wiley.

Pepitone, A., & Kleiner, R. (1957). The effect of threat and frustration on group cohesiveness. *Journal of Personality and Social Psychology, 54*, 192-199.

*Pepitone, E.A. (1980). *Children in cooperation and competition: Toward a developmental social psychology.* Lexington, MA: Lexington Books.

Petrie, B. (1971a). Achievement orientations in adolescent attitudes toward play. *International Review of Sport Sociology, 6*, 89-99.

Petrie, B. (1971b). Achievement orientations in the motivation of Canadian university students toward physical activity. *Journal of the Canadian Association of Health, Physical Education, and Recreation, 37*, 7-13.

Philibert, P. (1987). Relation, consensus, and commitment as foundations of moral growth. *New Ideas in Psychology, 5*, 183-195.

Phillips, D.P. (1983). The impact of mass media violence on U.S. homicides. *American Sociological Review, 48*, 560-568.

Piaget, J. (1923). *The language and thought of the child.* New York: Harcourt, Brace.

Piaget, J. (1962). *Play, dreams, and imitation in childhood.* New York: Norton.

Piaget, J. (1965). *Moral judgment of the child.* New York: Free Press. (Original work published 1932)

Piaget, J. (1970a). Piaget's theory. In P. Mussen (Ed.), *Carmichael's manual of child psychology* (pp. 703-732). New York: Wiley.

Piaget, J. (1970b). *Structuralism.* New York: Basic Books.

Piaget, J. (1977). *The development of thought: Equilibration of cognitive structures.* New York: Viking.

Picou, J.S., & Curry, E.W. (1974). Residence and the athletic participation-education aspiration hypothesis. *Social Science Quarterly, 55*, 768-776.

Piliavin, J.A., Dovidio, J.F., Gaertner, S.L., & Clark, R.D. III. (1981). *Emergency intervention.* New York: Academic Press.

Piliavin, J.A., Dovidio, J.F., Gaertner, S.L., & Clark, R.D. III. (1982). Responsive bystanders: The process of intervention. In V.J. Derlega & J. Gzrelak (Eds.), *Cooperation and helping behavior: Theories and research* (pp. 279-304). New York: Academic Press.

Pomazal, R.J., & Jaccard, J.J. (1976). An informational approach to altruistic behavior. *Journal of Personality and Social Psychology, 33*, 317-327.

Pooley, J.C. (1989). Player violence in sports: Consequences for youth cross-nationally (Part 2). *Journal of the International Council for Health, Physical Education and Recreation, 25*, 6-11.

Power, C. (1979). *The moral atmosphere of a just community high school: A four-year longitudinal study.* Unpublished doctoral dissertation, Harvard University, Cambridge, MA.

Power, C. (1991). Lawrence Kohlberg: The vocation of a moral psychologist and educator. In W. Kurtines & J. Gewirtz (Eds.), *Handbook of moral behavior and development: Vol. 1. Theory* (pp. 25-33). Hillsdale, NJ: Erlbaum.

Power, C., Higgins, A., & Kohlberg, L. (1989). *Lawrence Kohlberg's approach to moral education.* New York: Columbia University Press.

*Preston, D.G. (1979). *A moral education program conducted in the physical education and health education curriculum.* Unpublished doctoral dissertation, University of Georgia, Athens.

Puka, B. (1986). The majesty and mystery of Stage 6. In W. Edelstein & G. Nunner-Winkler (Eds.), *Zur Bestimmung der Moral.* Berlin: Suhrkamp.

Puka, B. (1991). Toward the redevelopment of Kohlberg's theory: Preserving essential structure, removing controversial content. In W. Kurtines & J. Gewirtz (Eds.), *Handbook of moral behavior and development: Vol. 1. Theory* (pp. 373-393). Hillsdale, NJ: Erlbaum.

Purdy, D.A., & Richard, S.F. (1983). Sport and juvenile delinquency: An examination and assessment of four major theories. *Journal of Sport Behavior, 6*, 179-193.

*Qi, W.M. (1982). The development of cooperative competition and sportsmanship in China. In J. Partington, T. Orlick, & J. Salmela (Eds.), *Sport in perspective* (pp. 178-185). Ottawa, ON: Coaching Association of Canada.

Rabbie, J. (1982). The effects of intergroup competition and cooperation on intragroup and intergroup relations. In V. Derlega & J. Grzelak (Eds.), *Cooperation and helping behavior: Theories and research* (pp. 123-149). New York: Academic Press.

Radke-Yarrow, M., & Zahn-Waxler, C. (1984). Roots, motives, and patterns in children's prosocial behavior. In E. Staub, D. Bar-Tal, J. Karylowski, & J. Reykowski (Eds.), *The development and maintenance of prosocial behavior: International perspectives on positive morality* (pp. 81-90). New York: Plenum.

Radke-Yarrow, M., Zahn-Waxler, C., & Chapman, M. (1983). Prosocial dispositions and behavior. In P. Mussen (Ed.), *Manual of child psychology.* E.M. Hetherington (Ed.), *Vol. 4: Socialization, personality, and social development* (pp. 469-545). New York: Wiley.

Raths, L., Harmin, M., & Simon, S. (1966). *Values and teaching.* Columbus: Merrill.

Rausch, H. (1965). Interaction sequences. *Journal of Personality and Social Psychology, 2,* 487-499.

Rawls, J. (1971). *A theory of justice.* Cambridge, MA: Harvard University Press.

Rayner, R. (1992). Matching, attunement and the psychoanalytic dialogue. *International Journal of Psycho-Analysis, 73,* 39-54.

*Reddiford, G. (1981). Morality and the games player. *Physical Education Review, 4,* 8-16.

*Rees, C.R., Howell, F.M., & Miracle, A.W. (1990). Do high school sports build character? A quasi-experiment on a national sample. *Social Science Journal, 27,* 303-315.

Reimer, J., Paolitto, D.P., & Hersh, R.H. (1983). *Promoting moral growth: From Piaget to Kohlberg* (2nd ed.). Prospect Heights, IL: Waveland.

*Remigino, L.J., Smith, R., & Vanderbeck, H. (1974). Fair play. In R. Frost & E. Sims (Eds.), *Development of human values through sport* (pp. 84-96). Washington, DC: American Alliance for Health, Physical Education and Recreation.

Rest, J.R. (1979). *Development in judging moral issues.* Minneapolis: University of Minnesota Press.

Rest, J.R. (1983). Morality. In P. Mussen (Ed.), *Manual of child psychology.* J. Flavell & E. Markman (Eds.), *Vol. 3: Cognitive development* (pp. 556-629). 4th ed. New York: Wiley.

Rest, J.R. (1984). The major components of morality. In W. Kurtines & J. Gewirtz (Eds.), *Morality, moral behavior, and moral development* (pp. 356-629). New York: Wiley.

Rest, J.R. (1986). *Moral development: Advances in research and theory.* New York: Praeger.

Rest, J.R. (Ed.) (1994). Moral development in the professions: Psychology and applied ethics. Hillsdale, NJ: Erlbaum.

Reykowski, J. (1982). Motivation of prosocial behavior. In V. Derlega & J. Grzelak (Eds.), *Cooperation and helping behavior: Theories and research* (pp. 355-375). New York: Academic Press.

Reykowski, J. (1984, August). *Evaluative systems: Rules of change.* Address at the annual meeting of the American Psychological Association, Toronto.

*Richardson, D. (1962). Ethical conduct in sport situations. *Proceedings of the National College Physical Education Association for Men, 66,* 98-103.

Roberts, G.C. (1980). Children in competition: A theoretical perspective and recommendations for practice. *Motor Skills: Theory into Practice, 4,* 37-50.

Rokeach, M. (1968). *Beliefs, attitudes, and values.* San Francisco: Jossey-Bass.

Rokeach, M. (1973). *The nature of human values.* New York: Free Press.

*Romance, T.J. (1984). *A program to promote moral development through elementary school physical education.* Unpublished doctoral dissertation, University of Oregon, Eugene.

*Romance, T.J. (1988). Promoting character development in physical education. *Strategies, 1,* 16-17.

*Romance, T.J., Weiss, M.R., & Bockoven, J. (1986). A program to promote moral development through elementary school physical education. *Journal of Teaching in Physical Education, 5,* 126-136.

*Roos, R. (1986). Do rough games hinder kids' moral growth? *Physician and Sportsmedicine, 14,* 31-32, 34.

Rosen, B. (1980). Moral dilemmas and their treatment. In B. Munsey (Ed.), *Moral development, moral education, and Kohlberg* (pp. 232-265). Birmingham, AL: Religious Education Press.

Rosenhan, D.L., Salovey, P., Karylowski, J., & Hargis, K. (1981). Emotion and altruism. In J.P. Rushton & R.M. Sorrentino (Eds.), *Altruism and helping behavior: Social, personality, and developmental perspectives* (pp. 233-248). Hillsdale, NJ: Erlbaum.

*Royce, J. (1978). Physical training and moral education. In E.W. Gerber & W.J. Morgan (Eds.), *Sport and the body: A philosophical symposium* (pp. 247-250). Philadelphia: Lea & Febiger.

Rushton, J.P. (1980). *Altruism, socialization and society*. Englewood Cliffs, NJ: Prentice-Hall.

Rushton, J.P. (1982). Social learning theory and the development of prosocial behavior. In N. Eisenberg (Ed.), *The development of prosocial behavior* (pp. 77-105). New York: Academic Press.

*Sabock, R., & Kadingo, C. (1987). Sports and ethics: Survey indicates female athletes have proper behavioral attitudes. *Interscholastic Athletic Administration, 13*, 14-15.

Sagan, E. (1988). *Freud, women, and morality: The psychology of good and evil*. New York: Basic Books.

*Sage, G. (1980). Orientation toward sport of male and female intercollegiate athletes. *Journal of Sport Psychology, 2*, 355-362.

*Sage, G. (1985a). American values and sport: Formation of a bureaucratic personality. In D. Chu, J.O. Segrave, & B.J. Becker (Eds.), *Sport and higher education* (pp. 275-282). Champaign, IL: Human Kinetics.

Sage, G. (1985b). The effect of physical activity on the social development of children. *Academy Papers, 19*, 22-29.

Sage, G. (1986). Social development. In V. Seefeldt (Ed.), *Physical activity and well-being* (pp. 343-372). Reston, VA: American Alliance for Health, Physical Education, Recreation and Dance.

*Sage, G. (1988). Sports participation as a builder of character? *The World and I, 3*, 629-641.

Sage, G. (1990). *Power and ideology in American sport: A critical perspective*. Champaign, IL: Human Kinetics.

Salz, A.E. (1975). *Comparative study of personality of Little League champions, other players in Little League, and non-playing peers*. Unpublished master's thesis, Pennsylvania State University, University Park, PA.

Schafer, W.E. (1969). Participation in interscholastic athletics and delinquency: A preliminary study. *Social Problems, 17*, 40-47.

Schafer, W.E. (1971). *Sport, socialization, and the school: Toward maturity of enculturation*. Paper presented at the Third International Symposium on the Sociology of Sport, Waterloo, ON.

Schafer, W.E. (1972). Participation in interscholastic athletics and delineuncy. In K. Polk & W.E. Schafer (Eds.), *Schools and delinquency* (pp. 91-101). Englewood Cliffs, NJ: Prentice-Hall.

Schmitz, K. (1976). Sport and play: Suspension of the ordinary. In M. Hart (Ed.), *Sport in the sociocultural process* (pp. 35-48). Dubuque, IA: Brown.

Schwartz, S.H. (1977). Normative influences on altruism. In L. Berkowitz (Ed.), *Advances in experimental social psychology*, Vol. 10 (pp. 222-279). New York: Academic Press.

*Scott, J. (1973). Sport and the radical ethic. *Quest, 19*, 71-77.

Searle, J.R. (1969). *Speech acts*. Cambridge, MA: University Press.

Sears, R.R., Rau, L., & Alpert, R. (1965). *Identification and child rearing*. Stanford, CA: Stanford University Press.

Secord, P.F. (1959). Stereotyping and favourableness in the perception of Negro faces. *Journal of Abnormal and Social Psychology, 59*, 309-315.

*Seefeldt, V. (1982). *The code of ethics for youth sport coaches*. East Lansing, MI: Institute for the Study of Youth Sports.

Segrave, J.O. (1981). Athletics and delinquency: Review and reformulation. *Journal of Sport Psychology, 2*, 82-89.

Segrave, J.O. (1983). Sport and juvenile delinquency. In R. Terjung (Ed.), *Exercise and Sport Sciences Review, 2*, 161-209.

Segrave, J.O., & Chu, D.B. (1978). Athletics and juvenile delinquency. *Review of Sport and Leisure, 3*, 1-24.

Segrave, J.O., & Hastad, D. (1982). Delinquent behavior and interscholastic athletic participation. *Journal of Sport Behavior, 5*, 96-111.

Segrave, J.O., & Hastad, D. (1984). Interscholastic participation and delinquent behavior: An empirical assessment of relevant variables. *Sociology of Sport Journal, 1*, 117-137.

Segrave, J.O., Hastad, D., & Moreau, C. (1985). An investigation into the relationship between ice hockey participation and delinquency. *Sociology of Sport Journal, 2*, 281-298.

Selman, R.L. (1976). Social-cognitive understanding: A guide to educational and clinical practice. In T. Lickona (Ed.), *Moral development and behavior* (pp. 299-316). New York: Holt, Rinehart and Winston.

Selman, R.L. (1980). *The growth of interpersonal understanding.* New York: Academic Press.

*Seymour, E.W. (1956). Comparative study of certain behavior characteristics of participant and non-participant boys in Little League baseball. *Research Quarterly, 27*, 338-346.

Shaffer, D.R. (1986). Is mood-induced altruism a form of hedonism? *Humboldt Journal of Social Relations, 13*, 195-216.

Shantz, C.U. (1975). The development of social cognition. *Review of child development research, 5*, 257-323. Chicago: University of Chicago Press.

Shantz, C.U. (1983). Social cognition. In P.H. Mussen (Ed.), *Handbook of child psychology: Vol. 3. Cognitive development* (pp. 495-555). New York: Wiley.

*Shea, E.J. (1978). *Ethical decisions in physical education and sport.* Springfield, IL: Charles C Thomas.

Sheehan, T.J., & Alsop, W.L. (1972). Educational sport. *Journal of Health, Physical Education and Recreation, 43*, 41-45.

*Sherif, C.W. (1976). The context of competition. In D. Landers (Ed.), *Social problems in athletics* (pp. 18-36). Champaign, IL: University of Illinois Press.

*Sherif, M. (1966). *In common predicament: Social psychology of intergroup conflict and cooperation.* Boston: Houghton-Mifflin.

*Sherif, M. (1967). *Group conflict and cooperation.* London: Routledge & Kegan Paul.

*Sherif, M., Harvey, O.J., White, B.J., Hood, W.R., & Sherif, C.W. (1961). *Intergroup conflict and cooperation: The robbers cave experiment.* Norman: University of Oklahoma Press.

Sherif, M., & Sherif, C. (1969). *Social psychology.* New York: Harper & Row.

Sherrill, C. (1985). Integration of handicapped students: Philosophical roots in pragmatism, idealism, and realism. *Adapted Physical Activity Quarterly, 2*, 264-272.

Shields, D. (1986). *Growing beyond prejudices.* Mystic, CT: Twenty-Third Publications.

*Shields, D.L., & Bredemeier, B.J. (1984). Sport and moral growth: A structural developmental perspective. In W. Straub & J. Williams (Eds.), *Cognitive sport psychology* (pp. 89-101). Lansing, NY: Sport Science Associates.

*Shields, D.L., & Bredemeier, B.J. (1986). Morality and aggression: A response to Smith's critique. *Sociology of Sport Journal, 3*, 65-67.

*Shields, D.L., & Bredemeier, B.J. (1989). Moral reasoning, judgment, and action in sport. In J. Goldstein (Ed.), *Sports, games, and play: Social and psychological viewpoints* (pp. 59-81). Hillsdale, NJ: Erlbaum.

*Shinnick, P. (1982). Youth and athlete's rights. *Arena Review, 6*, 40-42.

*Shogan, D. (1988). Moral development of young people through sport: Is it an attainable goal? In P.J. Galasso (Ed.), *Philosophy of sport and physical activity: Issues and concepts* (pp. 319-323). Toronto: Canadian Scholars Press.

Shure, M.B. (1980). *Interpersonal problem solving in ten-year-olds*. Final grant report to the National Institute of Mental Health (Grant #R01 MH 27741).

Shure, M.B. (1982). Interpersonal problem solving: A cog in the wheel of social cognition. In F.C. Serafica (Ed.), *Social-cognitive development in context* (pp. 133-166). New York: Guilford Press.

Shweder, R. (1982). Review of Lawrence Kohlberg's *Essays on moral development, Vol. 1: The philosophy of moral development. Contemporary Psychology, 27*, 421.

Siedentop, D. (1972). *Physical education: Introductory analysis*. Dubuque, IA: Brown.

Siedentop, D., Mand, C., & Taggart, A. (1986). *Physical education: Curriculum and instruction strategies for grades 5-12*. Palo Alto, CA: Mayfield.

*Silva, J.M. (1983). The perceived legitimacy of rule violating behavior in sport. *Journal of Sport Psychology, 5*, 438-448.

*Simon, R.L. (1991). *Fair play: Sports, values, and society*. Boulder: Westview Press.

Simpson, E.L. (1974). Moral development research: A case study of scientific cultural bias. *Human Development, 17*, 81-106.

Sipes, R. (1973). War, sports, and aggression: An empirical test of two rival theories. *American Anthropologist, 75*, 64-86.

Sipes, R.G. (1975). War, combative sports, and aggression: A preliminary causal model of cultural patterning. In M.A. Nettleship, R. Dalegivens, & A. Nettleship (Eds.), *War: Its causes and correlates* (pp. 749-762). The Hague: Mouton.

Sipes, R.G. (1976). Sports as a control for aggression. In T.T. Craig (Ed.), *Humanistic and mental health aspects of sports, exercise, and recreation* (pp. 46-49). Chicago: American Medical Association.

Skarin, K., & Moely, B.E. (1976). Altruistic behavior: An analysis of age and sex differences. *Child Development, 47*, 1159-1165.

*Skubic, E. (1956). Studies in Little League and middle league baseball. *Research Quarterly, 27*, 97-110.

Smetana, J. (1981a). Preschool children's conceptions of moral and social rules. *Child Development, 52*, 1333-1336.

Smetana, J. (1981b). Reasoning in the personal and moral domains: Adolescent and young adult women's decision-making regarding abortion. *Journal of Applied Developmental Psychology, 3*, 211-226.

Smetana, J. (1990). Morality and conduct disorders. In M. Lewis & S. Miller (Eds.), *Handbook of developmental psychopathology* (pp. 157-179). New York: Plenum Press.

Smetana, J.G, Killen, M., & Turiel, E. (1991). Children's reasoning about interpersonal and moral conflicts. *Child Development, 62*, 629-646.

Smith, M.D. (1974). Significant others' influence on the assaultive behavior of young hockey players. *International Review of Sport Sociology, 9*, 45-56.

Smith, M.D. (1975). The legitimation of violence: Hockey players' perceptions of their reference groups' sanctions for assault. In R.S. Gruneau & J.G. Albinson (Eds.), *Canadian Review of Sociology and Anthropology, 12*, 72-80.

Smith, M.D. (1977). *Hockey violence: A test of the subculture of violence thesis*. Paper presented at the annual meeting of the Southern Sociological Association, Atlanta.

Smith, M.D. (1979). Towards an explanation of hockey violence. *Canadian Journal of Sociology, 4*, 105-124.

Smith, M.D. (1983). *Violence and sport*. Toronto: Butterworths.

Smith, R.E., Smoll, F.L., & Curtis, B. (1979). Coach effectiveness training: A cognitive-behavioral approach to enhancing relationship skills in youth sport coaches. *Journal of Sport Psychology, 1*, 59-75.

Snarey, J. (1985). The cross-cultural universality of social-moral development: A critical review of Kohlbergian research. *Psychological Bulletin, 97*, 202-232.

*Snyder, E.E., & Spreitzer, E. (1979a). High school value climate as related to preferential treatment of athletes. *Research Quarterly, 50*, 460-467.

*Snyder, E.E., & Spreitzer, E. (1979b). Orientations toward sport: Intrinsic, normative, and extrinsic. *Journal of Sport Psychology, 1*, 170-175.

Snyder, E.E., & Spreitzer, E. (1983). *Social aspects of sport* (2nd ed.). Englewood Cliffs, NJ: Prentice-Hall.

Sobesky, W.E. (1983). The effects of situational factors on moral judgment. *Child Development, 54*, 575-584.

Solomon, D., Watson, M., Battistich, V., Schaps, E., Tuck, P., Solomon, J., Cooper, C., & Ritchey, W. (1985). A program to promote interpersonal consideration and cooperation in children. In R. Slavin, S. Sharan, S. Kagan, R. Hertz-Lazarowitz, C. Webb, & R. Schmuck (Eds.), *Learning to cooperate, cooperating to learn* (pp. 371-401). New York: Plenum.

*Solomon, G. (1993). *Children's moral reasoning and their perceptions of gender stratification.* Unpublished doctoral dissertation, University of California at Berkeley.

Spitz, R. (1958). On the genesis of superego components. *Psychoanalytic Study of the Child, 13*, 375-404.

Spivack, G., Platt, J.J., & Shure, M.B. (1976). *The problem solving approach to adjustment.* San Francisco: Jossey-Bass.

Spreitzer, E., & Pugh, M.D. (1973). Interscholastic athletics and educational attainment. *Sociology of Education, 46*, 313-325.

Sroufe, L.A. (1983). Infant caregiver attachment and patterns of adaptation in preschool: The roots of maladaptation and competence. In M. Perlmutter (Ed.), *Minnesota Symposium in Child Psychology* (Vol. 16, pp. 41-81). Hillsdale, NJ: Erlbaum.

*Stanton, M. (1975). Judgments by secondary school pupils of rules of games and social actions. *Journal of Moral Education, 5*, 71-80.

Staub, E. (1974). Helping a distressed person: Social, personality, and stimulus determinants. In L. Berkowitz (Ed.), *Advances in experimental social psychology* (Vol. 7, pp. 293-341). New York: Academic Press.

Staub, E. (1978). *Positive social behavior and morality: Vol. 1. Social and personality differences.* New York: Academic Press.

Staub, E. (1979). *Positive social behavior and morality: Vol. 2. Socialization and development.* New York: Academic Press.

Staub, E. (1986). A conception of the determinants and development of altruism and aggression: Motives, the self, the environment. In C. Zahn-Waxler, E.M. Cummings, & R. Iannoti (Eds.), *Altruism and aggression: Biological and social origins* (pp. 135-164). New York: Cambridge University Press.

Staub, E., & Noerenberg, H. (1981). Property rights, deservingness, reciprocity, friendship: The transactional character of children's sharing behavior. *Journal of Personality and Social Psychology, 40*, 271-289.

*Stephens, D. (1993). *Goals orientation and moral atmosphere in youth sport: An examination of lying, hurting, and cheating behaviors in girls' soccer.* Unpublished doctoral dissertation, University of California at Berkeley.

*Stephens, D., & Bredemeier, B. (1992, November). *Toward an understanding of moral behavior in sport: An examination of lying, hurting, and cheating behavior in girls' soccer.* Poster presented at the Association for the Advancement of Applied Sport Psychology Conference, Colorado Springs, Colorado.

*Stephens, D.E., Bredemeier, B.J.L., Shields, D.L.L., & Ryan, M.K. (1992, May). *Relation of motivational and leadership variables to temptation to play unfairly.* Paper presented at the International Conference for Physical Activity, Fitness and Health, Toronto.

*Stern, B.E. (1972). *The relationship between participation in sports and the moral and political socialization of high school youth in Chile.* Unpublished doctoral dissertation, Stanford University, Stanford, CA.

*Stevenson, C.L. (1975). Socialization effects of participation in sport: A critical review of the research. *Research Quarterly, 46*, 287-301.

*Stevenson, C.L. (1985). College athletics and "character": The decline and fall of socialization research. In D. Chu, J.O. Segrave, & B.J. Becker (Eds.), *Sport and higher education* (pp. 249-266). Champaign, IL: Human Kinetics.

*Stoll, S.K. (1993). *Who says this is cheating? Anybody's sport ethics book.* Dubuque, IA: Kendall/Hunt.

*Stone, C.C., & Chambers, F. (1983). Educational aspects of moral and social development of athletes. In E.R. Hall & M.M. McIntyre (Eds.), *Olympism: A movement of the people* (pp. 251-259). Lubbock: Texas Tech University Press.

Strayer, J., & Eisenberg, N. (1987). Empathy viewed in context. In N. Eisenberg & J. Strayer (Eds.), *Empathy and its development* (pp. 389-398). Cambridge, England: Cambridge University Press.

Strayer, J., & Roberts, W. (1989). Children's empathy and role taking: Child and parental factors, and relations to prosocial behavior. *Journal of Applied Developmental Psychology, 10,* 227-239.

Sugden, J., & Yiannakis, A. (1982). Sport and juvenile delinquency: A theoretical base. *Journal of Sport and Social Issues, 6,* 22-30.

Sullivan, E.V. (1977). A study of Kohlberg's structural theory of moral development: A critique of liberal social science ideology. *Human Development, 20,* 352-376.

Sutherland, E.H., & Cressey, D.R. (1966). *Principles of criminology.* Chicago: J.B. Lippincott.

Sutton-Smith, B. (1971a). Boundaries. In R.E. Herron & B. Sutton-Smith (Eds.), *Child's play* (pp. 103-109). New York: Wiley.

Sutton-Smith, B. (1971b). Piaget on play: A critique. In R.E. Herron & B. Sutton-Smith (Eds.), *Child's play* (pp. 326-336). New York: Wiley.

Szajnberg, N.M., Skrinjaric, J., & Moore, A. (1989). Affect attunement, attachment, temperament, and zygosity: A twin study. *Journal of the American Academy of Child and Adolescent Psychiatry, 28,* 249-253.

Tajfel, H. (1957). Value and the perceptual judgement of magnitude. *Psychological Review, 64,* 192-204.

*Templin, T., & Allison, M. (1982). The sportsmanship dilemma. *Physical Educator, 39,* 204-207.

*Theberge, N., Curtis, J., & Brown, B. (1982). Sex differences in orientation toward games: Tests of the sport involvement hypothesis. In A. Dunleavy, A. Miracle, & O.R. Rees (Eds.), *Studies in the sociology of sport* (pp. 285-308). Fort Worth: Texas Christian University Press.

Thirer, J. (1978). The effect of observing filmed violence on the aggressive attitudes of female athletes and non-athletes. *Journal of Sport Behavior, 1,* 28-36.

Thoma, S.J., Rest, J., & Barnett, R. (1986). Moral judgment, behavior, decision making, and attitude. In J.R. Rest (Ed.), *Moral development: Advances in theory and research* (pp. 133-175). New York: Praeger.

*Thorkildsen, T. (1989). Pluralism in children's reasoning about social justice. *Child Development, 60,* 965-972.

Tjosvold, D., Johnson, D.. & Johnson, R. (1984). Influence strategy, perspective-taking, and relationships between high- and low-power individuals in cooperative and competitive contexts. *Journal of Psychology, 116,* 187-202.

Travers, T.H.E. (1979). Technology, tactics and morale. *Journal of Modern History, 51,* 264,286.

Trulson, M.E. (1986). Martial arts training: A novel "cure" for juvenile delinquency. *Human Relations, 39,* 1131-1140.

Turiel, E. (1975). The development of social concepts: Mores, customs, and conventions. In D. DePalma & J. Foley (Eds.), *Moral development: Current theory and research* (pp. 7-37). Hillsdale, NJ: Erlbaum.

Turiel, E. (1976). A comparative analysis of moral knowledge and moral judgment in males and females. *Journal of Personality, 44,* 195-209.

Turiel, E. (1977). Conflict and transition in adolescent moral development. II. The resolution of disequilibrium through structural reorganization. *Child Development, 48,* 634-637.

Turiel, E. (1978a). Social regulations and domains of social concepts. In W. Damon (Ed.), *New directions for child development. Vol. 1. Social cognition* (pp. 45-74). San Francisco: Jossey-Bass.

Turiel, E. (1978b). The development of concepts of social structure: Social convention. In J. Glick & A. Clarke-Stewart (Eds.), *The development of social understanding* (pp. 25-107). New York: Gardner Press.

Turiel, E. (1983). *The development of social knowledge: Morality and convention.* New York: Cambridge University Press.

Turiel, E. (1989a). Domain-specific social judgments and domain ambiguities. *Merrill-Palmer Quarterly, 35,* 89-114.

Turiel, E. (1989b). The social construction of social construction. In W. Damon (Ed.), *Child development today and tomorrow* (pp. 86-106). San Francisco: Jossey-Bass.

Turiel, E., & Davidson, P. (1986). Heterogeneity, inconsistency, and asynchrony in the development of cognitive structures. In I. Levin (Ed.), *Stage and structure: Reopening the debate* (pp. 106-143). Norwood, NJ: Ablex.

Turiel, E., Killen, M., & Helwig, C.C. (1987). Morality: Its structure, functions and vagaries. In J. Kagan & S. Lamb (Eds.), *The emergence of moral concepts in young children* (pp. 155-244). Chicago: University of Chicago Press.

Turiel, E., & Smetana, J. (1984). Social knowledge and action: The coordination of domains. In W.M. Kurtines & J.L. Gewirtz (Eds.), *Morality, moral behavior and moral development* (pp. 261-282). New York: Wiley.

Turiel, E., Smetana, J.G., & Killen, M. (1991). Social contexts in social congitive development. In W. Kurtines & J. Gewirtz (Eds.), *Handbook of moral behavior and development: Vol. 2. Research* (pp. 307-332). Hillsdale, NJ: Erlbaum.

Underwood, B., & Moore, B. (1982). Perspective-taking and altruism. *Psychological Bulletin, 91,* 143-173.

*VanDyke, R.R. (1980). Aggression in sport: Its implications for character building. *Quest, 32,* 201-208.

Vaughn, B.E. (1992). Attachment security and temperament in infancy and early childhood: Some conceptual clarifications. *Developmental Psychology, 28,* 463-473.

Vaz, E.W. (1982). *The professionalization of young hockey players.* Lincoln: University of Nebraska Press.

Vealey, R.S. (1989). Sport personology: A paradigmatic and methodological analysis. *Journal of Sport and Exercise Psychology, 11,* 216-235.

Vine, I. (1984). Moral maturity in socio-cultural perspective: Are Kohlberg's stages universal? In S. Modgil & C. Modgil (Eds.), *Lawrence Kohlberg: Consensus and controversy* (pp. 431-450). Brighton: Falmer.

Wagner, C., & Wheeler, L. (1969). Model, need and cost effects in helping behavior. *Journal of Personality and Social Psychology, 12,* 111-116.

Walker, L.J. (1980). Cognitive and perspective-taking prerequisites for moral development. *Child Development, 51,* 131-139.

Walker, L.J. (1984). Sex differences in the development of moral reasoning: A critical review. *Child Development, 55,* 667-691.

Walker, L.J. (1991). Sex differences in moral reasoning. In W. Kurtines & J. Gewirtz (Eds.), *Handbook of moral behavior and development: Vol. 2. Research* (pp. 333-364). Hillsdale, NJ: Erlbaum.

*Wandzilak, T. (1985). Values development through physical education and athletics. *Quest, 37,* 176-185.

*Wandzilak, T., Carroll, T., & Ansorge, C.J. (1988). Values development through physical activity: Promoting sportsmanlike behaviors, perceptions, and moral reasoning. *Journal of Teaching in Physical Education, 8,* 13-22.

*Webb, H. (1969). Professionalization of attitudes toward play among adolescents. In G. Kenyon (Ed.), *Aspects of contemporary sport sociology* (pp. 161-179). Chicago: Athletic Institute.

Weber, M. (1947). *The theory of social and economic organization.* Glencoe, IL: Free Press. (Original work published 1922)

*Weiblen, J. (1972). *Game rules and morality.* Unpublished doctoral dissertation, University of North Carolina, Greensboro.

Weidman, C.S., & Strayhorn, J.M. (1992). Relationships between children's prosocial behaviors and choices in story dilemmas. *Journal of Psychoeducational Assessment, 10*, 330-341.

*Weiss, M. (1987). Teaching sportsmanship and values. In V. Seefeltd (Ed.), *Handbook for youth sport coaches* (pp. 138-151). Reston, VA: American Alliance for Health, Physical Education, Recreation and Dance.

*Weiss, M.R., & Bredemeier, B.J. (1983). Developmental sport psychology: A theoretical perspective for studying children in sport. *Journal of Sport Psychology, 5*, 216-230.

*Weiss, M.R., & Bredemeier, B.J. (1986). Moral development. In V.E. Seefeldt (Ed.), *Physical activity and well being* (pp. 373-390). Reston, VA: American Alliance for Health, Physical Education, Recreation and Dance.

*Weiss, M.R., & Bredemeier, B.J. (1991). Moral development in sport. *Exercise and Sport Science Reviews, 18*, 331-378.

Weiss, P. (1969). *Sport: A philosophic enquiry.* Carbondale: Southern Illinois University Press.

Weston, D.R., & Turiel, E. (1980). Act-rule relations: Children's concepts of social rules. *Developmental Psychology, 16*, 417-424.

*Wilkerson, M., & Doddler, R. (1982). Toward a model of collective conscience and sport in modern society. *International Journal of Sport Psychology, 13*, 268-275.

*Wilkerson, M., & Doddler, R. (1987). Collective conscience and sport in modern society: An empirical test of a model. *Journal of Leisure Research, 19*, 35-40.

Winnick, J. (Ed.) (1990). *Adapted physical education and sport.* Champaign, IL: Human Kinetics.

Wispe, L. (1986). The distinction between sympathy and empathy: To call forth a concept, a word is needed. *Journal of Personality and Social Psychology, 50*, 314-321.

Wohl, A. (1970). Competitive sport and its social functions. *International Review of Sport Sociology, 5*, 117-124.

Wohl, A. (1979). Sport and social development. *International Review of Sport Sociology, 14*, 5-18.

Wolf, D. (1972). *Foul: The Connie Hawkins story.* New York: Warner.

Yiannakis, A. (1980). Sport and deviancy: A review and reappraisal. *Motor Skills: Theory into Practice, 4*, 59-64.

Yiannakis, A. (1981, November). *Athletics, delinquency, and the deterrence hypothesis.* Paper presented at the Second Annual Convention of the North American Society for the Sociology of Sport, Forth Worth, Texas.

*Zaichkowsky, L.D., Zaichkowsky, L.B., & Martinek, T.J. (1980). Moral development. In L.D. Zaichkowsky, L.B. Zaichkowsky, & T.J. Martinek (Eds.), *Growth and development* (pp. 139-153). St. Louis: Mosby.

*Zeigler, E.F. (1984). *Ethics and morality in sport and physical education: An experiential approach.* Champaign, IL: Stipes.

Zillman, D., Johnson, R.C., & Day, K.D. (1974). Provoked and unprovoked aggression in athletics. *Journal of Research in Personality, 8*, 139-152.

Zimmerman, B.J., & Blom, D.E. (1983). Toward an empirical test of the role of cognitive conflict in learning. *Developmental Review, 3*, 18-38.

Photo Credits

Index

About the Authors

Brenda Jo Light Bredemeier and David Lyle Light Shields developed the first ongoing research program in the area of morality and physical activity. Together, they have been studying this topic since 1983. They have also collaborated on numerous book chapters and journal articles pertaining to sport and morality. David and Brenda were married in 1987.

Brenda Bredemeier earned her PhD in physical education with a concentration in social psychology of sport from Temple University in 1979. She conducts workshops both in the U.S. and internationally on assessing moral reasoning and on promoting character development through sport and physical education. She is a consultant for the National Collegiate Athletic Association (NCAA) and is certified through the Association for the Advancement of Applied Sport Psychology as a sport psychology consultant.

Brenda has served as a Dean in the College of Letters and Science at the University of California at Berkeley since 1987. She has also been a professor for the university's Department of Human Biodynamics since 1979. Brenda enjoys a variety of nature activities, playing with children, and reading.

David Shields received his PhD in 1983 from The Graduate Theological Union in Berkeley, California. He has given presentations on the topic of morality and sport at several conferences and offered seminars at the University of California at Berkeley on how to conduct and score moral interviews.

David is a research associate and lecturer in peace and conflict studies at the University of California at Berkeley. He is also the associate director of the Unitas Ecumenical Campus Ministry in Berkeley. David's favorite leisure-time activities include swimming, water skiing, and reading.